Cinema's Strangest Moments

Cinema's Strangest Moments

Extraordinary but true tales from the history of film

Quentin Falk

ROBSON BOOKS

First published in Great Britain in 2003 by Robson Books, The Chrysalis Building, Bramley Road, London, W10 6SP

An imprint of Chrysalis Books plc

British Library Cataloguing in Publication Data
A catalogue record for this title is available from the British Library.

ISBN 1 86105 673 7

Typeset by FiSH Books, London WC1
Printed by Creative Print & Design (Wales), Ebbw Vale

For Anna

Contents

The 1930s

The 1940s

The 1950s

The 1960s

The 1980s

Cinema's Strangest Moments

The 2000s

INTRODUCTION

Ever since pictures started moving more than 115 years ago, Strange But True has been a recurring theme in any discussion about, or reportage of, films and filmmakers. One of the strangest stories of them all still surrounds the unexplained disappearance in 1890 of the French-born but Leeds-based pioneer inventor Louis Augustin Le Prince after boarding a train in Lyon. He was on his way to New York intending to demonstrate his patented film camera for the first time in public, but never even arrived in Paris.

Then there was the curious case of a piece of historic footage shot by Thomas Alva Edison, father of the motion-picture process, at his famous New Jersey studio, a hut covered in tarred paper known as the Black Maria. A seventeen-second archive fragment of that session, probably in 1894, clearly shows Edison's assistant, W K L Dickson, playing a violin alongside a large cone. It was clearly an attempt to create synchronised sound. Yet it would be decades before a cylinder of that violin music was finally tracked down, and eventually another new millennium when the award-winning American film and sound editor Walter Murch managed successfully to 'marry' that age-old fiddling and creaky monochrome image thanks to the latest high-tech digital equipment.

This survey begins in 1895, when the public first began to champion a new art form that would become unarguably the greatest of the twentieth century and certainly seems to show precious little sign of diminishing in the twenty-first. From black and white 'flickers' in the picture houses of yore to the ear-splitting, eye-boggling entertainments served up in today's multiplexes, cinema remains one of the great, even occasionally profitable, crowd pleasers, and can sometimes embrace art too.

1

These three hundred stories – some well known, others hopefully more unfamiliar to all but the most die-hard movie buffs (who should get out more often) – span silents to the very latest blockbusters. There are, for which I must now apologise, too few foreign-language films represented and there is, I admit, a bias towards the last thirty or so years during which I have been a film journalist and critic. Also, I have sometimes stretched the word 'Strange' to embrace both 'Funny Peculiar' and, depending on your sense of humour, 'Funny Ha-Ha'.

Ever since reporting from my first-ever location visit in the Home Counties on a long-forgotten Anglo-American thriller called *Blind Terror* (1971), starring Mia Farrow and Paul Nicholas, I have collected film anecdotes and since compounded the felony on film sets all over the world – from Alice Springs and Tokyo to Simi Valley and Sicily – as well as at festivals such as Cannes, Teheran, San Sebastián and Berlin.

These stories are often the result of research for other various books as well as my journalism for magazines and newspapers such as *Screen International, Academy, Exposure, Sight & Sound*, the *Daily Mail*, the *Sunday Mirror*, the *Sunday Telegraph*, the *Guardian* and *Observer*. I've also indulged (at times been submerged) in the copious reading of an unhealthy number of biographies and memoirs written by or about directors, producers, cameramen and stars. These sources, though not necessarily the eventual outcome of some anecdotes following careful fact-checking, can be found in an extensive bibliography. All film dates refer to the year that the film was released originally in the UK.

Though often as trivial, these real-life yarns of 'Love and Pain and the Whole Damn Thing' – to borrow the useful title of an otherwise moderate 1972 film with Maggie Smith – not to mention frequent helpings of Death, purport to be rather more substantial than just a catalogue of the so-called 'bloopers' and continuity errors that seem regularly to pepper every movie production.

But how many of these stories are actually true, or how many are simply perpetuating well-trodden myths? I offer a pair of world-weary quotes to cover my potential embarrassment. The veteran actor Boris Karloff was being interviewed on the British set of his latest film, *Corridors of Blood* (1958), when he offered this piece of advice to a callow young writer: 'Wait until I'm dead. . . then make it up!' And from John Ford's *The Man Who Shot Liberty Valance* (1962), comes this invaluable piece of advice: 'When truth becomes legend, print the legend.'

My very special thanks go to Anwar Brett and Stephanie Billen for help often above and beyond. Also to Dora Dobson, Peter Duffell, Guy East, Ben Falk, Alan Frank, Philip French, Marianne Gray, David Hall, Peter Hannan, Jamie Harcourt, Iain Johnstone, Mark Kermode, Mike Molloy, Ronald Neame, Michael Pickwoad, Ben Robinson, Mark Shivas, Ian Soutar, Richard Tedham, Adrian Turner, Ivan Waterman and David Young for their extra-special recall.

Finally, I'd like to thank my long-suffering agent, Jane Judd, as well as Jeremy Robson and his editorial team at Robson Books for suggesting *Cinema's Strangest Moments* and seeing it through to completion.

Little Marlow 2003

BEFORE 1920

TRAIN OF EVENTS
A TRAIN ARRIVING AT A STATION (1895)

The arrival of cinema could not have been more dramatic. Indeed some would say that it also represented the birth of the horror film.

When the Lumière Brothers opened the first movie theatre on 28 December 1895, in the basement of a Paris café, there were several short films on the bill, but the one that caused the biggest stir featured a simple scene of a train arriving from Marseilles and pulling into the platform at La Ciotat station in Provence.

Recorded by the brothers during their family holiday in July the same year, the innocent-sounding footage caused a sensation with audience members ducking behind their seats, convinced that the engine was about to run them over. For the price of one franc each, the Parisians had in effect witnessed the first screen 'monster'.

It is interesting to note that the success of this short prompted a number of spin-offs, including 'Phantom Rides', whereby audiences sat in a mock railway carriage surrounded by a screen that displayed moving scenery recorded by a camera that had been mounted on the front of a real train.

Early movies featuring trains included *A Kiss in the Tunnel* (1900), *La Tunnel Sous La Manche* (1907) and the seminal picture *The Great Train Robbery* (1903), which prompted D W Griffith, excited by the new medium, to make his version of the story, *The Lonedale Operator* (1911).

The film industry would continue to exploit the dramatic value of trains with the scene of a fair maid tied to a rail track becoming a cliché of silent cinema. An exciting 'train' of events had indeed been set in motion by a film that would scarcely raise an eyebrow if shown in cinemas today.

FOUR-LEGGED FRIEND

RESCUED BY ROVER (1905)

Here's the film – all 425 feet of it (that's approximately seven minutes) – that probably first established another favourite screen cliché, 'Never act with children or animals.'

There's both in the pioneering British filmmaker Cecil Hepworth's popular short which originally cost under £8 to make and sold some four hundred prints.

Hepworth, who as early as 1897 had written *Animated Photography, or the ABC of the Cinematograph*, told the story of a kidnapped child rescued by a wily pooch.

Often credited as the UK's first major fiction film, it was, at the same time, probably the definitive 'home movie'. Hepworth's wife, who wrote the story, played the mother, his eight-month-old baby daughter was the heroine and his dog, Blair, was the canine hero. With no titles, the tale was simply told by means of authentic visual flair.

SHOT DOWN UNDER

THE STORY OF THE KELLY GANG (1906)

Generally considered to be the world's first commercial feature film – and promoted on its release in the UK as 'the longest film ever made' – this Australian-made flicker followed the last days of the local antihero Ned Kelly.

At a time when a usual evening's programme consisted of one-reel shorts, *The Kelly Gang* comprised no fewer than four reels running to more than forty minutes.

The full print no longer exists – some nine minutes only of the footage survives – but it seems to have been an ambitious production that was able to persuade the museum in Victoria to lend it the actual armour worn by Kelly during his exploits a quarter-century before.

It was filmed on location in Victoria over six months, and the cast included Elizabeth Veitch, Ollie Wilson and Frank Mills. Costing only £450, the film went on to make a handsome profit, and helped establish Australia – temporarily at least – as a base for major film production.

The latest Aussie-produced version of the story, this time round costing megadollars and with Heath Ledger as the wily bushranger, arrived in 2003. And, as also the current production base for the *Star Wars* and *Matrix* sequels, Australia is firmly back at the cutting edge of global filmmaking.

HOORAY FOR HOLLYWOOD

THE SQUAW MAN (1913)

Modern Hollywood – and all that it entails – was born the year Cecil B DeMille travelled west to make his pioneering western based on the play by Edwin Milton Royle.

Until that time the film industry had largely been based on the East Coast, where the old money and infrastructure was, but DeMille's vision and the success of his film inspired a mass migration to a quiet LA suburb that would soon become the beating heart of the American film industry.

The Squaw Man was the result of a concerted effort by DeMille, Jesse Lasky and Samuel Goldfish (later Goldwyn) to make a success in the film business after reaching a dead end in the depressed New York theatre.

Money was tight, but the prospect of shooting in the much more temperate climate on America's West Coast, with the range of scenery it offered combined with the cheaper real estate and labour costs, seemed tempting.

Dustin Farnum was signed to play the lead and New York-based Winifred Kingston was cast opposite him, but the rest of the actors were drawn locally and included Hal Roach, who would later become a great comedy director in his own right.

Stumbling through production, learning as he went, DeMille might lay claim to have made one of early cinema's first 'classics', a film enthusiastically described by *Variety* as 'a masterpiece'. More than that, he helped inspire a new generation of Americans to go west, and help found the movie capital of the world.

Hollywood itself was a vast region noted primarily for its citrus groves before this. After a prime piece of real estate was acquired by the developer Harvey H Wilcox in the 1870s, his wife Daeida named it 'Hollywood' after an estate in Illinois. Despite its name, holly is not indigenous to the area.

FACE OF THEM ALL
SIXTY YEARS A QUEEN (1913)

You're unlikely to have heard of Rolf Leslie. He was a busy British actor during the silent era who specialised in strong background character roles. He once appeared as Abraham Lincoln and also played 'The Old Man' in a dozen other films.

His finest hour has to be in this re-creation of some of the great events during Queen Victoria's long reign. However, the clearly versatile Leslie didn't get to play any of the showier roles, such as Prince Albert, the Duke of Wellington, Gladstone or even, in perhaps daring drag, Victoria herself.

No, he's credited instead with no fewer than '27 Characters', none of them specified, which not only confirmed his versatility but also earns him a place at number one in the all-time multiple-roles chart.

Starrier names such as Alec Guinness, in *Kind Hearts and Coronets* (1949), and Eddie Murphy, in *Nutty Professor II: The Klumps* (2000), who jointly tie with eight roles each, seem positively restrained by comparison.

IN HARM'S WAY
THE BIRTH OF A NATION (1915)

Although he had been directing films for only six years, the former stage actor David Wark Griffith had already built his reputation as a rising star of this bright new medium. His 1915 epic, all three hours of it, established him as one of the first truly great film directors, able to balance grand scale with intimate, impassioned storytelling.

The Birth of a Nation was based on the racy, racist play, *The Clansman*, by the Reverend Thomas Dixon, a rather partial account of the South's mistreatment at the hands of the victorious North after the American Civil War.

The tale held personal echoes for Griffith, a Southerner himself, who had grown up in Kentucky and heard stories of the war at his father's knee. Setting about the story, Griffith persuaded his favourite cameraman, Billy Bitzer, to shoot it for him, knowing that Bitzer's technical expertise, inventiveness and nerve would help to make this picture something remarkable.

Yet as trusted a collaborator as Bitzer was, Griffith was not above putting him and his assistant cameraman, Karl Brown, in harm's way for the sake of a good shot.

The risk of being trampled by horses during enormous battle scenes that had the bulky, wooden-cased, hand-cranked Pathé camera in the thick of the action was par for the course. When the bombs, fireworks and squibs went off, Bitzer, Brown and others were similarly heavily involved.

A colourful character who gloried in the name Fireworks Wilson was in charge of all these 'special effects', and he was a man whose extravagant moustache might have been his most remarkable feature were it not for the fact that he had only one arm. As he explained the intricacies of his craft to the bemused crew, a fizzing fuse ran down between his teeth as he matter-of-factly chatted away.

Holding the live explosives under his one good arm, he assured onlookers that everything was perfectly safe, and that he had never had an accident in his life.

'But the silent witness of his stump,' Karl Brown explained many years later, 'convinced me that it had not been nibbled off by mice.'

The film was credited with encouraging a revival of the Ku Klux Klan, who featured prominently in the film and used it as a recruiting tool. Despite this, it had seemingly received an official endorsement when it became the first film to be screened in the White House.

'It is like writing history with lightning,' President Woodrow Wilson said, 'and my one regret is that it is all so terribly true.' Wilson would later distance himself from the film and his remarks about it.

However, the furore surrounding this groundbreaking movie inspired Griffith to write a pamphlet entitled *The Rise and Fall of Free Speech in America* (sadly out of print today) and begin work on his next masterpiece, *Intolerance*.

THE 1920s

FUNNY BUSINESS
ROBIN HOOD (1922)

Douglas Fairbanks had just finished filming his swashbuckling adventure, whose lavish centrepiece was a fantastic castle set – believed to be the biggest ever constructed in Hollywood – when he was approached by his old friend and business partner, Charlie Chaplin.

Chaplin asked him if he could use the castle for a sequence in his next film. Bemused, Fairbanks wondered what on earth Chaplin was up to. The little comic showed him. The drawbridge was lowered and Chaplin emerged from inside the castle carrying a kitten. He put it out, then collected a bottle of milk, a newspaper and some letters and went back in with the drawbridge closing slowly behind him.

Fairbanks laughed, but refused permission.

REACH FOR THE SKY
THE WOMAN WITH FOUR FACES (1923)

Our hero (Richard Dix) is languishing in jail when his girlfriend (Betty Compson), disguised as his mother, arrives to tell him that help will come from above.

It did, literally, for, as the prisoners are later playing baseball in the yard of San Quentin, a plane flies in with a ladder, which he then climbs to freedom.

The trouble was, authorisation to shoot at the top-security jail was still on its way by car when the plane, with the cameraman on board, arrived to begin filming the hazardous scene. It was made even more hazardous when a guard began firing his rifle at the plane, thinking that it was a daringly authentic escape plan.

HANGING AROUND
SAFETY LAST (1924)

Considering he was a man famous for the death-defying stunts in his highly popular silent films, Harold Lloyd was not especially keen on heights. And yet none of his films was more popular, or famous, than his clock-hanging antics after a dizzying climb up a skyscraper.

The plot was inspired by a craze in the 1920s for such 'human fly' antics, freestyle and unassisted climbs up the sides of buildings by publicity-hungry characters – some of whom returned to the ground the fast way.

In the story, Lloyd was a small-town guy whose stories of success in the big city inspire his girl to come and visit, leading to all sorts of complications that end in his climbing the side of the department store in which he works to claim a thousand-dollar prize.

Aside from the fact that Lloyd had reportedly hidden his eyes when he saw someone scaling the side of the Brockman Building in LA, he was the man audiences believed could do it for real. But audiences did not know of their hero's disability – the loss of the thumb and forefinger on his right hand after a movie publicity stunt went disastrously wrong.

Thereafter he always wore a glove on the hand, and despite being a supremely talented athlete had to cede certain physical challenges to stuntman Harvey Parry. Even on *Safety Last*, safety was an important issue: 'He gave me every precaution that I wanted in climbing buildings and so forth,' Parry reported.

False sets were constructed on top of the high buildings, which were shot from such an angle that the one blended seamlessly with the other; yet if either Lloyd or Parry was to fall he would have a drop of only fifteen feet before hitting the safety pads.

The final tragic irony is that when the film opened someone thought a fitting publicity stunt would be to have a real 'human fly' scale a building. The poor guy made it successfully to the 32nd floor before slipping and falling to his death.

CHARIOTS OF FIRE
BEN-HUR (1925)

Some twenty years after its publication in 1880, there had been a spectacular stage version – complete with chariot race conducted on a treadmill – of General Lew Wallace's novel subtitled 'A Tale of the Christ'. A one-reel film followed in 1907.

Plans to remake *Ben-Hur* on an altogether more lavish scale would take so long to instigate that one wag joked that it might eventually win an award for being 'the Best Film of 1940, if there isn't a world war in the meantime'.

After endless false starts, including constant changes of cast and directors, the final permutation reported for duty in Italy – Ramon Novarro as Judah, Francis X Bushman as Messala, and Fred Niblo, director.

But Niblo was effectively a spectator, and an increasingly horrified one at that, as the film's two big set pieces – the sea battle and the chariot race – were directed by the action specialist B 'Breezy' Reeves Eason.

With footage already scrapped once from a disastrous earlier attempt to shoot the sea battle at Anzio, south of Rome, cameras now started turning at Livorno off the coast of northern Italy.

When the pirate vessel rammed the Roman war galley, the slave extras – many of them nonswimmers who had lied to get work –

began to panic and jumped overboard, especially when fire started spreading through the ship. Opinion seems divided as to the final casualty rate.

Then it was back to Rome and the Colosseum set for the chariot chase in which the resulting carnage – some one hundred horses believed dead – was more obvious. One of the equine fatalities occurred when Novarro's chariot crashed and Bushman's rode over the wreckage. The actor was uninjured.

Finally, in Italy, after fire tore through a property warehouse, the production relocated back to Hollywood to resume filming the chariot race. An urgent call went out for extra assistants to take charge of the huge crowds.

One was a young man from Alsace-Lorraine who had started working recently at Universal, where his mother's cousin was head of the studio. He was given a toga and a set of signals so that he could get his section of the crowd to cheer on cue.

The name of the 23-year-old was William Wyler, who, 34 years later, would win his third Oscar for directing... altogether now, *Ben Hur*.

THE MIND'S EYE

THE BATTLESHIP POTEMKIN (1925)

In film as in most other endeavours, advances are slow and painstaking. Occasionally, though, there are great leaps forward, momentous declarations of new ideas that take hold and spread their influence far wider than ever intended.

So it was with Sergei Eisenstein's classic Soviet drama. The intent of this suitably political tale of sailors who inspire a revolt against the cruelty and oppression of the tsar's rule in 1905 was simple: a celebration of the individual's heroism over the unjust cruelty of an evil regime.

So far, so familiar. Just how Eisenstein achieved many of the most harrowing sequences, shot and edited in such a way as to sustain the tension throughout a greater portion of the film's 75-minute running time, is like a masterclass in film theory.

The director used montage to spectacular effect, intercutting between scenes and sights that created a fresh image of the whole. A baby crying, a woman screaming, a Cossack's blade slashing downward – three separate sequences that, when run together, immediately imperil the innocent victim of a heinous crime.

Another pioneering Soviet director, Lev Kuleshov, was an influential figure on Eisenstein, and gave his name to the Kuleshov Effect, which creates an emotional context from otherwise unrelated scenes edited together in this way.

Ironically, it was the lack of resources at Soviet Film that led Kuleshov and his students to pay such attention to detail. At one point they simply experimented with a print of D W Griffith's *Intolerance*, arranging the scenes and shots in a different order to create a different effect each time.

Those teachings found perfect expression in Eisenstein's masterpiece, a film whose influence continues to this day in ways that are both obvious and sublime. Perhaps the most memorable sequence involves a pram trundling out of control, down the Odessa steps while all around is chaos and carnage. It has been much imitated since, notably by Brian De Palma in a station sequence Scene in *The Untouchables* (1987) and the Zucker Brothers, altogether less seriously, in the third of their *Naked Gun* films.

WHERE THE MOUTH IS
WINGS (1927)

The first ever Best Picture to receive the Cedric Gibbons-designed gold-plated statuette (yet to be nicknamed 'Oscar') was actually released two years before the inaugural Academy Awards ceremony in the Blossom Room of the Hollywood Roosevelt Hotel on 16 May 1929.

The director William A Wellman, who was a nineteen-year-old pilot in the Lafayette Flying Corps during World War One, was in a perfect position to recreate authentic-look aerial action in his silent classic, filmed on location in Texas with the US Army's full cooperation.

He also found himself doubling as a stuntman both in the air and, later, quite literally on the ground. After the extras, playing German soldiers in retreat, first balked at the prospect of being trampled by advancing American troops, Wellman had to show them the way.

THE UNKINDEST CUT
UN CHIEN ANDALOU (1928)

Perhaps the strangest scene in cinema – a close-up shot of the slicing of an eyeball – came about as a result of a surreal collaboration between two visionary Spaniards, the filmmaker Luis Buñuel and the artist Salvador Dalí.

While staying with Dalí at his house, Buñuel told him about a dream he had in which a cloud sliced the moon in half 'like a razor blade slicing through an eye'. Dalí had had his own disturbing dream and the pair decided there and then to create a revolutionary, low-budget short film using images from their subconscious minds.

Audiences were spared nothing. In the opening sequence, we see Buñuel sharpening the blade of a razor and cutting his fingernail to prove its sharpness. He leaves the room and looks at the full moon. As in the dream, a cloud moves to bisect the moon. Buñuel forces open a woman's eye, the cloud cuts across the moon and the razor slices the eye (actually a calf's eye) apart. Needlessly shocking as the scene still seems to many, it is to others the key to the whole, disjointed enterprise.

As the French film maker Jean Vigo would put it, 'Can there be any spectacle more terrible than the sight of a cloud obscuring the moon at its full? The prologue can hardly have one indifferent. It tells us that in this film we must see with a different eye. Er, all right.

LOVE ON THE RUN
THE KISS (1929)

This searing courtoom drama about adultery and murder was MGM's, and their star Greta Garbo's, last silent film.

After the first day's shooting of scenes making love to her young leading man Lew Ayres, Garbo was anything but silent. She turned to her French director, Jacques Feyder, and said, 'I wonder if you would mind introducing me to this boy – we have not met.'

Owing to some oversight, 21-year-old Ayres, three years Garbo's junior, hadn't been presented to the star before they were required to embark on their passionate affair in front of the camera. From then on, after every love scene, Garbo would look at Ayres and smile, saying, 'Have we met?'

A year later, with the posters trumpeting 'Garbo Talks!', audiences heard the reclusive star speak on screen for the first time in the title role of *Anna Christie* (1930). Those huskily delivered lines were, 'Gimme a whisky! Ginger ale on the side. And don't be stingy, baby.'

SOUNDS RIDICULOUS
HIS GLORIOUS NIGHT (1929)

The talkies were already two years old when John Gilbert, one of the silent screen's greatest heart-throbs, co-star of Garbo and Gish, was properly heard for the first time by cinema audiences in this glossy froth based on a Molnar play.

The result was, contrary to the film's title, quite inglorious, spelling the beginning of the end for the visually dashing actor who drank himself to death six years later.

According to the film historian Kevin Brownlow, early recording on sound films meant that voices tended to be a raised an octave or two. The best results generally came from booming baritones.

In the case of light tenor voices like Gilbert's, the result was something approximating a squeak – 'more Mickey Mouse than Don Juan'. Even Gilbert's most die-hard fans had to giggle, and so his romantic image was effectively blown from that moment on.

HITCH IN TIME
BLACKMAIL (1929)

Described by *The Guinness Book of Movie Facts & Feats* as 'The first feature-length talkie made in Britain' (as opposed to 'Britain's first all-talking feature', *The Clue of the New Pin*, released three months earlier), this Hitchcock thriller was also, intriguingly, the first British film to be dubbed.

An adaptation of Charles Bennett's play, which had run very successfully in the West End during 1928, Hitchcock's silent version of *Blackmail* was almost complete by the following April, starring John Longden, Donald Calthrop and Anny Ondra, a Polish-born, Czech-raised actress, as the ingénue.

What then seems to have happened is that a temporary sound stage was set up at BIP's Elstree Studios and it was suggested to Hitch that he reshoot some of the scenes with dialogue as well as record a live music score and offstage sound effects.

This was fine in theory, but the main problem was the lovely Ondra. Her thick foreign accent – no problem when she had filmed Hitchcock's silent *The Manxman* (1929) – was patently ludicrous for an English shopkeeper's daughter.

Hitch's solution was to hire 25-year-old Joan Barry, who, according to the great director, 'did the dialogue standing outside the frame, with her own microphone, while Miss Ondra pantomimed the words'.

In a sense, Ondra had the last laugh because, although she was dubbed out by Barry, the substitute voice proved far too refined ('more Royal Family then East End shop girl', said one critic) for such a down-to-earth role.

Luckily, Hitch's pioneering trickery elsewhere in the film helped to compensate for this oral, and aural, glitch.

THE 1930s

REACHING OUT
ALL QUIET ON THE WESTERN FRONT (1930)

The first great Hollywood talkie – based on the World War One veteran Erich Maria Remarque's 1929 pacifist novel – was an audacious subject, considering it was made at the height of the Depression and seen from the German point of view.

The director Lewis Milestone sought out former German army officers living in the Los Angeles area to add authenticity to the filming, especially to the training-camp scenes where they helped drill the extras. The battles, featuring some two thousand extras, were recreated on a twenty-acre ranch at Irvine, south of LA.

The final moment of the film – as young Paul (Lew Ayres) is mortally wounded as he reaches out to grasp a butterfly – had been suggested to the director by the uncredited ace cameraman, Karl Freund. It's Milestone's own hand in that memorable shot.

DRILLING DANCERS
WHOOPEE! (1930)

When Sam Goldwyn hired Busby Berkeley to direct musical sequences in this musical comedy he may not have fully realised what sort of a chance he was taking. Berkeley was, after all, neither a trained dancer nor a choreographer.

But he had enjoyed considerable success on Broadway in the late 1920s, and, as talking pictures gripped Hollywood, anyone with a successful track record in the theatre found plentiful opportunities on America's West Coast. And film at last gave him a chance to make his mark in a medium that could give full rein to his burgeoning imagination.

For the trademark Berkeley sequence – a beautifully timed kaleidoscopic routine of arms, legs, heads, props and anything else that took his fancy – enabled him to draw upon the defining experiences of his earlier life and subsequent career.

Both bore fruit in *Whoopee!*. After enlisting in the army in World War One, he trained as an aerial observer, hence his appreciation of overhead shots that captured elaborate patterns played out on huge studio soundstages. Furthermore, he was also called upon to choreograph large, trick parade-ground drills involving hundreds of soldiers.

The ranks of Sam Goldwyn's contract dancers, the Goldwyn Girls, as they were known, would benefit (or some might say suffer) from the unlikely military origins of Berkeley's screen career. He would create ever more ambitious set pieces in ever more successful musicals – *42nd Street* (1933), *Gold Diggers of 1933* (1933) and *Dames* (1934) among them.

GRAPEFRUIT STARTER
THE PUBLIC ENEMY (1931)

A piece of shameless fruit abuse was the making of the public's favourite gangster in this disconcertingly violent tale of the underworld.

Borrowing from a real-life incident in which the brutal Chicago mobster Hymie Weiss had rubbed an omelette in his whining girlfriend's face, the writers decided a grapefruit half would prove less messy but equally effective.

There are a couple of versions of how James Cagney, as the gleefully vicious Tom Powers, committed this citric assault on the hapless Mae Clarke, playing his mistress. Cagney began by throwing the grapefruit at Clarke, but it was generally agreed that this could be bettered. Cagney and the director then got in a huddle, after which they asked Clarke if they could rub the fruit in her face. The actress agreed to 'one take only'.

A less congenial version was that, after Clarke had arrived on set pleading a bad cold, she asked Cagney if he'd fake the shot. Cagney agreed and worked out a suitable angle with the cameraman.

The director would have none of it, claiming, rightly, this to be the best scene in the film. So, despite Clarke's sore nose and subsequent off screen fury, Cagney grapefruited her with proper zeal.

SIDESHOW SENSATION
FREAKS (1932)

This horror masterpiece by the director Tod Browning was notable for many reasons, the most extraordinary being the fact that it was banned in Britain for more than thirty years.

Browning had started his career in circus before moving into vaudeville and then motion pictures. By 1916 he was starring in *Intolerance* as well as serving as assistant director to D W Griffith.

A dozen years later he had forged a successful partnership with the legendary horror star Lon Chaney, and was all set to direct the great man in *Dracula* when Chaney tragically died. Bela Lugosi took on the role, and made an indelible impression as the Prince of Darkness. The year after that hit, the director tackled a grim tale based on a short story entitled 'Spurs'.

In Browning's film, a group of so-called circus sideshow freaks live in harmony together. Only when one of their number is threatened by the beautiful but manipulative trapeze artist (Olga Baclanova), in cahoots with the circus strongman, do they exact a grisly revenge.

The power of the piece comes from Browning's use of real sideshow 'freaks': midgets, Siamese twins, 'the Pinheads', folk with all manner of physical disfigurements – most memorably Randian the Living Torso – populate a film that daringly asks the audience to challenge its own conceptions of beauty and goodness.

The climactic scene is a horror classic in its own right, with this hitherto benign community setting off on a lightning-lit journey of vengeance.

Some found it be to be too much, the British censors among them, rejecting the film out of hand when it was submitted to them in July 1932.

Their reaction was the same twenty years later, despite the fact that the interim had borne witness to real-life horror on a global scale, not to mention the hundreds of horror movies deemed legitimate entertainment for British audiences.

It was only in September 1963 that the censor gave his grudging approval, allowing the submitted print to be released with an X certificate and no cuts made. There is no record of what Browning thought of this. He died the year before his finest film was passed for public viewing in the UK.

DEADLY DECISION
A FAREWELL TO ARMS (1932)

Although Ernest Hemingway would become hunting pals with its star Gary Cooper, he wasn't exactly a fan of this mangled adaptation of his World War One novel.

After taking various liberties along the way with 'Papa' Hemingway's story, the director Frank Borzage finally arrived at the climactic deathbed scene between star-crossed lovers, ambulance driver Cooper and nurse Helen Hayes.

Deciding to hedge his bets, Borzage shot two versions and then let cinema managers decide which one they wanted to show. In one, as Coop comforts the dying Hayes to the strains of a Wagner aria, she miraculously recovers. Cue bells ringing and doves swooping upward.

In the other, she doesn't.

The happy ending was the preferred pick. However, when the film was rereleased in 1948, Hayes more accurately died in Cooper's arms.

GORILLA TACTICS
KING KONG (1933)

When Fay Wray was promised 'the tallest, darkest leading man in Hollywood' for her next film, she immediately conjured up visions of Clark Gable.

She was not so much disappointed as 'appalled' after she actually read the script sent to her by co-directors Merian C Cooper and Ernest Schoedsack. When she discovered that her co-star was to be a rampaging giant gorilla, she thought it must be a practical joke.

Wearing a blonde wig to cover her normal auburn hair and nestling fearfully in an eight-foot-long giant hairy paw as she was cranked up high above the studio floor at RKO-Pathé, scream queen Wray soon discovered it was no laughing matter.

The filmmakers had, in fact, been strictly accurate about the 'darkest' bit. But Kong, cinema's favourite monster, who tears New York apart after being hijacked from remote Skull Island to the Big Apple, turned out to be merely eighteen inches high.

That was the size of the main model used for the very effective stop-frame animation sequences that climaxed dramatically on top of the Empire State Building.

Alberta-born Wray, who because of the instant success of King Kong would be stuck with the blonde image for the rest of her film career, could have been excused for looking distracted as she tussled with the mighty simian.

In the midst of her role as Ann Darrow, she was also hopping from set to set filming scenes for two other Hollywood chillers, *Doctor X* and *The Most Dangerous Game*.

Unlike her co-star who plunged to his death from New York's

highest skyscraper, Wray was, at the time of writing this book, still alive, well and aged 95.

THE LAST LAUGH
IT HAPPENED ONE NIGHT (1934)

In Hollywood's Golden Age, MGM was the studio that ruled the roost. And Louis B Mayer ruled Metro like a tsar, unafraid to punish his biggest stars if they stepped out of line. Clark Gable was one such, a hugely popular leading man who had the temerity to check himself into hospital citing exhaustion and overwork rather than take on the next picture on the studio production line.

As punishment, Mayer put him on suspension at MGM and lent him out to the comparatively tiny Columbia Studios – which tells you something of the pecking order then in Hollywood – where he was cast in a film that no one had much faith in.

The story for *It Happened One Night* was purchased for just $5,000, and was based on a magazine short story. Frank Capra, its director, was keen on it but a string of leading ladies had turned it down, Claudette Colbert accepting the role of an errant heiress only after Columbia doubled her usual salary.

Somehow the chemistry between the stars, the director and the screen worked, and the film slowly built up a big audience following. The impact of the film might be measured by the male film fans who responded to the scene in which Gable took off his shirt and revealed that he did not wear a vest. Demand for the undergarment dwindled alarmingly as a result.

But the story had one final twist, on Oscar night that year. Twelve films were nominated for Best Picture, but none could match *It Happened One Night*, which became the first of only three films to date (the others are *One Flew Over the Cuckoo's Nest* and *The Silence of the Lambs*) ever to win the Big Five – Film, Director, Screenplay, Actress and, most satisfyingly in this case, Actor for Gable.

Mayer's punishment had backfired spectacularly, as Gable returned with his reputation – and MGM salary – greatly enhanced.

A STAR IS BORN
CAPTAIN BLOOD (1935)

When Robert Donat withdrew from playing the intrepid swashbuckler – because of his recurring asthma or a contract dispute, depending which version you believe – Warner Brothers then screen-tested no fewer than 22 actors for the role.

History records that Errol Flynn snared his first major Hollywood role, but just two days into shooting he was struck down with malaria, which had plagued him ever since his globetrotting days in New Guinea.

Told that filming would have to be halted if he left for the day, Flynn downed a bottle of brandy and carried on working. That evening he was summoned to see the studio boss Jack Warner, who accused him of being drunk on set.

Flynn exploded with anger and told him he'd quit the film straightaway if he wasn't given an immediate pay rise. Warner, who knew from the earliest buzz in filming that he had a star in the ascendant, immediately increased Flynn's weekly stipend from $150 to $750.

WHAT A DUMB PUCK
A MIDSUMMER NIGHT'S DREAM (1935)

Kids will be kids, so you can't really blame fourteen-year-old Mickey Rooney for wanting to let off some steam while he was playing Puck in Warner Brothers' lavish all-star (James Cagney, Olivia de Havilland, Dick Powell) screen version of the Bard's jolliest play, filmed entirely on indoor studio sets.

Yes, he did have a reputation for being accident-prone, so, before shooting started, Rooney, who'd been a film star since the age of six, was warned not to play football or baseball or do any high diving for fear of injury.

However, his contract said nothing about playing in the snow so, about a third of the way into filming, he persuaded his mother to take him to a snowy California resort, where he and his friends hired a large toboggan.

Moments later, they piled into a large Jeffery pine and Rooney, in the front, found himself flat on his back in the snow with his leg twisted up round his chin. He grabbed it angrily and yanked it back down again. He'd broken his femur, but his instant reaction, before he passed out with the pain, managed at least to re-set the break. With his leg in a big temporary splint he returned rather shamefaced to the studio to be greeted by an apoplectic Jack Warner, who threatened to break his other leg.

Although they tried to shoot round him as much as possible, Rooney, leg-cast hopefully hidden, still had some crucial scenes. In order to move through the forest, he was pushed on a tricycle by hidden stagehands.

And for one speech he had to raise and then drop his injured leg through a hole cut in the platform while doing knee bends with his good leg. What a young trouper!

THE VALLEY OF DEATH

THE CHARGE OF THE LIGHT BRIGADE (1936)

The climactic charge in this rather fanciful re-creation of a foolishly heroic moment during the Crimean War was filmed in the San Fernando Valley.

Sadly, certainly for many of the horses involved in the production, it did indeed prove to be an authentic Valley of Death thanks to the 'Running W' method of felling galloping quadrupeds.

It consisted of attaching trip wires to all four legs and the wires were then connected to wooden posts hammered into the ground below the camera line. Once a horse had run its appointed distance, the wire would go taut and bring it down. The result here was that during the sequence more than fifty horses were badly injured, many of them having to be destroyed.

After a vigorous campaign by the American Society for the Prevention of Cruelty to Animals, the American Humane Association eventually stepped in and the 'Running W' was outlawed.

TAKING THE HELM
MARY OF SCOTLAND (1936)

Both fiercely single-minded individuals, it's perhaps not surprising that Katharine Hepburn and John Ford worked together only once, although they would remain life-long friends (and, it's rumoured, sometime lovers). The Bryn Mawr-educated actress and the hard-drinking Irish director, whom she called 'Sean' (his birthname), collaborated at times explosively on this notional slice of English history.

Matters came to head when they were shooting a crucial scene between Mary and her lover, later her husband, Bothwell (Fredric March). Ford thought there was far too much dialogue and that it slowed everything down, so he suggested to Hepburn that they drop it altogether. The actress was dumbfounded, claiming it was the best scene in the film. With that, he said, 'Well, if you like it so much, why don't you shoot it?' and stomped off the set.

Either he was trying to call her bluff or else genuinely thought she was up to directing it. Whatever the real reason, Hepburn asked the cameraman Joe August if he was prepared to stick around. When both he and co-star March agreed, she directed for the one and only time in her career.

INDIAN LOVE CALL
THE PLAINSMAN (1936)

The tyrannical director Cecil B DeMille didn't think much of the young Irish-Mexican actor playing a Cheyenne warrior in his sprawling western. The twenty-year-old Anthony Quinn, who had had one previous walk-on film role, was attempting to sing an Indian song and DeMille told his star Gary Cooper, 'I don't think the kid's going to work out.'

Coop, impressed with what he thought were Quinn's authentic Native American looks, urged DeMille to give the 'kid' another chance. A year later, Quinn married the director's daughter, Katherine.

STAR-CROSSED OLDIES
ROMEO AND JULIET (1936)

First, you must try to erase from your mind's eye the very idea of star-crossed teenagers – Leonardo DiCaprio and Claire Danes, Leonard Whiting and Olivia Hussey, for example – as etched in more recent versions of the much-filmed play. In comparison this was a positively geriatric take on the romantic tragedy. Or, as Joan Crawford was reported to have said after watching Leslie Howard, 43, and Norma Shearer, 32-year-old mother-of-two, 'Christ, I couldn't wait for those two old turkeys to die...'

To be fair, Howard was at first very wary of accepting the role because of the age question, something that had finally persuaded first-choice Brian Aherne, ten years Howard's junior, to steer clear. After that, it seemed the middle-aged die was cast. John Barrymore (Mercutio) was 54 and Basil Rathbone (Tybalt), 44. At 73, C Aubrey Smith, as Lord Capulet, was just old.

Long sunk into alcoholism, Barrymore seemed much older than his years. He was often late, regularly forgetful of his lines and had a tendency to insert the odd foul-mouthed addition to the original text. They even contemplated replacing him with William Powell, 44, but Barrymore's old friend remained loyal.

The fated couple must have been feeling positively ancient when they finally got the play's most famous duologue – the balcony scene – in the can. It took five weeks to film and the balcony itself had to be reinforced during shooting when it began to crack under the actors' weight.

EPIC THAT NEVER WAS
I, CLAUDIUS (1937)

Forty years before the BBC's award-winning twelve-part drama based on Robert Graves's novels *I, Claudius* and *Claudius the God* was the promise of a marvellous film version of the same sprawling Roman saga. But as Bill Duncalf's fascinating mid-sixties TV documentary would title it, this was to be *The Epic That Never Was*.

As with almost every significant British movie of the period, this story also begins and ends with Alexander Korda and his filmmaking empire at Denham Studios.

Baldly, the film, directed by Joscf von Sternberg, was a month and a day into shooting when co-star Merle Oberon, who was playing mischievous Messalina to Charles Laughton's stammering cripple Claudius, was involved in a car crash on her way to a fitting. Within hours of the accident, producer Korda suspended the production indefinitely.

A careful trawl of the various, indeed varying, accounts of those far-off events – from von Sternberg's own memoir to biographies of Laughton and Korda – suggests an altogether more tangled tale behind the decision so summarily to shelve a stillborn masterpiece.

Korda had already directed the temperamental Laughton twice (in *The Private Life of Henry VIII* and *Rembrandt*) but couldn't face a third heavyweight bout. However, he knew the role was tailor-made for Laughton, just as the film would also be the perfect 'vehicle' for Oberon (who'd become the second Mrs Korda in 1939).

So he hired von Sternberg, he of the jodhpurs, riding boots and occasional turban, to direct because he felt that the autocratic Austrian would take no nonsense from Laughton. Another more practical reason might have been that he still owed Marlene Dietrich the final part of her salary on another Korda production, *Knight Without Armour*, and she said she'd waive the money if he hired her mentor.

If Laughton was pleased to see von Sternberg at the helm – and he certainly considered the filmmaker an 'artist' – that didn't seem to be reflected in his endless agonising over the right way to play the role. Everything from the limp to the voice seemed to be part of some daily torture as Laughton visibly struggled with the performance to the increasing frustration of both director and producer.

It seems that the car accident was the final straw and certainly the insurance payout helped the perpetually cash-strapped Korda recover some much-needed funds.

The evidence of just what might have been can be glimpsed in some of the 25 minutes of surviving footage on show in Duncalf's superbly mounted 1965 documentary. As well as Oberon, there was 35-year-old Flora Robson playing the octogenarian empress Livia, Emlyn Williams as mad Caligula, John Clements as Messalina's lover, and Robert Newton as Cassius.

Above all, there was Laughton himself who, although he might, as some reports suggest, have driven von Sternberg into psychiatric care, was clearly creating something exceptional.

As his biographer Simon Callow puts it, 'We can see that Laughton was struggling to give life to a performance of unprecedentedly searing pathos, to show a man mocked and spurned though sensitive, gentle and intelligent; a simple enough character who, by the intensity of his inner feeling, he was transfiguring into a paradigm of pain, a Dostoevskian creation, almost too painful to watch.'

HI HO, HI HO!
SNOW WHITE AND THE SEVEN DWARFS (1937)

Difficult to imagine it now, but this timeless cartoon classic – the first-ever full-length animated feature film – was once derided as 'Disney's Folly'. Many doubted that Walt could pull off such an unprecedented technical and artistic challenge and, when it looked as though the film was going to cost around six times its estimated budget, even the patience of his bank finally began to run out. Disney was staring into the abyss of financial ruin.

Joseph Rosenberg, who handled the studio accounts at the Bank of America, questioned why he should keep advancing cash for this celluloid money pit.

In a last desperate effort to keep the film going, Walt and his brother Roy offered to screen a showreel of available footage for Rosenberg who watched their efforts in stony silence. Walt feared the worst, until the banker was back in his car and about to drive off. 'That thing,' he said, 'is going to make you a hatful of money.'

PHOTO FINISH
WINGS OF THE MORNING (1937)

Never count your race horses...Britain's first Technicolor film involved a gypsy horse winning the Derby. They used a genuine racehorse in the film for the scenes leading up to the big race with real-life champion jockey Steve Donoghue aboard riding for all his worth.

All they had to do then was show the real Derby winner as it passed the winning post and the audience would assume it was the film horse.

Trouble was, the film horse was a chestnut and for the first time in, well, donkey's years, a grey won the classic. In the end, they had to fake it with close-ups.

39

CREATING A STORM
THE HURRICANE (1937)

Charlie Locher was an aspiring young actor when, legend has it, someone from the Goldwyn Studio spotted the tall, athletic-looking 22-year-old working at a nearby garage and thought he had star potential.

Charles H Locher had done bit parts in some ten films working as Locher, Charles Loucher and even Lloyd Crane. With titles like *Women Must Dress*, *Charlie Chan In Shanghai* and *The Amazing Exploits of the Clutching Hand*, they were hardly A-list assignments.

But suddenly he was being paraded before Goldwyn and the director John Ford for the role of hunky Terangi, a courageous South Sea islander whose plans to marry a Tahitian princess are interrupted, first by cruel fate and then by the climactic hurricane of the title.

Based on the best-selling book by Charles Nordhoff and James Norman Hall, who had also written *Mutiny on the Bounty*, it was to be the studio's most expensive and prestigious production of that year.

According to Goldwyn's official biographer, A Scott Berg, who spent eight years researching his project with unrestricted access to the mogul's archives, Ford took one look at Charlie and said, 'I can take that boy and make something of him.'

Starring alongside established names like Raymond Massey, C Aubrey Smith, Mary Astor, John Carradine, Thomas Mitchell and lovely young Dorothy Lamour, as his bride-to-be, Locher started work on the lavish film that culminated in $250,000 worth of spectacular set-destroying special effects on the back lot at United Artists.

But he was no longer called Locher. The studio had renamed him Jon Hall, using his middle name. But hold on, wasn't the name of one of the original authors Hall, too? Surely just coincidence?

What Berg's otherwise meticulously researched tome doesn't tell us is that Charles Hall Locher was actually the writer's nephew and, even more serendipitously, the real-life son of a Tahitian princess. His cousin was the great cinematographer

Conrad L Hall, who in 2003 would posthumously win his third Oscar, for *Road To Perdition*.

Sadly, Jon Hall, too, wouldn't live to enjoy his cousin's acclaimed hat-trick. After *The Hurricane*, he appeared in a series of increasingly forgettable easterns and westerns, married three times and even directed a horror called *Beach Girls Vs The Monster*.

In 1979, suffering from bladder cancer, he committed suicide by shooting himself in the head.

A CLOSE MISS
ANGELS WITH DIRTY FACES (1938)

If you live by the machine gun... Playing cocky Rocky Sutton who ends up turning yellow – or does he? – on Death Row, James Cagney narrowly escaped a real bullet in the head.

The director Michael Curtiz wanted Cagney to stand at an open window raking bullets at the street below. Fire would be returned, crossing the right side of the window, just missing him. Remember, these were still the days before special-effect exploding caps.

Cagney, who had survived a near miss during a piece of machine-gunnery in *The Public Enemy*, objected, telling Curtiz they could superimpose the shots later, and walked away from the scene.

So they carried on without him. One of the bullets proceeded to hit the window's steel border and was deflected onto the wall where Cagney's head would have been.

Interestingly, Cagney based one of his most memorable roles on two real-life characters from the tough Yorkville district of New York in which he gew up. One was a local pimp whose catchphrase was 'Whadda ya hear? Whaddya say?'; the other, a childhood friend called Peter Hessling, who, like Rocky, ended up in the electric chair at Sing Sing.

PULLING RANK
CLIMBING HIGH (1939)

Jessie Matthews, Britain's favourite singing-and-dancing star of the period, was shooting this breezy musical at Pinewood Studios when she suddenly noticed a tall dark man standing at the back of the set watching the filming. Like many other stars, she tended to dislike unidentified visitors coming to the set during shooting, so she mentioned it to the director, who then asked his assistant to tell the stranger to go away.

The 'gofer' asked the man if there was anything he wanted. 'No,' he replied pleasantly, 'nothing in particular.' And, with that, he walked away without another word.

'Did you ask his name?' said the director. 'Yes,' replied the assistant, 'I believe he said it was Rank.' That's J Arthur Rank, who just happened to own Pinewood.

COSTUME DRAMAS
THE FOUR FEATHERS (1939)

Shooting on location in Sudan, the production – the third remake of A E W Mason's ripping yarn – employed hundreds of locals for the spectacular battle sequences, a fact that gave the already agitated director Zoltan Korda even more headaches.

Recreating the climactic Battle of Omdurman, he instructed the extras to charge towards the camera and then die on cue, as if shot by British rifles. They all did as requested, except for one old man who resolutely refused to fall down dead.

Slowly, Korda's blood pressure rose, as take followed take and the old man stayed standing. Eventually, he asked him, through interpreters, why he would not die. The old man explained that he fought in the original Battle of Omdurman forty years earlier and having survived that was damned if he would 'die' at the hands of the British now.

Accuracy was the byword of the production – but not necessarily, it seems, at the cost of visual spectacle. For example, there's a particularly splendid ball scene for officers of the regiment. Military advisers, on hand to check that every detail of dress was correct, sent co-stars Ralph Richardson and John Clements to Savile Row to be properly kitted out.

'But what is this blue uniform?' producer Alexander Korda spluttered when the sequence was about to be shot. It was absolutely accurate, he was assured, since the ball was taking place in a private house and not the mess. 'But this is Technicolor!' barked Korda, with some finality, so the officers had to get changed into more camera-friendly red uniforms instead.

The wonderfully colourful Sudan battle footage, filmed by Jack Cardiff and Osmond Borrodaile, would, incidentally, get several more leases of reel life: in a yet another remake, *Storm Over the Nile* (1955), once again directed by Zoltan Korda, as well as unrelated films like *Zarak* (1956), *Master of the World* (1961) and *East of Sudan* (1964).

SINGING LESSON
THE ICE FOLLIES OF 1939 (1939)

Not even the introduction of a climactic Technicolor sequence after an hour and a half of monochrome could do much for a dreary attempt to spice up MGM's usually surefire musical format.

The fans of the co-star Joan Crawford, who were led to believe that they'd be enjoying their favourite Hollywood actress singing half a dozen songs in the film, discovered that four of those tunes were eliminated before release while the other two were dubbed by a professional singer.

The temperamental Ms Crawford put it about that Jeanette MacDonald, the studio's more famous diva, had pressured the studio bosses into dropping her contribution for fear of competition.

ASHES TO ASHES
GONE WITH THE WIND (1939)

There are enough 'strange but true' stories about this American Civil War saga to fill a book – many already have – so the focus here is essentially on the night of 10 December 1938 – the night the producer David O Selznick decided that Atlanta would go up in flames.

Though the money and crew were in place, the cast, apart from Clark Gable as Rhett Butler, weren't yet fully finalised – least of all the key role of Scarlett O'Hara – but Selznick felt he needed a big publicity coup to justify all the column inches already expended on an as-yet theoretical movie epic.

Overseen by George Cukor, the first of some six directors to come and go from (and, on occasion, return to) the project, the Burning of Atlanta got under way at 8.20 p.m. at Selznick (Pathé) Studio, the old RKO lot.

The fire would not only ignite one of the most successful and award-laden films in history, but would also reduce to ashes the last remnants of some old movies, such as pieces of first-century Jerusalem built for DeMille's *The King of Kings* (1927), the high wall that defended the natives of Skull Island in *King Kong* (1933) and the ruins of *The Garden of Allah* (1936).

Fitted with false fronts, carefully dressed and photographed in the dark, old Hollywood, instead of being bulldozed, was cleverly recycled to aid the big blaze, which got Selznick's magnum opus – which wasn't due to begin principal photography for another month and a half – off to the best possible start.

But the excitement of that first night wasn't quite over yet. As the producer gazed excitedly on the inferno, his agent brother Myron came up behind him, touched Selznick's arm and said, 'David, I'd like you to meet Scarlett O'Hara.'

Selznick said later, 'When my brother introduced her [Vivien Leigh] to me, the dying flames were lighting up her face. I took one look and knew she was right – at least right as far as her appearance went, and right as far as my conception of how Scarlett O'Hara looked. I'll never recover from that first look.'

A LITTLE HOARSE
MR SMITH GOES TO WASHINGTON (1939)

James Stewart was understandably apprehensive as the time approached for him to film a 23-hour filibuster speech in the US Senate, the climax of Frank Capra's comedy-drama classic.

Playing a naïve young senator who discovers corruption in high places, Stewart became even more concerned when Capra made it clear he didn't feel the actor was achieving a necessary hoarseness during the vocal marathon.

So Stewart sought out a doctor who he hoped might give him something to resemble, albeit temporarily, a sore throat. The prescription was regular doses of dichloride of mercury which induced inflammation and a noticeable rasp. Filming the speech took three weeks.

SETTLING SCORES
THE OLD MAID (1939)

The firing of Humphrey Bogart after just four days into his unlikely role as a romantic hero barely registered on the Richter scale compared with the positively seismic intensity of the on- and off-screen clashes between the two leading ladies.

Bette Davis and Miriam Hopkins had, as they say, 'a history'. Their rivalry went back to their time together in the theatre, when insecure Hopkins was the star and newcomer Davis, six years her junior, was the bright ingénue. Hopkins had treated her badly then, and now that had been fuelled into something more like bitter resentment, especially as Davis had just won a Best Actress Oscar for *Jezebel*, a role that Hopkins coveted, having played it on the stage.

In her film assignment straight after *Jezebel*, Davis was rumoured to have had a brief affair with the director who just happened to be Hopkins's husband. And, to add yet more frisson, bisexual Hopkins probably fancied Davis, which made the adultery even harder to take.

Now they were cast together as cousins in a shamelessly soapy saga set against the background of the Civil War in America's Deep South.

On the first day of shooting, Hopkins arrived on set wearing one of Davis's costumes from *Jezebel*, and then proceeded to do everything she could to undermine her during filming.

This included refusing to make eye-to-eye contact and, during one scene on a couch, moving further and further back so that Davis had to face away from the camera in order to look at her. And, just when it seemed Davis had completed a particularly tough scene, Hopkins would apologise and ask for a retake, claiming a button had popped or one of her hairpins had fallen out.

As for Davis, she vented her resulting frustration on everyone but Hopkins, hoping simply to act her off the screen. The verdict of audiences and critics suggests that she succeeded triumphantly.

MAL DE MER
RULERS OF THE SEA (1939)

Frank Lloyd, director of that salty epic *Mutiny on the Bounty* (1935), needed a British leading lady for his latest ocean-going tale – about the first steamship crossing of the Atlantic. He found her in Margaret Lockwood, who was briefly, and unhappily, in Hollywood playing second banana to ten-year-old Shirley Temple in *Susannah of the Mounties*.

Homesick for England, Lockwood was persuaded to stay on but warned Lloyd that she was 'the world's worst sailor'. Homesickness was soon overtaken by something altogether more physically violent as she filmed her shipboard scenes off the coast of California.

In fact she became so ill that her footage had to be scrapped altogether and then reshot later against back projection.

MAKING FEELGOOD
WUTHERING HEIGHTS (1939)

After all its well-documented casting problems, illness and injury, rivalries and temperament, the completed Hollywood version of Emily Brontë's classic – boasting imported Yorkshire heather on 450 acres of recreated Californian 'moors' – was finally sneak-previewed to a suburban audience.

They hated it, especially the way the film ended with the camera lingering on Cathy's (Merle Oberon) dead body, with a distraught Heathcliff (Laurence Olivier) at her bedside. They were also confused by the story's various twists and turns.

How to make resolutely downbeat into 'feelgood'? After rehiring Flora Robson to add a helpful narration, the producer Sam Goldwyn suggested helpfully that perhaps the star-crossed couple could be shown reunited in heaven.

The director William Wyler was horrified and refused to have anything to do with it. With the two stars having departed Los Angeles, Goldwyn hired the director H C Potter to film star doubles from behind walking hand in hand to heaven. The shot was superimposed over a suitably imposing Yorkshire crag.

This time round, American audiences loved it. Goldwyn would say later that he 'made' *Wuthering Heights* while Wyler merely 'directed' it.

RAINBOW ENDS

THE WIZARD OF OZ (1939)

L Frank Baum Jr's 1900 bestseller had been filmed twice before, as a one-reeler in 1910 and as a seventy-minute feature in 1925, with a cast including Oliver Hardy as the Tin Man.

In February 1938, MGM announced its new musical version with fifteen-year-old Judy Garland as Dorothy, but that was only after attempts to get 20th Century-Fox to lend out their resident moppet Shirley Temple had failed.

Like *Gone with the Wind*, the subsequent production – at 23 weeks, the longest at that point in Metro's history – proved to be another case study in Strange But True.

Buddy Ebsen (later to become best known as patriarch of the rustic Clampett clan in TV's *The Beverly Hillbillies*) quit as the Tin Man after two weeks' shooting because the inhalation of his make-up caused lung problems.

Margaret Hamilton, playing the Wicked Witch of the West, literally caught fire and was badly burned in an effects accident during her spectacular departure from Munchkinland. Her stunt double Betty Danko did the broomstick ride, which also ended in near disaster when the broomstick pipe exploded.

Although Victor Fleming had sole credit, three other directors were also involved in the production – Richard Thorpe, George

Cukor and finally, after Fleming had gone to take over a similarly director-plagued *Gone with the Wind*, King Vidor. Vidor was responsible for the black-and-white Kansas sequences that open and close the film.

To name but a few.

But no entry about this much-loved musical can be complete without mention of its most enduring item – Harburg/Arlen's 'Over the Rainbow', sung by Garland.

In view of all the film's other comings and goings it probably comes as no surprise to discover that the Oscar-winning song very nearly didn't make it to the final cut because the film was felt to be too long.

THE 1940s

FAST TALKING
HIS GIRL FRIDAY (1940)

When the director Howard Hawks set about remaking Charles MacArthur and Ben Hecht's classic play, *The Front Page*, he caused a near scandal when he changed the sex of ace reporter Hildy Johnson from male to female. In all previous stage versions, as well as the 1930 film adaptation, the story had – and has in all versions since, until a new National Theatre production in 2003 – been a wisecracking tale of a battle of wills between a hard-bitten editor and his top male reporter.

Hawks had always admired MacArthur and Hecht's writing, and during a read-through of the play one night he invited a female party guest to read the Hildy Johnson role, instantly realising he had struck on something. Hecht, for one, was amenable to the change. When Hawks called him for advice, Hecht explained that he was stuck on a storyline, and if Hawks would help him he would gladly assist the director.

Casting Cary Grant as Walter Burns, editor of *The Morning Post*, Hawks handed the role of Walter's top reporter – and ex-wife – to Rosalind Russell. That was good. What made the film special was the ratatat delivery of some blisteringly funny dialogue.

'If you ever listen to some people talking,' Hawks said, 'especially in any scene of any excitement, they all talk at the same time. All it needs is a little extra work on the dialogue ... so they can overlap it. It gives you a sense of speed that actually doesn't exist.'

Running the completed film for real newspaper reporters who had expressed horror that a much-loved classic had been tampered with in this way, Hawks also showed them the original *Front Page* movie again. He got the reaction he wanted. 'My God,' they said, 'your picture is so much faster.'

PLAYING ADOLF
NIGHT TRAIN TO MUNICH (1940)

Generally credited – or in this particular case uncredited – with portraying Hitler on screen for the first time, certainly in a non-comic way, was the British character actor Billy Russell in Carol Reed's wartime thriller.

Russell, who'd appeared a couple of years earlier in Reed's *Penny Paradise*, was better known as a musical-hall star but had become increasingly noted for his likeness to the Führer.

His turn as Hitler proved to be a one-off, unlike Illinois-born Bobby Watson, who, born a year before Adolf, played him in no fewer than seven films, including *The Nazty Nuisance* (1943), *The Hitler Gang* (1944), *The Miracle of Morgan's Creek* (1944) and *The Story of Mankind* (1957).

TAKING THE BLAME
TWENTY-ONE DAYS (1940)

Readers of *The Spectator* in January 1940 might have been rather surprised to see their film critic Graham Greene's much-admired weekly column end with this humiliating *mea culpa*: 'Let one guilty man, at any rate, stand in the dock, swearing never, never to do it again.'

Greene, who supplemented his meagre income from writing novels such as *The Man Within*, *Stamboul Train* and *A Gun For Sale* with screenwriting and film reviewing, was confessing his participation in an adaptation of John Galsworthy's short story, 'The First and the Last'. It co-starred Laurence Olivier and Vivien Leigh as young lovers – during filming they were in the first flush of their own scandalous real-life love affair – caught up in an absurdly melodramatic tale of murder, blackmail and legal corruption.

'For the rather dubious merits of the original ["peculiarly unsuited for film adaptation", he had admitted earlier in the review] the adaptors [he and director Basil Dean] have substituted incredible coincidences and banal situations. Slow, wordy and unbearably sentimental...' Such self-flagellation from a critic must surely remain unsurpassed.

Then Greene further tantalised his readers with this rather cryptic observation: 'I wish I could tell the extraordinary story that lies behind this shelved and resurrected picture, a story involving a theme song, and a bottle of whisky, and camels in Wales...'

Filmed in 1937, *Twenty-One Days*, a Korda production, was eventually released more than two years later in the wake of Leigh's worldwide success in *Gone with the Wind*. Emboldened by drink – which probably accounts for the 'bottle of whisky' reference – Greene and Dean composed a song to accompany a cheery Southend location sequence. In the event it wasn't used.

And those camels? That had to do with the fact that the original producer was taken off the film because he had to arrange the delivery of said mammals to a location in the Welsh hills near Harlech for another Korda production, *The Drum*, actually set in and around India's turbulent North-West Frontier.

APING ADOLF
THE GREAT DICTATOR (1940)

It was Alexander Korda who, in 1937, first suggested to Charlie Chaplin that he should do a story about Hitler based on mistaken identity; and, because Hitler had the same moustache as the little tramp, Chaplin could play both characters.

Did Korda – or, for that matter, Chaplin – know that Hitler and Chaplin had been born within a week of each other in 1889? Chaplin didn't think much more about the film idea until Hitler was almost on the last lap to world war.

For his first-all sound film, Chaplin played the dual roles of gibberish-spouting Adenoid Hynkel, dictator of Tomania, and a nameless Jewish barber.

Warned on both sides of the Atlantic about the suitability of such an enterprise at a time when both Britain and America were still somewhat equivocal about Hitler and his long-term threat, Chaplin firmly maintained that the German leader should be laughed at. He later admitted he would never have gone ahead (Britain would declare war on Germany after filming began) had he known at the time about the burgeoning Holocaust.

As well as drawing attention to the coincidence of their birth dates and moustaches, a recent television documentary called *The Tramp and the Dictator* also pointed up other strange parallels between the two men, among them that Hitler actually was a tramp a few years before Chaplin became one professionally.

The programme also provided anecdotal evidence that Hitler had watched *The Great Dictator* not once but twice.

AN UNEASY PEACE
49TH PARALLEL (1941)

When in a Canadian Hutterite camp... The Austrian actress Elizabeth Bergner had been hired to provide some token female relief in this otherwise mostly macho wartime drama of five stranded U-boat men trying to escape across the border into the US (America wasn't in the war at this point).

She was playing a Hutterite, one of a strict rural community of Lutherans. After marriage, the men never shave and the women all wear simple black dresses with white spots and are forbidden luxuries such as makeup.

Filming on overseas location in one of their camps, the British crew had to tread carefully so as not to offend their hosts. However, the exceedingly grand Bergner, an Oscar winner and also portrayer of *Catherine the Great*, probably felt she wasn't subject to such strictures.

One day she was sitting on the steps of the unit caravan, dressed in costume, cigarette in her mouth, painting her fingernails red, when a Hutterite woman happened to pass. Incensed by this spectacle, she snatched the cigarette, trampled it on the ground and smacked the actress's face.

Pandemonium ensued as the Hutterites vied with Bergner to appear the more outraged. Once peace was haltingly restored, Bergner finished her role and then disappeared.

Summoned to complete her scenes back in England, she refused so Glynis Johns was given the role, which was then filmed entirely in the studio using back-projection.

TELLING THE TRUTH
A YANK IN THE RAF (1941)

This cheerful flagwaver – in truth a 'vehicle' for two glamorous co-stars, Tyrone Power and Hollywood's most famous pair of legs, Betty Grable – sadly had its dark side. Although it was principally filmed in California with various members of the local Raj – such as Reginald Gardiner, John Sutton and Donald Stuart – roped in for their pukka accents, the studio, 20th-Century Fox, wanted to get some authentic dog-fighting Spitfire footage.

A British-based camera crew were hired and, with suitable permissions granted, began to get some fighter action even if their borrowed planes could be requisitioned at any time for the real thing.

Problems loomed when Hollywood decreed it needed film of the fighters lined up in V formation – something the Brits knew, but Fox clearly didn't, would simply not happen in wartime for security reasons.

That didn't faze the powers-that-be, and during a sequence in which cameraman Otto Kanturek and his crew were shooting ten

Spits in a tight V, one of the fighters accidentally sliced through the tail of the camera plane, an Anson. The fighter pilot bailed out safely while Kanturek and his entire crew were killed instantly.

Ronald Neame, who'd been the chief cameraman on the project until he had to quit fortuitously for another assignment – ironically, *One of Our Aircraft is Missing* – recently revealed how Fox tried to cover up the truth of the accident.

In a press release issued by the studio, it hyped how Kanturek had been filming the Spitfires when they ran into a 'convoy of German fighters', one of which 'bore down on the tail of Kanturek's plane, which was unarmed, and riddled it with machine-gun fire. The ship crashed to earth, killing Kanturek [along with his assistant], and the pilot...'

Neame claims very little of the UK-shot footage was included in the final film, which, strange to relate, then went on to win an Oscar for its special effects.

IN THE STARS
ALL THAT MONEY CAN BUY (1941)

Also known as *The Devil and Daniel Webster*, this delicious fantasy about greed and ambition was directed by German-born William Dieterle, who made a habit of wearing white cotton gloves when he was working. His crews reasoned that he must have some sort of dirt or germ phobia.

One day he was shooting a street scene and the road was very muddy. As the cameras were about to roll he noticed that there wasn't mud on a certain part of a carriage wheel, so he quickly peeled off a glove, dipped his hand in the mud and then rubbed some of it on the wheel.

Then he wiped his hands on his trousers, put his glove back on and continued working. It turned out that Dieterle, who was also a great believer in astrology, simply wore the gloves out of superstition.

The readings couldn't, however, prevent an injury soon after filming began to Thomas Mitchell, who was playing the playfully diabolical Mr Scratch. His replacement, Walter Huston, duly won an Oscar nomination for his performance, so perhaps it was all in the stars.

CREATING PANIC
CITIZEN KANE (1941)

When Orson Welles made his film debut with the film consistently voted the greatest ever made, he had no first-hand experience of movies. The twenty-five-year-old 'boy wonder' was already a stage veteran, and perpetrator of one of the most amazing incidents in modern American history, when his radio version of H G Wells's *War of the Worlds* panicked a significant portion of the listeners into fleeing from their homes.

By comparison, *Citizen Kane* stirred fewer American citizens, but it did upset the man upon whom the flawed, fabulous, charismatic hero was based. William Randolph Hearst was a right-wing newspaper baron (there's another kind?) and the script by Herman J Mankiewicz charted the rise and fall of a man who shared many of Hearst's qualities and failings.

Welles received a co-writing credit, too, although this seems little more than his contractual right as head of the Mercury Theater company, which formed the backbone of the production.

Mankiewicz, a wily, hard-drinking Hollywood veteran, fought hard to get his screen credit, and even secured top billing. When the film won an Oscar for its screenplay, Mankiewicz was there to collect the prize, Welles was not. 'I am happy to accept this award in Mr Welles's absence,' 'Mank' said, 'because the script was written in Mr Welles's absence.'

He may have overstated his contribution to the scenario and dialogue, but Welles's talents shone elsewhere. He had arrived in

Hollywood a few years earlier and was proclaimed as the saviour of the industry. Resentment was in plentiful supply, and even those who worked closely with him often had cause to hate him. At the same time, he could bring out the best in others, and on *Citizen Kane* used his inexperience in film as a positive thing, encouraging his key creative colleagues to come up with fresh, daring ideas.

Getting the finished film released was another matter. However good Welles and the rest felt it to be, word had already reached Hearst that the film was a thinly veiled, highly critical version of his own life.

He set to work to see to it that the movie should never come out, his many papers and radio stations sowing the seeds of dissent against Welles and the movie. He even seems to have been behind questions to the draft board, asking why young Orson hadn't been drafted into the armed services in a time of war.

Finally his friend Louis B Mayer came up with an offer of $805,000 to the studio behind *Kane*, RKO, for the master print and all copies of the film to be burned. Head of production George Schaefer politely declined.

CASUALTIES OF WAR
IN WHICH WE SERVE (1942)

Noël Coward's stirring account of a wartime naval tragedy had a real-life tragedy of its own while filming at Denham Studios.

They were shooting the scene of an explosion on a gun turret. One shot had been completed successfully but another was required, if possible before lunch, which was imminent.

In the hurry, the flash powder was placed in the breech, which had not sufficiently cooled, causing it to ignite. This in turn triggered the remainder of the charge, ending in a large explosion, seriously injuring three electricians and killing the 'gaffer' (chief electrician) Jock Dymore.

UP IN SMOKE
NOW, VOYAGER (1942)

This is, for some, the ultimate 'chick flick', in which, thanks to the counselling of a sympathetic shrink – and some nifty makeup effects – Bette Davis is transformed from a dowdy, beetle-browed spinster into an attractive, stylish 'catch'.

During a South American cruise, she and unhappily married Paul Henreid begin an affair conducted under a romantic Warner Bros studio moon.

Naturally, the relationship's doomed and, in a climax that had the world's women awash with tears, Henreid lights two cigarettes in his mouth, then hands one to Davis, who utters the immortal line: 'Oh, Jerry, don't let's ask for the moon – we have the stars.'

Henreid often claimed to have invented the ciggie business and it duly became a fad with the public following the film's huge success.

In fact, it seems more likely that Davis might have originated it since, ten years earlier, she and George Brent, with whom, incidentally, she had a brief affair, had done that same suggestive mouth-to-mouth in *The Rich Are Always With Us*.

DRUNK IN CHARGE
TALES OF MANHATTAN (1942)

The all-star cast list – Henry Fonda, Charles Laughton, Rita Hayworth, Ginger Rogers, Paul Robeson, Ethel Waters and Edward G Robinson, to name but a few – for this episodic comedy-drama about the life and times of a tailcoat should also have included the name of the veteran comedian W C Fields.

Fields, who co-wrote and starred in the fifth sequence playing opposite that incomparable stooge, Margaret Dumont, was apparently drunk – so what else was new? – throughout filming, and as a result the perfectionist director Julien Duvivier refused to take credit for the section.

The studio, Fox, eventually called the sequence 'inappropriate' and dropped it, although another explanation for its deletion (it has been restored to the American VHS release) was that the film simply ran too long.

WAVING THE FLAG
MRS MINIVER (1942)

When this patriotic film broke box office records, Prime Minister Winston Churchill is said to have described it as more powerful than a flotilla of battleships in propaganda terms.

Certainly the charming story of a plucky English family enduring the hardships of war helped to persuade many ordinary Americans, newly involved in the war following Pearl Harbor, to understand just what they were fighting for.

Jan Struther, the writer behind the original 'Mrs Miniver' newspaper columns in *The Times*, was assumed to have much in common with her goody-goody housewife creation and toured America as a kind of ambassador for Britain, giving lectures about Anglo-American relations.

In truth, though, Struther was not the happily married woman she appeared to be but involved in a secret affair with a Jewish refugee in flight from Nazi Austria. She eventually divorced her husband Tony and married Dolf Placzek in 1948, setting up home in New York.

Greer Garson, who played Mrs Miniver, was no moral paragon, either, being caught up in a relationship with 23-year-old Richard Ney, who played her son.

There were strange echoes of reality in the plotline of the sequel, *The Miniver Story* (1950), however. The makers decided to kill Mrs

Miniver off, giving her cancer, but Struther took legal action against MGM because she was angry that they were closing the door to further sequels.

Eerily, she was herself to die of breast cancer followed by a brain tumour in 1953. When earlier that year the tumour was misdiagnosed as Ménière's disease, she quipped, 'Or Miniver's disease?'

GETTING THE HUMP
ROAD TO MOROCCO (1942)

The biggest laugh in the third in a series of seven comic buddy-buddy movies starring Bob Hope and Bing Crosby – third-choice teaming after Fred MacMurray and Jack Oakie, and George Burns and Gracie Allen – was earned by a scene-stealing camel.

The quadruped was meant to sneak up behind Hope and Crosby and give them each a lick on the cheek. The intended joke was that each should think the other had kissed him.

Then the camel decided to improvise. After kissing Hope, he promptly spat in his face. The comedian staggered back while Crosby and the rest of the set collapsed with laughter.

Expecting the director David Butler to order another take, Hope was firmly told that the hilarious scene was 'in the can'.

PLAY IT, SAM
CASABLANCA (1942)

When the actors began assembling on 25 May 1942 to start shooting what would become arguably the most quotable (and misquoted) film of all time, the script in their hands was anything but. A final script was not approved until weeks before shooting was finished and nobody knew how the picture would end until just before the last scene was shot.

With its place so firmly set in the hearts and minds of film lovers, it is perhaps pointless to speculate on how different it might all have been with, instead of Bogie and Bergman, the romantic pairings of Ronald Reagan and Ann Sheridan or George Raft and Hedy Lamarr.

And what if the film's composer Max Steiner had had his way and successfully blocked the use of the song, 'As Time Goes By', in favour of one of his own ditties?

Now firmly part of the film's lore, the song was actually written more than a decade earlier by Herman Hupfeld for a stage revue and later incorporated into the play, *Everybody Comes To Rick's*, which inspired the film.

The use of the song in the film is inextricably linked with the performance of Arthur 'Dooley' Wilson, who played Sam, the nightclub pianist-singer. The only problem was that Wilson, an experienced vocalist in nightclubs and on stage – and, incidentally, the only member of the cast ever to have been to Casablanca – couldn't play the piano.

Pianist Elliot Carpenter had been hired to record the piano tracks, which Wilson would mime. But, according to Frank Miller, who wrote a fiftieth-anniversary commemorative book on the film, 'Wilson had to be able to hear the piano and [Michael] Curtiz [the director] had decided to have dialogue overlap the music, even in shots where Wilson was clearly seen at the piano.

'The man in charge of playing back Carpenter's piano tracks followed standard procedure. When there was no dialogue, he played the prerecorded music at full volume. But, without the playback, Wilson was totally lost.

'Curtiz finally came up with a solution to the problem. He had Carpenter installed at a piano just out of the camera range so he could play as the camera rolled. Wilson could hear the music and sneak occasional peeks at Carpenter's playing to match his hand movements.'

Contrary to some wilder reports, it is Wilson's own singing on the soundtrack.

BREAST OF EVERYTHING
THE OUTLAW (1943)

American Air Force chiefs were waiting anxiously to see Howard Hughes's design for a revolutionary and highly secret medium-range bomber capable of flying at a speed of 450 m.p.h. Meanwhile, the eccentric tycoon and film mogul was more preoccupied with accentuating the breasts of his latest starlet to create maximum big-screen impact.

Hughes's movie project was a new version of the Billy the Kid western legend and he'd signed up unknown Jane Russell, a $30-a-week part-time receptionist to a chiropodist, to play Rio, the Latin-looking love interest, opposite Jack Beutel, Walter Huston and Thomas Mitchell.

Although nineteen-year-old Russell was already well endowed (38–22–36), Hughes felt that the camera simply wasn't maximising her cleavage. His dissatisfaction reached its apogee during the film's most notorious scene, when Russell's wrists were tied between two trees and she was required to writhe sensuously in a desperate bid to break free.

'We're not getting enough production out of Jane's breasts,' complained Hughes to the wardrobe department and especially to Gregg Toland, the Oscar-winning cinematographer of films such as *Wuthering Heights*, *Grapes of Wrath* and *Citizen Kane*.

As World War Two continued to rage outside the studio, Hughes – who had taken over directing the film from the veteran Howard Hawks, who was frustrated with the mercurial producer's constant intervention – sat down at his desk patiently to design his own patented cantilever bra employing the kind of aerodynamics that were the more usual stock-in-trade of Hughes Aircraft.

Russell, just starting out on a career that would later burgeon properly as a brunette sex goddess in films such *The Paleface* and *Gentlemen Prefer Blondes*, docilely accepted the spectacularly redesigned bra. But, as she'd explain later, she never actually wore it for the scene in question.

'When I tried it on,' she said, 'it was uncomfortable, ridiculous. Obviously what he [Hughes] wanted was today's seamless bra, which didn't exist then. I just put on my own bra, covered the seams with tissues, pulled the straps over to the side, and then put on my own blouse.'

Hughes never spotted the switch as they filmed the horse opera, which got nicknamed 'A Tale of Two Titties'.

SUFFERING FOR ART
HENRY V (1944)

Responding to a plea from the Ministry of Information to make a big propaganda film for the war effort – these were still the dark days of 1943 – Laurence Olivier took on the mantle of producer-director and star as well as helping devise its unique take on Shakespeare's play.

He also, quite literally, suffered for his art. Filming battle scenes (including the Agincourt charge) in the neutral Republic of Ireland, where extras were plentiful and aerial bombardment absent, Olivier sustained a number of injuries.

Take the time he was required to demonstrate how he wanted a soldier to drop out of a tree onto a horseback rider below. He did it, spraining his ankle in the process, but someone managed to disguise the accident (and his tearful pain).

Then he wanted a French (for the French, read Germans) horseman to ride at the camera brandishing a spear, pulling away at the last minute. Unfortunately, the horse collided with the camera rig, part of which then painfully and bloodily pierced Olivier's upper lip and gum before crashing down on his right shoulder.

As he recalled in his memoirs, there were times during the filming when he was walking around the battlefield with a crutch, his arm in a sling and bandage round his face. He'd grow a moustache to help disguise his slight facial disfigurement.

The only other serious accident during filming was to a horse, which lost its eye.

WHISTLING IN THE DARK
TO HAVE AND HAVE NOT (1944)

One of the sexiest come-on lines in film history has to be Lauren Bacall's propositioning of Humphrey Bogart in this wartime romantic drama set in the Caribbean. Purring huskily, 'You know how to whistle, don't you, Steve? You just put your lips together – and blow,' the nineteen-year-old cover girl became an overnight film sensation.

Whether this come-on would have had quite the same effect on Bogart – and the world, for that matter – if the painfully nervous Bacall had intoned the immortal line in her 'little high nasal voice', as mentor director Howard Hawks described it, is rather doubtful.

Before shooting started, Hawks changed her original name Betty (as in Betty Joan Perske) to Lauren (the Bacall with an 'l' added was from her mother's maiden name) and told her to start reading aloud regularly to lower the tone of her voice.

In order to compound the vocal huskiness, which would become one of her trademarks – and a further attraction to a swiftly besotted Bogie, who married Bacall a year later – she'd perform shouting and screaming exercises throughout filming.

Intriguingly, her great line wasn't in the original screenplay although she did perform it at her screen test, and it was added to the script.

A SHAW THING
CAESAR AND CLEOPATRA (1945)

It's one thing to carry coals to Newcastle, quite another to take the Sphinx to Egypt. This once costliest of all British films started shooting six days after D-Day and just four days before the first V-1 flying bombs began to rain over southern England.

George Bernard Shaw, who had been born forty years before the official birth of moving pictures, was nearly ninety when he fully collaborated with exotic Hungarian émigré Gabriel Pascal in the film production of his 1907 play, following their work together on *Pygmalion* and *Major Barbara*.

The bulk of the film, co-starring Claude Rains and Vivien Leigh, was shot at Denham Studios, but Pascal desperately wanted to send a second unit to Egypt – remember, there was still a war on – to film the battle scenes. J Arthur Rank, alarmed at spiralling costs, thought this quite unnecessary.

However, GBS's contract had stipulated that not one word of his screenplay was to be changed and it was argued that the fulfilment of this clause required the inclusion of footage from Egypt. Rank stuck to his guns, while Pascal urgently sought help from the venerable author.

Shaw's swift retort was a short sharp postcard: 'What!!! Cut out the first act!!! Throw Rains at the audience's head before it knows who he is, or where they are!! Spoil a £300,000 ship for a ha'porth of tar?' It worked and soon the production set sail for Egypt.

The Egyptian army lent them 1,250 troops and 250 horses for the battle, while a Denham-manufactured Sphinx – not the Great Sphinx, to be sure, but rather what Cleo describes to Caesar as 'a dear little kitten of the Sphinx' – was assembled in the desert at Beni Ussef outside Cairo.

The film, eventually released well into the new peace, ended up costing a staggering £1.3 million and was described by Rank as a 'disastrous loss'.

FISHY SUBSTITUTE

JOHNNY FRENCHMAN (1945)

The whimsical tale of friendly rivalry between Breton fishermen and a Cornish harbourmaster was scripted to include the spectacular netting of a shoal of grey mullet.

It was the habit of this particular fishy specimen to appear off the coast of Land's End about six times a year in enormous numbers. Almost the entire male population of the nearby village of Sennen would then wade into the sea waist-deep and trawl in the fish using a large net.

A couple of Sennen villagers were put on the production payroll to pass on news of any impending mullet invasion, but nothing was heard. The filmmakers later learned of at least two successful trawls while shooting was in progress elsewhere. No explanation was given.

Just as Mevagissey had to double for both Brittany and, authentically, Cornwall, because there was still a war on, so the modest pilchard had to stand in for the elusive grey mullet.

GIVING CREDIT
OBJECTIVE BURMA! (1945)

It was not so much the making of but the aftermath of the filming of a stirring wartime drama that drove a rather bitter wedge into the 'special relationship' between allies Britain and America.

The undeniably powerful story told how Errol Flynn, as Major Nelson, led fifty US paratroops on a daring raid behind enemy lines to destroy a Japanese radar station.

The implication was that Flynn and his tiny force had somehow single-handedly liberated Burma. The closing credits belatedly paid tribute to 'the men of the American, British, Chinese and Indian Armies, without whose efforts Burma would still be in the hands of the Japanese'.

The fact that America came first in the list and that there was no acknowledgement in the film of Britain's remarkable contribution to perhaps World War Two's nastiest theatre was simply too much for some of the UK press. A cartoon in the *Daily Mirror* pictured a uniformed Flynn sitting in a studio chair with his name on it while the ghost of a British soldier is telling him, 'Excuse me, Mr Flynn, you're sitting on my grave!'

When it was trumpeted that Flynn himself had sat out the war, some of the criticism, especially from fellow actors, became very personal. In fact, Flynn, still a British Empire citizen at the outbreak of war, had desperately tried to get into the services but had been rated 4F because of recurrent malaria, a heart murmur and a slight case of TB.

Following its opening in September 1945, the film was withdrawn in the UK and not reissued again until 1952 with a prologue added lauding the British contribution to the campaign.

BITS AND PIECES
THE GREAT MORGAN (1946)

The oft-heard criticism that there are no new stories in Hollywood movies has been around longer than you might think.

A classic example of studio parsimony came with this inconsequential tale starring the scene-stealing character actor Frank Morgan, perhaps best known for playing the Wizard of Oz.

In this hastily cobbled-together film, he played a befuddled producer let loose and creating havoc in a studio editing room. Ostensibly there to supervise the editing of his own production, he gets the footage mixed up with scenes and outtakes from other MGM movies and 'comedy' reigns.

The cinematic equivalent of bubble and squeak, this was a fleeting journey through the leftovers of past musicals and dramas, with stars such as Eleanor Powell unwittingly starring in it. Not deemed acceptable for American audiences, the film was released abroad only.

UNDER SURVEILLANCE
NOTORIOUS (1946)

Hitchcock loved the notion of a device, often irrelevant, that helped propel the plot of a suspense film and its characters.

But he could have little idea that his choice of 'McGuffin' – a term said to have been originally coined by the screenwriter Angus McPhail – on *Notorious* would pique the interest of the FBI and lead them to keep him under surveillance for six months.

Cary Grant is hot on the heels of a Nazi kingpin hiding in Rio de Janeiro, when he gets involved with the man's much younger wife, played by Ingrid Bergman. Only towards the end of the story do the many twists reveal the identity of the Nazi and the means by which he intends to help the Nazi cause in the last days of the war.

It was by means of uranium, which the man kept hidden in his wine cellar – an element that Hitch selected by chance but that turned out to be a crucial ingredient in the then top-secret production of the atom bomb. Hence the interest of J Edgar Hoover.

BROTHERS AT WAR
A NIGHT IN CASABLANCA (1946)

Joyously spoofing one of the greatest romances in movie history, the Marx Brothers made their way to North Africa four years after Humphrey Bogart and Ingrid Bergman had their bittersweet parting.

When word of the movie reached Warner Bros' head, Jack L Warner, he immediately set his lawyers on Groucho and co., demanding that they remove the word 'Casablanca' from the title of their film.

Groucho responded in typical fashion, firing off letters of his own asking – among other things – if Warner's now owned the rights to the Moroccan capital, whether he really felt audiences

71

would be unable to distinguish Harpo Marx and Ingrid Bergman, as well as offering a baffling array of ever more outrageous synopses.

His *coup de grâce* was then to counteraccuse Jack Warner of copyright infringement, reminding the tough mogul that the Warner was OK, but to call themselves 'Brothers' was a step too far. 'Professionally,' Groucho wrote, 'we were brothers long before you were.' Exasperated, Warner gave up the fight.

KEW THE ACTION
THE OVERLANDERS (1946)

Ealing Studios planned to make ten films in Australia – in the event they made just five – of which this wartime epic about a cattle drive across the Outback was the first.

When the director Harry Watt took the raw footage back to Ealing, there was concern that, although the action was great and the performances excellent, the story simply didn't hang together.

A number of editors tried to work their various magic but to no avail until, with the distinct threat that the film might be scrapped altogether, supervising editor Leslie (father of Barry) Norman stepped into the frame.

What the film lacked, recalls Barry, 'was linked shots, moments that would ease the transition from one scene to another without a lurching jolt.

'There was no chance of going back to Australia to shoot them so Dad took a camera unit to Kew Gardens and there filmed footage of water, plants, grass waving in the wind. This stuff he used as the scene breakers Harry had forgotten to shoot.

'There was one sequence in particular when the cattle smelled water ahead and grew restless. The cattle were filmed in Australia, the water they could smell at Kew.'

FURIOUS CARY-ON
THE BACHELOR AND THE BOBBYSOXER (1946)

Shirley Temple was, as they say, 'all-growed-up' when, aged eighteen, she played the second half of the title to Cary Grant's suave playboy artist. She hadn't though lost her impish sense of humour, which used to keep casts and crew (mostly) amused when she was toiling away on film after film as a ring-curled moppet.

Fed up with the daily wrangles about everything from dialogue to stage directions between Grant, director Irving Reis and co-star Myrna Loy, Temple started kidding about on set one day during yet another hiatus. Grant was the particular target of her acute mimicry and the crew roared their approval until suddenly they went silent as the actor was spotted stone-faced observing the impromptu sideshow.

The producer summoned Temple, telling her that Grant had threatened to quit the film unless she was fired. The only way out would be a suitably abject personal apology. Grant accepted it and, as Temple recalls in her memoir, *Child Star*, was turning to leave when he stopped and said, 'By the way, it was a pretty good imitation.'

SCREEN TEST
GREAT EXPECTATIONS (1946)

In the days before mass communication, the notion of a nationwide, let alone global, casting search for a new young actor was tricky, to say the least. John Mills had already been signed up to play the older Pip in what would result in perhaps the best ever Dickens film adaptation, but they still needed a youngster to play the character as a child.

Finding no one suitable by conventional methods, the producers came up with what may be a unique casting 'call'. They made a short film of Mills looking into the camera and asking if the audience out there – in seven hundred Rank cinemas where the plea was screened during each programme – knew someone who would be perfect for the role.

Naturally, the production office was flooded with letters and photographs. Eventually the shortlist was narrowed to just six. The lucky winner was thirteen-year-old Anthony Wager from north London, son of a plumber and an aspiring actor.

After his film debut, Wager would go on to play other juicy juvenile roles in *Fame Is the Spur* and *Hungry Hill* before making a less celebrated transition to adult acting.

LUST IN THE DUST
DUEL IN THE SUN (1947)

Probably most famous for his memos, often pages-long documents in nit-picking detail to his hirelings about every aspect of their projects, the producer David O Selznick was also no mean practitioner of publicity himself. To get the ball rolling on this sprawling sultry western, quickly nicknamed 'Lust in the Dust', he came up with one of his best-ever campaigns.

First he obtained lists of the names of bartenders in cities and towns all over the States and then hired teams of workers to write by hand a letter to each individually extolling a great new western they'd just seen in California starring Jennifer 'Boy, is she an eyeful' Jones (who also happened to be Selznick's wife).

The letter was then simply signed simply, say, 'Joe', which could probably account for any number of regulars in bars across the nation.

This was followed up with an America-wide poster campaign of a ten-foot-high Jones with her blouse suggestively ripped from one shoulder, the idea being that other bar regulars would be further jolted after their epistolary reminder. It worked a dream and the film became a big hit.

BEATING THE SPIVS
BRIGHTON ROCK (1947)

The Boulting Brothers always knew they were likely to have censorship problems with their often startlingly realistic version of Graham Greene's vivid novel about thirties' gang warfare on the south coast. The BBFC (the C stood in those days for Censorship rather than Classification) was particularly concerned in that postwar period by what it saw as the proliferation of so-called 'spiv' films.

Having been recently appointed assistant script examiner by the ageing BBFC Secretary Brooke Wilkinson – who'd been virtually blind for ten years – Miss Madge Kitchener took extreme exception to some of the 'sordid' gangland realities in Greene's own screenplay. She also pointed out that 'Brighton Town Council may not appreciate having this unpleasant and sinister tale located in their holiday resort.'

Though it had been heavily censored at script stage, the Boultings reinstated all Miss Kitchener's suggested deletions and the film was surprisingly passed uncut, razor slashings and all.

But, whether because of her admonition or the filmmakers' feeling that they needed some sort of compromise to ensure full cooperation from the locals, a faintly apologetic preface was added at the front of the film.

Smacking slightly of a rather tatty tourist brochure, it read: 'Brighton today is a large, jolly, friendly seaside town in Sussex exactly one hour's journey from London, but in the years between the wars behind the Regency terraces and crowded beaches there was another Brighton of dark alleyways and festering slums. From here, the poison of crime and violence, gang warfare began to spread until the challenge was taken up by the police. This is a story of that other Brighton – now happily no more.'

In the States, the film was retitled *Young Scarface*. Any resemblance between the chilling teenage thug Pinkie and the chubby white-bearded old chap who'd play Santa Claus in Hollywood nearly fifty years later seems almost to be coincidental – even if they did both go by the name of Richard Attenborough.

RESTORATION RUCKUS
FOREVER AMBER (1947)

The studio, 20th Century-Fox had already poured $2 million – an astronomical sum for those days – into Kathleen Winsor's Restoration bodice-ripper when the studio head Darryl F Zanuck decided to call a halt to filming. With more than half the film shot, he was deeply unhappy with the director, John M Stahl, and with his leading lady, pert, Welsh-born Peggy Cummins, 21, in her big Hollywood break.

So he fired both of them and turned instead to Otto Preminger to rescue the project. Preminger had hated the book but, furnished with an enormous salary and *carte blanche* to remake the material, he dived in with some enthusiasm.

He didn't get it quite all his own way. Preminger wanted to cast Lana Turner as the gorgeous, pouting, defiantly décolleté Amber, mistress to Charles II. However, Zanuck insisted on a dyed-blonde Linda Darnell, perhaps best known to that date, ironically, as the Virgin Mary in *The Song of Bernadette*.

With the hiatus in filming, there were bound to be other casualties. Vincent Price, playing the hero's best friend, had to move on to another commitment.

Following the summary dismissal of Cummins, there was at least some consolation for the old country with the casting of TV's future Robin Hood, Richard Greene, in the Price role.

BACK IN THE SWIM
MIRANDA (1948)

Long before Daryl Hannah quite literally made a *Splash!* as a comely mermaid in the successful eighties comedy of that name, Glynis Johns was required to do much the same in this popular

76

British-made fishy precursor. The main problem was to give the actress a convincing-looking tail.

The wardrobe and props department, not to mention several couturiers, came up with various versions, but they were either too ugly or too impractical. More worryingly, they tended to drag Johns underwater.

Eventually, the producers went to the Dunlop company, who had designed apparatus for frogmen during the war, and they finally came up with a tail of very light rubber, filled with water,

This proved fine for the swimming scenes but looked clumsy when comely Miranda had to sit on a rock and sing siren songs. So they then produced a second tail complete with a convenient curve.

One of the end credits for the film read, 'Tail by Dunlop'.

A NOSE TOO FAR

OLIVER TWIST (1948)

Alec Guinness, with just one film role behind him, persuaded David Lean he should be screen-tested as the villainous Fagin. The director was rightly sceptical that the rather slight 34-year-old could transform himself successfully.

Working with the makeup artist Stuart Freeborn – with whom he would be subsequently closeted for three hours every morning during filming – he turned up for inspection looking uncannily like a Cruikshank drawing of Dickens's massively beaky old Jewish miser and was hired on the spot. He couldn't have known the potential storm he was unleashing.

Any actual reference to Fagin's race was excised from the adaptation, but Guinness's fruity portrayal simply proved too much for various countries, who then read what they wanted to into the characterisation.

The film was banned on its initial release in both Israel and Egypt – in Israel for being anti-Semitic, and in Egypt for making Fagin too sympathetic. There were riots in Berlin and a walk-out in Austria.

The reaction in the United States, where the film was expected to make an award-winning splash, was even more extreme. After various American Jewish organisations – though by no means all – laid into *Oliver Twist*, its Radio City Music Hall opening was postponed indefinitely.

The film would not appear on US screens until 1951 – with ten minutes of Fagin's scenes chopped from the original British release.

A FIRE ESCAPE

THE THIRD MAN (1948)

The film once voted the Greatest British Film of All Time very nearly became the Film That Never Was.

The ace Austrian cutter Oswald Hafenrichter was editing the film one evening when he popped out for a bite to eat with his assistant, Edith. According to John Glen, then a seventeen-year-old assistant sound editor, who years later would direct five James Bond films, 'Some film had been left draped over the sound head, which used to get very hot. The film heated up and eventually exploded, causing a huge fire in the cutting rooms.

'Ossie rushed back and tried to get into the room. We did our best to restrain him, but he broke free and waded in through the thick smoke. He emerged, not with any of the precious film but with his smouldering jacket. It had been hand-woven in Austria and was very dear to him.'

A great deal of the film had been lost in the fire. According to Glen, almost eight reels – virtually the whole film – had to be reprinted from the negative which was, thankfully, intact.

'Virtually every editor that was free was drafted to recut the film from scratch,' recalled Glen.

It seemed that one of the assistant editors had been particularly meticulous and kept an exhaustive record of the original cuts, code numbers and all, and so the film could be reassembled to match exactly Hafenrichter's work print.

WAITING FOR INSPIRATION
THE LOVABLE CHEAT (1949)

Is it possible that a classic example of European theatrical high art was inspired by an obscure American B-movie? The Irish playwright Samuel Beckett was an avowed fan of the silent screen legend Buster Keaton's work, and may well have seen this odd movie adaptation of a Balzac play.

Keaton played a small role, as Goulard, a man who awaits the return of a partner who never arrives. As the partner was called Godot, the idea is an intriguing one, but was not the only connection between the writer and the US comic, dubbed 'the Great Stone Face'.

In 1965 Beckett wrote a short with Buster Keaton in mind, a twenty-minute silent entitled *Film*, in which Keaton did indeed star.

STICKS AND STONES
HOME OF THE BRAVE (1949)

The late forties were a fertile period for hard-hitting, Hollywood-style social realism with subjects tackled such as anti-Semitism (*Gentleman's Agreement*, *Crossfire*), mental illness (*The Snake Pit*) and racism (*Pinky*, *Intruder in the Dust*).

Based on Arthur Laurents's play (which actually dealt with anti-Semitism), this uncompromising drama tells the powerful story of a black American GI (newcomer James Edwards) who suffers more from abuse from his own army colleagues than from the enemy during World War Two.

Unprecedented for a major studio film, it took a mere three months from concept to release. Mostly shot behind studio locked doors, this was the first American film to be planned, written, cast and produced in secret.

The producer-director Stanley Kramer insisted everyone from cast to crew pledge complete confidentiality. It was also the first major Hollywood film to use controversial language such as 'nigger', 'boogie', 'shine' and 'nigger lover'.

THE 1950s

GIVEN THE BIRD
TREASURE ISLAND (1950)

Robert Newton's incomparably fruity, eye-rolling turn as Long John Silver is one of the most imitated performances in cinema history. Getting it on film at all was a performance in itself.

The old sea dog's left leg ended at the knee, so Newton wore a padded three-quarter-length coat, which had to hide his leg strapped up uncomfortably behind him. He also had to wear a partial wig with side-whiskers under his tricorn hat, walk with a crutch and balance a parrot on his shoulder.

Filming in Technocolor required a lot of light, so the studio (Pinewood) was often extremely hot. Newton regularly dripped with perspiration.

Came the day when, out on location in nearby Black Park, Newton was required to rush through the bracken, hopping along one-legged with the use of the crutch, the parrot perilously perched. Every time the shot was attempted, the parrot found it impossible to cope with the erratic shoulder movements and fell off. As a matter of expediency, it was decided to give the bird something it could cling to by sewing on pieces of sashcord, painted gold to resemble epaulettes.

Newton set off, but once again the parrot failed to stay on board, despite much wing flapping. As a last resort it was decided to camera-tape the parrot's feet to the sash cord and paint the tape gold to conceal it. Newton lunged forward. The bird couldn't fall because of the tape, but it couldn't stay upright, either. In desperation, it grabbed the nearest means of support, which happened to be Newton's ear. The powerful beak took hold, resulting in a torrent of unscripted dialogue from the injured star.

SHOT IN THE DARK
SUNSET BOULEVARD (1950)

One of the most damning, bitter and yet fondly remembered Hollywood film satires is packed with in-references and ironic twists. The story of a forgotten film star from the silent era who takes up with a dissolute, opportunistic young screenwriter and puts in motion her misguided plans for a triumphant comeback contained enough sex, scandal and all-round bad behaviour for it to have been torn from Hollywood's own history pages.

But in fact the story, written by Billy Wilder, Charles Brackett and the film critic D M Marshman Jr, was an original one.

Wilder had wanted Montgomery Clift to play the feckless toyboy of the older star, but Clift got cold feet – perhaps too uncomfortable over the perceived parallels in his own fling with the ageing singer Libby Holman. Fred MacMurray and Gene Kelly passed, too, before William Holden grabbed the opportunity with both hands.

The role of Norma Desmond was harder to cast, requiring someone who could fill the shoes of this larger-than-life character without having an ego that would balk at playing the slightly pathetic older woman.

Mae West could not be tempted; the silent star Pola Negri could barely be understood through a thick Polish accent; and 'America's sweetheart', Mary Pickford, would surely not consider so base a character as this.

In the end, at George Cukor's suggestion, Wilder and Brackett offered the role to Gloria Swanson, who had been a star at Paramount in the 1920s but hadn't appeared in a film for almost ten years.

While her character had enjoyed a successful collaboration with the legendary director Cecil B DeMille in the story, so too had Swanson in real life. DeMille is seen on the set of his latest production, *Samson and Delilah*.

When Max, her former husband and now her butler, plays back a film he had directed her in during her pomp, Max (played by Erich von Stroheim) is actually screening *Queen Kelly*, a film that he – von Stroheim that is – had directed Swanson in many years before.

And in a sad, detached scene, in which Norma plays bridge with some of the few friends she has left, those fleeting cameos were filled by fellow veteran players Buster Keaton, H B Warner and Anna Q Nilsson.

As if the film were not already eerie enough with its effective blend of fantasy and reality, its opening suitably sets the right tone: we see the body of a young man floating head down in a swimming pool. His voice (Holden's) then begins to narrate the story in flashback.

An altogether weirder opening was shot, then rejected, after a preview screening. This was set in a morgue, where various corpses, being toe-tagged by attendants, are discussing how they died. Wilder's film is dark – but not that dark.

BEEFING UP THE ACTION
THE BRAVE BULLS (1951)

Most available prints of this account of the life and times of a Mexican matador (Mel Ferrer) now run about eight minutes longer than the original-release version, which was deemed too gruesome for audiences at the time.

The technology devised to capture the authentically bloody flavour of the story was perhaps crude but yet remarkably effective.

One of the real bullfighters was fitted out with a harness on which was mounted a small 16mm camera with a good wide-angle lens. You could see his cape moving in front of the camera and the bull charging him. Horns almost brushed the lens.

For other shots, they took a bull's head, mounted it on the handlebars of a bicycle and then, with a camera set up on the seat of the bike and filming through the horns, it would 'charge' Ferrer.

They even dug a pit with a trapdoor near the bullring through which, after receiving cues by phone link, they were able to shoot through the hooves.

CALL OF THE WILD
AN OUTCAST OF THE ISLANDS (1951)

Billeted at a remote guesthouse in the far north of Sri Lanka, the cast and crew of this elegant adaptation of Conrad's novel were plagued nightly by the incessant barking of wild dogs. Eventually the director Carol Reed persuaded his producer, Leigh Aman, to complain to the management about the increasing problem of sleep deprivation.

In the evening, when they had returned from their jungle location, Reed and co. were informed that about 150 dogs had been shot, so things should be more peaceful. Naturally, the animal lover Reed was shocked, because as he'd simply wanted the dogs to be quietened, not killed.

That night, the howling was greater than ever and, mysteriously, the star Trevor Howard's shoes and socks disappeared as well as Aman's. They were eventually discovered in bushes half a mile away.

That was the last anyone saw or heard of wild dogs, but a theory persisted about the presence of canine ghosts.

FROM OUTER SPACE
THE DAY THE EARTH STOOD STILL (1951)

They needed a giant actor to play the towering robot Gort, who, together with his alien master Klaatu, arrives on Earth to warn mankind about the dangers of atom-bomb testing.

After an exhaustive search for a suitable candidate to fill the big, shiny, metallic-looking (actually foam-rubber) bodysuit, the film-makers found their Gort quite literally on the doorstep.

Somebody suddenly remembered Lockard 'Lock' Martin, the seven-foot-seven doorman at Grauman's Chinese Theater – the one with all the starry hand- and footprints outside – on Hollywood Boulevard.

The problem was that Lock wasn't very strong, and wearing the suit even for only half an hour at a time was exhausting.

For a scene where Gort has to pick up and carry Patricia Neal (playing an earthly widow who befriends Klaatu), they had to use a crane, wires and even (for the reverse shot) a lightweight dummy to get away with the shot.

FORGING AHEAD
MOULIN ROUGE (1952)

Using a special rig to strap his calves back so that he could wear shoes on his knees, Jose Ferrer often went through considerable torment to play the 'vertically challenged' Paris painter, Toulouse-Lautrec.

But for close-up shots of Lautrec's hand, drawing scenes in the background, they used the French artist Marcel Vertes, who had made a living after World War One by creating very good forgeries of Lautrec's work.

ON THE LINE
HIGH NOON (1952)

One of the most quoted images in screen history came about by accident, and almost ended in tragedy. The shot of the approaching train, from a dot on the horizon to the moment when it filled the screen, establishes the impending threat that the western hero Gary Cooper must face.

The director, Fred Zinnemann, and his cinematographer, Floyd Crosby, lay on the tracks, while the rest of the crew waited a few hundred yards away. They captured the steam train moving relentlessly up the track, when suddenly the white steam coming out of the engine turned black.

Both were pleased with the shot, but did not know that this was a signal that the engine's brakes had failed. Suddenly realising that it was not going to stop, they stood up, and got the camera caught on the tracks. All at once the train was upon them, smashing the camera and leaving Zinnemann and Crosby looking aghast.

Amazingly the magazine containing the film remained intact. The film was developed and provided the shot used.

MONEY INTO NOTHING
WILLIAM TELL (1953)

You won't find this epic retelling of the Swiss legend about an apple-splitting Alpine hero who took on the Austrian occupying hordes in any film guide.

Starring Errol Flynn, who as producer sank $500,000 of his own money into the lavish project, it was to have marked the film-directing debut of the Oscar-winning British cinematographer Jack Cardiff.

But money problems, exacerbated by some darker dealings at the Italian end of the project, dogged an ambitious production from the outset. Shooting slowed to a trickle as cast and crew weren't paid, then halted completely when the cameras were seized as collateral for various unpaid bills. All that remained on a lovely location in Val d'Aosta, with Mont Blanc soaring high in the background, was the perfect re-creation from scratch of a stone-built village with fifty fourteenth-century houses and a church.

Perhaps the writing was on the wall from the moment during pre-production when Flynn was shown the screen test of an eighteen-year-old bit-part actress called Sofia Lazzaro.

'Sorry,' said the famous womaniser, apparently unmoved by those lips and those eyes. 'I can see nothing in this girl – nothing at all.'

Soon after that, Lazzaro became Loren and the rest, as they say, is history.

TURNING OFF THE LIGHTS
GENEVIEVE (1953)

The story of two young couples and their unofficial old crocks' rivalry on the annual London–Brighton Veteran Car Rally is rightly remembered as a British box-office classic of frothy fun.

Actually making the film during miserable winter weather, with mobile generators endlessly firing up blazing arc lights to give the illusion of a balmy summer's weekend, was altogether less cheery.

After frequent soakings, exacerbated by 'perfectionist' director Henry 'Corny' Cornelius's reliance on repeated 'takes', one of the stars, Kay Kendall, finally cracked and laid into him one day with her prop parasol, screaming, 'You miserable little bastard!'

Kendall, like her co-stars Kenneth More, John Gregson and Dinah Sheridan, thought the film would be a disaster and throughout shooting sought ways of trying to quit the project.

The final straw came when – More recalled in his autobiography – the production hit cash problems. 'Having overcome trouble with the weather, we went into the studio – and seven-eighths of the way through the film, the company ran out of money.

'We were well over budget because of Corny's insistence on repeating each shot so many times. To cut all possible costs, the insurance company [who had to pay up against such a contingency] had their men prowling round the studio switching off any lights that were not needed.'

EYE FOR SUCCESS
HOUSE OF WAX (1953)

Though not the first commercial 3-D feature (that honour belongs to the forgettable *Bwana Devil* made a year earlier) this is certainly the most successful – rendered even more memorable by the fact it was directed by a man with only one eye.

Sporting one of Hollywood's finest black eye-patches, André de Toth had written about the possibilities of three-dimensional film-making as early as 1946.

But when his name came up later, in the inevitable rush to capitalise on the available technology, the head of the Warner Brothers studio instantly ruled him out with, 'You're half-blind. How in the hell can you make a 3-D picture?'

De Toth was, however, very persuasive and, with a promise to keep his eye-patch pocketed, he embarked on this luridly colourful remake of the studio's own *Mystery of the Wax Museum* made twenty years earlier.

Apart from an on-set blaze during filming, which nearly did for cast and crew, the film was also directly responsible for setting its star, Vincent Price, on a new course as cinema's premier horror-meister.

Much further down the bill playing a deaf mute was a young stone-faced actor called Charles Buchinsky, barely distinguishable from the surrounding waxworks. His subsequent change of surname to Bronson signalled the beginning of another momentous change of fortune.

NICE CUP OF TEA
THE SEEKERS (1954)

Everything stops for tea. Or so the union demanded, even when it might jeopardise a crucial shot.

A skeleton British crew, on location in New Zealand to provide some authentic colour for this period colonial epic – which included a Maori battle fought on the back lot at Pinewood – was in Rotorua to shoot the big geyser, which blows off just once a day.

With the budget tight and the schedule even tighter, everything was ready, including the star Jack Hawkins, when the production's shop steward blew the whistle.

Apparently, the producer had been late providing the morning tea wagon. No char, no shot. By the time the ensuing row had subsided, nature, no respecter of tea breaks, intervened and the geyser blew unrecorded.

GETTING THE GIRL
HELL AND HIGH WATER (1954)

It may have earned an Oscar nomination for its special effects but otherwise this Cold War submarine adventure was remarkable only for being the first in a succession of films to star the movie mogul Darryl F Zanuck's various high-profile mistresses.

The womanising head of 20th Century-Fox was fifty and married with three children when he fell headlong for Bayla Wegnier, a Polish-born, French-raised former beauty contestant nearly half his age.

Changing her name to Bella Darvi – the new surname combining parts of his and his wife Virginia's first names – Zanuck tried unsuccessfully to launch an acting career for her with *Hell...* followed by *The Egyptian* and *The Racers*.

Her greatest success, though, as the writer-director Nunnally Johnson once remarked, was that she managed to get Zanuck into bed. 'Until then,' he quipped, 'Darryl thought it was somethin' you did on a desk.'

Zanuck's next squeeze was the sultry singer Juliette Greco, the same age as Darvi but with at least the advantage of having some performing experience as a cabaret artiste. Yet, despite appearances in Zanuck productions such as *The Sun Also Rises*, *Roots of Heaven*, *Crack in the Mirror* and the presciently titled *The Big Gamble*, she too signally failed to make the big-screen grade.

Zanuck was no more successful, cinematically speaking, with the Czech-born French model Irina Demick, who was more than thirty years his junior. Her appearances in films such as *The Longest Day* and its unofficial sequel, *Up From the Beach*, barely registered.

The insatiable producer was then well into his sixties when he met nineteen-year-old Genevieve Gillaizeau, yet another French model for whom her new mentor had starry ambitions. As Genevieve Gilles, she made just one film for him, *Hello-Goodbye*, a saccharine romance as trite as its title. It duly bombed. Zanuck died nine years later, in 1979, with his wife of 55 long-suffering years by his bedside.

BLOWING IN THE WIND
THE SEVEN-YEAR ITCH (1955)

Ask any discerning buff to name the single most iconographic image in film and he or she would probably cite an ecstatic-looking Marilyn Monroe and her billowing skirt in Billy Wilder's New York comedy.

The shot we see in the film as Monroe gets to cool down in unorthodox style on a steamy summer's night in Manhattan is mild compared with what an estimated five thousand New Yorkers saw earlier as they watched the shooting live on their city streets.

It was just past one o'clock in the morning on the corner of Lexington Avenue and 52nd Street when, with jostling crowds straining to see Hollywood's latest sex goddess, Monroe stood over a street grate and let the draft from a fan below do its sexy damnedest.

It took no fewer than fifteen takes to reveal her shapely legs and her white panties (two pairs, actually) to the satisfaction of the filmmakers – and the crowds. And perhaps even more to the satisfaction of the fan operators, who had allegedly taken bribes to let some lucky spectators get an even closer look.

However, the footage would prove unusable and so they all had to meet up again on a sound stage back at the Fox Studios in Hollywood for a mock-up of the New York street scene. This time Monroe's skirt lifted more modestly to just above knee level before cutting to a shot of her happy face.

The Big Apple location would have a rather sad coda. Monroe's jealous husband, Joe DiMaggio, apparently so incensed by the sight of this public ogling of his wife, took it out brutally on her later. Three weeks later, their separation was announced.

PULLING THE RUG
NOT AS A STRANGER (1955)

'It wasn't a cast so much as a brewery,' remarked Robert Mitchum of his co-stars in this soapy drama about the medical profession. Broderick Crawford, Myron McCormick, Lee Marvin and Frank Sinatra, not to mention Mitchum himself, could be counted as peers among the Hollywood drinking classes.

Shooting was often raucous and downtime for the actors more so. But nothing was quite as spectacular as the day chunky Crawford decided to fight back after being needled once too often by scrawny Sinatra.

According to Edward Anhalt, who wrote the screenplay with his wife Edna, Crawford attacked Sinatra, held him down, tore off his hairpiece and began eating it. Mitchum, who tried to break up the fight, was eventually thrown through a window by Crawford for his pains.

When Crawford then began choking on the fake hair, the film's technical adviser was called in to help the actor vomit up the 'rug'.

Anhalt added, 'I don't know whether they were trying to save him or the hairpiece, because it was the only one they had. Anyway, it was mangled and they couldn't use it, so filming had to be postponed for I don't know how long, until Sinatra could be fitted for a new toupee.'

CONQUERING HERO
TO HELL AND BACK (1955)

In 1945, Audie Murphy, the son of a poor Texas sharecropper, was barely 21 and yet had become America's most decorated combat soldier of World War Two. Four years later, and a year after he had taken his first faltering steps in pursuit of Hollywood stardom, he published his best-selling biography, *To Hell and Back*.

It was a clearly only a matter of time before there would be a movie version and, with Murphy's growing screen popularity, just as obvious that the babyface hero would be required to play himself.

Murphy, now thirty, was altogether less convinced, claiming it was 'a lousy book because it was a lousy war'. Naturally, he wanted any film to be a success, 'but I'm not sure', he said, 'the public will accept me in the role. I don't think I'm the type – maybe Tony Curtis would do.'

With approval over cast and script, he signed on. There were to be two scenes requiring the war hero to cry. When his mother died in 1941, Murphy had cried solidly for three days and swore then he'd never shed another tear. Although recreating the scene was profoundly moving for him, he still couldn't manage to blub.

The next occasion was the sequence in which his best friend Lattie 'Brandon' Tipton was killed in France straight after a German machine-gun post treacherously offered its surrender. In his grief, then rage, Murphy went beserk, single-handedly killing 23 of the enemy, earning himself the first in a succession of his country's highest decorations for valour.

Although they changed the reality of Tipton (played by Charles Drake) dying in his arms because it was felt to be 'too corny', the scene triggered the required response. Murphy's lips quivered and his eyes filled up.

TWO ON A ROLE

THE MAN WITH THE GOLDEN ARM (1955)

One of Hollywood's oddest, indeed more unlikely, acting rivalries was for a while between Frank Sinatra and Marlon Brando, nine years his junior. On the face of it they couldn't have been more dissimilar. Sinatra, the spindly crooner, and Brando, the powerfully built Method actor.

But after Ol' Blue Eyes won an Oscar for *From Here to Eternity* – a year or so after 'Mumbles' (as Sinatra called him) had won his first for *A Streetcar Named Desire* – he was suddenly a contender and the two seemed to be in direct competition for the same roles.

Sinatra was the producer Sam Spiegel's first choice to play Terry Malloy, the inarticulate boxer-turned-longshoreman, in *On the Waterfront*, but to his fury – although $18,000 was eventually paid by way of compensation – lost out to Brando when the Columbia studio chief Harry Cohn played God.

He was even more peeved when Brando, a self-confessed non-singer, got the star part of Sky Masterson – a role Sinatra coveted – in *Guys and Dolls*. So it seemed almost like masochism when Sinatra finally agreed to play the film's second banana, Nathan Detroit.

It was then *mano a mano* when Otto Preminger sent them each fifty pages of script for *The Man with the Golden Arm*, promising that the rest would follow soon. The role was a junkie with a crippled wife. Sinatra agreed on the spot, while Brando's agent, without showing his client the work in progress, said they'd wait for the completed script.

Sinatra's reward for quick thinking was not just the juicy part of Frankie Machine in one of the more controversial films of the decade but also an Oscar nomination. Not to mention putting one over 'Mumbles'.

Brando would, however, have the last Oscar laugh. Years later, Preminger was offered *The Godfather* to direct and wanted Sinatra to play Don Vito Corleone. Sinatra wanted no part of the ageing mafioso – perhaps it was a bit too close to home – and so passed. Preminger quit too.

Brando, who by then was at a stage of his career when he couldn't get arrested, eventually got the part and, of course, won the Academy Award (his second) for Best Actor.

WHAT A SHOWER
DOCTOR AT SEA (1955)

Gorgeous, pouting Brigitte Bardot, perhaps best remembered for her image-defining sex siren role in ...*And God Created Woman*, was to be found auditioning her assets a year earlier on this side of the Channel in the unlikely setting of this inoffensive home-grown family comedy.

Bardot, barely twenty, was playing a French cabaret performer stranded on a cargo ship in the Tropics. Series regular Dirk Bogarde, alias Dr Simon Sparrow, suddenly discovers Bardot while she's taking a shower in his cabin. With characteristic British reserve, filming of the actress was to take place from the other side of the shower curtain with her naughty bits properly covered up.

However, because of the way the set was lit, the camera was able to pick out the outline of the modesty garments, which, frankly, looked foolish on film.

With a complete lack of inhibition, BB came to the rescue. She stripped off completely and presented herself naked before an agog crew. For censorship purposes, the scene was shot through a semi-transparent shower curtain.

Word of the scrumptious starlet whizzed round the studio like wildfire and often the stage at Pinewood was bulging at the seams with everyone sneaking in to try to have a look at this continental sensation.

CZAR OF Z-MOVIES

PLAN 9 FROM OUTER SPACE (1956)

The weird and sometimes rather wonderful bargain-basement film career of the maverick writer/producer/director/transvestite Edward D Wood Jr – generally regarded as 'the world's worst filmmaker' – was enjoyably immortalised in Tim Burton's affectionate biopic, *Ed Wood* (1994), starring Johnny Depp.

But no mere re-creation could have really done proper justice to the actual reality – fore and aft of camera – of Wood's schlock masterwork, lowlier even than his *Glen or Glenda* (1953), *Bride of the Monster* (1955), *Night of the Ghouls* (1958) or *The Sinister Urge* (1960).

The alternative title – *Grave Robbers From Outer Space* – probably tells you all you need to know about the flimsy plot for this absurd slice of cheapo sci-fi, which was shot over four to six days in November 1956.

Partly financed by some local churches on condition that the cast be baptised before filming, it was meant to have starred Bela Lugosi but by the time Wood eventually got his cash for the production the drug-addicted old actor was terminally hospitalised. Luckily, Wood had already shot a scene with Lugosi in a graveyard, so this footage was inserted and Lugosi's other scenes were undertaken by Wood's chiropractor, Dr Tom Mason, shielding his face with a cloak.

The otherworldly special effects were a mixture of model kits and Cadillac hubcaps, cardboard cutouts, balsa wood and piano wire. And, yes, it showed.

Ever the cock-eyed optimist, Wood would always describe *Plan 9*, which eventually got a brief release in 1959, as his 'pride and joy'.

Ironically, for *Ed Wood*, Tim Burton's tribute to the perpetually cash-strapped director, the cost alone of re-creating those old sets totalled more than Wood spent on all his films put together.

WHALE OF A TIME
MOBY DICK (1956)

With Disney's *Treasure Island* vessel, the *Hispaniola*, purchased, then remodelled as *Pequod*, a suitably salty cast signed up and, the little southwest Ireland coastal town of Youghal standing in for New Bedford, Massachusetts, the only thing left was to find a great white whale convincing enough to torment Herman Melville's Captain Ahab (Gregory Peck).

Since no *living* creature would suffice, the production built a ninety-foot-long beast made of a plastic and rubber skin over a steel frame and weighing many tons. Electronic controls would enable it to dive, surface, spout and slap its tail against the side of a boat. Several of these expensive creatures were constructed.

The creation was, however, so huge and heavy that it constantly broke the cables used to tow it out to sea. One day, while filming off Fishguard, Peck was on the model whale's back when a sudden squall blew up and a fog bank rolled in just about the time the actor lost sight of the motor launch towing the beast with an underwater line.

Peck recalled, 'The towline snapped and I was in the fog in a squall in waves that were ten to fifteen feet high, alone on a slippery rubber whale. And I thought, What a way to go! But I yelled and they were able to find me in the fog. I got off that whale in a hurry. The whale itself was never found.'

The close-up climactic scenes of Peck lashed to the thrashing, harpooned whale – actually a revolving drum inside a section of model whale head and body – were filmed in a large tank at

Elstree Studios. Concerned that they might miss some of his genuine anguish, Peck eschewed a stunt double and was nearly drowned for his pains.

DUST TO DUST
THE CONQUEROR (1956)

If you were casting a twelfth-century historical epic about the marauding Mongol warrior Genghis Khan, surely the last star you'd pick for such a role would be a drawling western hero like John 'Duke' Wayne.

If Wayne, in a part originally envisioned for Marlon Brando, seemed misguided, the absurdity was then compounded by equally daft dialogue in which the Tartar princess Susan Hayward was required to say stuff like, 'I am consumed with want of him', while the Duke helpfully contributed the legendary, 'You're beautiful in your wrath.'

Yet this recreated nonsense pales in the shadow of one of cinema's darker tales connected with the already doomed production. Of the 220 people the director Dick Powell brought to St George, Utah – doubling for the Gobi Desert – 91 would come down with cancer later in their lives, a number three times the actuarial average.

These included Wayne and Hayward as well as their co-stars Pedro Armendariz and Agnes Moorehead, not to mention Powell.

Most of the eventual victims had admittedly been heavy smokers, but an altogether more sinister explanation has since been offered with the revelation that radioactive dust had permeated the location following the testing of no fewer than eleven atomic bombs a year earlier some 150 miles to the west.

As if breathing in the wind-blown dust daily wasn't bad enough, the filmmakers then trucked more than sixty tons of the local dirt back to Hollywood to make sure the studio-shot scenes had the same colour and texture.

BREATHING DIFFICULTIES
TRIBUTE TO A BAD MAN (1956)

After signing up to play a tough cattle baron, Spencer Tracy agreed enthusiastically with the director Robert Wise that the production should try to seek out some unfamiliar western locations. Wise and his team went off on a recce and came up with some glorious country over 8,000 feet up in the Rockies about 250 miles southwest of Colorado.

Hard-drinking Tracy, whose insecurities meant he would ask to be released from his commitment just before the start of shooting on almost every film in which he was involved, was even more concerned this time round. He was concerned about everything from the height of his co-star, the rangy Irene Papas, to the location itself. However, he informed Wise that he would actually arrive early in order to acclimatise properly.

When he proved a no-show, Wise began filming without him, concentrating on scenes involving Papas and the young newcomer, Robert Francis. Five days later, Tracy turned up, checked into his motel and then disappeared again. This time he went AWOL for eight days before suddenly flying back into a local airport. Worried about the after-effects of an operation for the removal of a cyst on his cheek, and terrified about contracting skin cancer, he shot four scenes but with increasing difficulty because of lack of breath.

Becoming irascible with his co-stars and dictatorial with the director, the double-Oscar winner complained constantly about the altitude and insisted on a change of location.

By now, Wise had reached the end of his tether and demanded successfully that the studio replace a mortified Tracy. When the first-choice replacement, Clark Gable, proved unavailable, MGM managed to sign up James Cagney, who still had another film to finish.

During the hiatus, Robert Francis filled in the time by taking flying lessons, only to be killed when his trainer plane crashed. His place was taken by Don Dubbins. As for Tracy, he moved on to his next film, *The Mountain*, which was, strange to relate, filmed 12,500 feet up near Chamonix in the Alps.

DANCE OF DEATH
THE SEVENTH SEAL (1956)

Also known as *Det sjunde inseglet*, this is the early masterpiece of the Swedish filmmaker Ingmar Bergman: an allegory about life and death famously featuring a chess match between a medieval knight and the Grim Reaper – wittily spoofed, among its many parodies, in *Bill & Ted's Bogus Journey* (1991).

The film's other best-recalled scene is the so-called 'Dance of Death' ending, in which the Reaper dances off with some travellers under a dark cloud.

This was, Bergman would later admit, a piece of luck. Most of the actors and crew had left the location for the day because of a gathering storm when the director spotted a 'strange cloud' and got his cameraman to set up. A few electricians and a couple of tourists were swiftly filmed instead dancing off to catch the scene on film.

Bergman also owned up to another – less fortunate – blink-and-you'll-miss it moment. In the witches' forest, you can spot the light from the window of a high-rise city apartment nearby.

KEEP YOUR HAIR ON
THE MAN WHO NEVER WAS (1956)

Before the days of enthusiastic 'chameleon' actors, when you hired a Hollywood star you also got the stock image.

With three Oscar-nominations to his credit, Indiana-born Clifton Webb had perfected the role of the WASP, and waspish, intellectual American, complete with neat moustache.

On the face of it, he seemed a strange choice to play a real-life true Brit, Lt Commander Ewen Montagu QC, Navy reservist and Intelligence genius, who hatched a brilliant diversionary plan – Operation Mincemeat – to fool Hitler during World War Two.

When Webb was told that British navy officers weren't permitted to wear moustaches, he offered this ultimatum: 'Either the moustache stays, or I go back to the States.'

After consultation with the senior service, the compromise reached was that the actor could wear a full beard, which, happily, satisfied Webb.

Incidentally, the first famous (disembodied) voice you hear in the film is that of Winston Churchill, who authorised the successful operation. Except that it wasn't Churchill: instead, it was an uncanny impersonation of the great man by a thirty-year-old comic just beginning to make his way in films – Peter Sellers.

CREATING A SPLASH
THE INCREDIBLE SHRINKING MAN (1957)

The director Jack Arnold was having trouble creating the giant water drops for his low-budget sci-fi classic – until he remembered his misspent youth, part of which was spent filling condoms with water and dropping them on luckless passers-by.

Result – a large wheel was fixed on the sound-stage ceiling, which revolved, dropping the water-filled condoms attached to it one by one, which, as they fell, were dead ringers for enormous drops of water.

The punchline, said Arnold, was that Universal, as usual, assigned an auditor to check the production budget when the film was completed. He queried the charge for condoms. 'We had a terrific wrap party' was Arnold's straight-faced response.

ADDING SOME EXTRAS
THE CAMP ON BLOOD ISLAND (1957)

By the time they'd cast this inexpensive wartime drama set in a brutal Japanese PoW camp – recreated on the back lot at Bray Studios – the production still needed another twenty Japanese extras to play soldiers and prison guards.

The Crowd Artists' Association had only some half a dozen Japanese on their books, so, after a brainwave, the filmmakers eventually trawled London's few Japanese restaurants to make up for the shortfall.

There were later echoes of this in the altogether more lavishly produced *55 Days At Peking* (1963), the 1900-set story of the Boxer Rebellion.

At a time when it was reckoned there were perhaps no more than one hundred Chinese in the whole of Spain, the producer Sam Bronston somehow managed to assemble a mighty supporting cast of suitable-looking Orientals at his Madrid studio by stripping the Chinese restaurants and laundries of Europe.

'I'm told,' the film's star Charlton Heston recalled in his memoirs, 'you couldn't get a decent Chinese meal in any European capital the rest of that summer [1962].'

THE BOY WONDER
MAN OF A THOUSAND FACES (1957)

Robert Evans (born Robert J Shapera) was lying one morning by the pool at the Beverly Hills Hotel buffing up his perma-tan when a man called Marti Arrogue came over to him and told him he'd be perfect for an important role in a new film.

Arrogue was making the overture on behalf of his wife, the Oscar-winning actress Norma Shearer, whose late husband, Irving

Thalberg, was going to be featured in a biopic about the silent screen star Lon Chaney.

Shearer had observed Evans for a couple of days and – with casting approval of the actor selected to play Thalberg – reckoned that the 24-year-old Evans bore a remarkable resemblance to the *young* movie mogul. 'Would you', she asked him, 'consider playing Irving?'

Evans, a sometime actor and model, was now running a successful New York clothes business in partnership with his brother.

Thinking it all had to be some sort of joke, Evans, who was due to fly back to New York in the evening, went along with it, only to be press-ganged into a meeting at Universal Studios that very afternoon with producer Robert Arthur, director Joseph Pevney and the film's star, James Cagney.

The company quickly moved through onto a set that was a replica of Thalberg's office and, in something of a dream, Evans did a screen test with Cagney.

Back in the hotel and all packed and ready to head for the airport, Evans received a call from Arthur, who told him, 'Congratulations!' and that he'd 'be needed in wardrobe tomorrow'.

One headline of many excited industry headlines summed it up perfectly: BIG SPLASH: NY BUSINESSMAN DIVES IN POOL AND COMES OUT A MOVIE STAR!

Evans would appear in just three more films before becoming a producer at the turn of the sixties. A decade later, at forty, he was head of worldwide production at Paramount Pictures, very much a sort of latterday Thalberg.

RUNNING INTO DANGER

THE PRIDE AND THE PASSION (1957)

The filming in Spain of this costly adaptation of C S Forester's *The Gun,* set during the Napoleonic wars, had its fair share of problems

– from mustering ten thousand extras to curbing the worst excesses of Frank Sinatra's absurd Spanish accent.

But nothing was quite as potentially hazardous as the moment when Sophia Loren, making her American film debut after Ava Gardner turned down the role, was nearly killed for real while shooting the scene in which she was meant to be killed in the film.

During the destruction of the walls surrounding the city of Avila, Loren is seen running through the chaos, terror etched on her lovely face. The terror, it seems, was authentic, because Loren was so close to one of the exploding mines that the cork and sand momentarily blinded her.

She stumbled, nearly fell, rubbed some of the sand out of her eyes and then continued the assigned run. Had she faltered and fallen at this point, the entire sequence would have been ruined, since the wall couldn't have been blown up again. The trouper continued her panic-stricken flight until the exact point at which she was supposed to fall dead.

ANYTHING FOR PUBLICITY
INTERPOL (1957)

A near-disastrous publicity stunt involving co-star Trevor Howard was to prove more exciting than anything on screen in this mediocre international police-chase thriller.

The press had been mustered one morning in Frankfurt to watch how, despite being given a ten-minute start, a speeding car containing Howard would be swiftly apprehended by the authorities. With a police driver at the wheel of his red Mercedes, Howard's car sped off until it came to a halt behind a queue of cars near the centre of the city.

Howard's driver had been given previous permission to take avoiding action, and so pulled out of the orderly line and around a traffic cop, who unfortunately hadn't been informed of the developing stunt. All he knew was that the previous day there had been a big bank robbery from which the baddies has escaped in...you've guessed it, a red Merc.

Seeing a police car in hot pursuit, the lawman pulled out his gun and starting firing at Howard's vehicle. Eventually the police cars homed in on the Mercedes, which eventually careered to a stop beside a railway line.

Apparently, Howard, told that the press would be waiting at the point of capture, was now meant to jump out of the car and run. To everyone's horror, he set off across the railway's electrified lines but remained unharmed. The resulting press coverage was, to say the least, extensive.

FACING THE FUTURE
RAINTREE COUNTY (1957)

About a month into shooting studio scenes on this poor man's *Gone with the Wind*, Montgomery Clift was driving home after a dinner party at his co-star Elizabeth Taylor's house in the Hollywood Hills when he blacked out, lost control of the car and crashed into a telegraph pole.

Rushing to the scene of the accident, Taylor and another dinner guest, Rock Hudson, helped pull a badly injured Clift from the wreck.

According to one report, 'his face, swollen to the size of a football, was unrecognisable, and two teeth were stuck in the back of his throat. There were terrible lacerations on the left side of his face where a nerve had been severed. His nose, jaw and sinus cavity were broken and he was badly concussed.'

Determined to get back into action, Clift, already addicted to drink and drugs, slowly recovered in hospital by sipping martinis through a straw and popping painkillers. Although he had recurring back pain, he didn't, miraculously, require plastic surgery. Just nine weeks after the terrible accident, he was filming again.

Watch the film today and it's a bit, as some critics have pointed out, like watching a real-life *Picture of Dorian Gray*. In most of the studio-set scenes he is still the almost impossibly handsome Clift of best movie memory. In the location footage, filmed in Kentucky and Mississippi, it's like the attic version of Dorian, with the left side of Clift's face virtually immobile, mouth grotesquely twisted.

Said to be distraught by the loss of his legendary looks, Clift removed all the mirrors from the house he rented in Hollywood, draped the windows with black curtains and received visitors only rarely.

COR BLIMEY, MISSUS!
WITNESS FOR THE PROSECUTION (1957)

The history of cinema is littered with monstrous assaults on the Cockney accent, principally by denizens of Hollywood who, although they should have known better, decided to have a go anyway with hilariously dire results: Bette Davis in *Of Human Bondage* (1934), Joan Bennett in *Man Hunt* (1941), Dick Van Dyke in *Mary Poppins* (1964), and Don Cheadle (who at least had the decency to remain uncredited) in *Ocean's 11* (2001) – to name just four of the more reckless screen perpetrators of East End inflection abuse.

Marlene Dietrich ought, by all that's Bow Bells, be added to the list for her extraordinary turn in the witness box in this enjoyable version of Agatha Christie's twist-packed stage whodunnit. Playing the German refugee wife of the accused (Tyrone Power), she disguises herself as a Cockney prostitute, giving evidence at the Old Bailey to provide an alibi for him.

The 55-year-old Berlin-born actress tackled the Cockney challenge with gusto, using her co-star Charles Laughton (b. Scarborough, Yorkshire) as her principal voice coach.

An off-screen chum, Noël Coward, also gave her a few pointers. He would note in his diaries, 'It is not easy to teach Cockney to a German glamour-puss who can't pronounce her Rs, but she did astonishingly well.' So well, in fact, she deserves to be excluded from the list of Cockney shame.

If cinemagoers were pleasantly surprised by La Dietrich's split personality in the film they perhaps groaned at the rather shameless way her more famous persona was gratuitously woven into the plot.

In a lavish flashback sequence designed to show how Power first met his wife, Dietrich undergoes several layers of filter as she's filmed belting out a tune in the Red Devil club – *The Blue Angel* was, of course, her breakthrough film nearly thirty years earlier – and even contrives to flash one of her famous legs.

TESTING TIME
GIDEON'S DAY (1958)

John 'I make westerns' Ford decided he needed a break from Hollywood. Declaring that 'Scotland Yard is the British equivalent of the wild west', he crossed the Atlantic to make a cosily dramatic day-in-the-life of a workaholic police inspector (Jack Hawkins).

The script, which veered between thrills and farce, required one of the cop characters to have a passion for cricket and be constantly distracted by the progress of a crucial test match.

Ford queried this, suggesting that not only was the idea 'silly' but Americans tended to consider cricket a 'soft game'. However, he eventually gave in, with one proviso: 'You play it against the Australians, don't you? So let's have Australia winning, it may help our takings out there.'

MADE IN WALES
THE INN OF THE SIXTH HAPPINESS (1958)

You'll always get a welcome in the hillside, especially when wild Wales is required to double for altogether more exotic foreign climes.

This big-budget version of the missionary Gladys Aylward's inspiring life was always planned to be shot in Taiwan. Until, that is, there was a clash between the Nationalist leader Chiang Kai-shek and the filmmakers, led by the American director Mark Robson, about the story content.

Chiang Kai-shek, desperate to promote a new image for his Republic of China, didn't want any reference to the past and in particular objected to the film's poignant historical depiction of 'bound feet' among young Chinese women.

So Robson, Ingrid Bergman, Robert Donat and company decamped instead for a Chinese walled city recreated at Nantmor at the foot of Cwm Bychan valley near Beddgelert in Snowdonia.

Ten years later, the same area was once again requisitioned to 'play' China in *The Most Dangerous Man in the World* (1969), starring Gregory Peck, just a year after it – the Pass of Llanberis, to be exact – had also done doughty duty as the North-West Frontier during a rare location outing for the regulars in *Carry On . . . Up The Khyber* (1968).

PAIN IN THE ARTS
LUST FOR LIFE (1958)

When collaborators describe the director as a 'perfectionist', that's usually a euphemism for nit-picking obsessive.

In this biopic of the tortured artist Vincent van Gogh (Kirk Douglas), there's a scene near the end where he's seen painting in a wheat field shortly before he commits suicide. The production had purchased a suitable field from a French farmer and placed a cherry tree in the foreground.

Weighing several tons, the mature tree took some planting. Top-heavy with leaves and branches, it had to be supported with piano wire to prevent it from falling over. This achieved, the shot was lined up with the framing reproduced to recreate exactly what van Gogh would have seen when he was painting the original picture.

The director Vincente Minnelli took a look through the lens and shook his head, clearly displeased. The tree was in the wrong place, he told the crew: they must move it three feet to the left. When they pointed out to him that it might be easier just to move the camera instead, Minnelli demurred, firmly. It had to be the tree.

Talk of the cost and the probable loss of a day's shooting couldn't budge him and so the tree was laboriously extricated and replanted a yard away.

During the course of the operation it fell over, losing a couple of branches and a few thousand leaves – but the 'perfectionist' filmmaker got his shot.

READY FOR THE CHOP
A TALE OF TWO CITIES (1958)

The original plan was to shoot some scenes on this umpteenth version of Dickens's classic about the French Revolution in the beautiful Provence town of Avignon – until someone realised that the schedule was smack bang in the middle of the summer tourist season.

So the filmmakers settled instead on Bourges, further to the north in central France, an unexciting town despite its beautiful thirteenth-century Gothic cathedral. It was empty, too, because, it being harvest time, the locals were out in the fields all day.

They badly needed French peasants for the crowded guillotine scenes. Nearby was an American Army base and a contract was drawn up for US servicemen to be extras, a concession being they'd be allowed to bring their own water.

The main problem was that what turned out to be a bunch of mostly six-foot soldiers would have to cram themselves into five-foot-eight peasant outfits.

Orders were issued (as were tomatoes for throwing), for them to 'shake your fists and cry, "Death to the aristocrats!"' On the first take, a cry was distinctly heard, 'Hang the bum!'

When the scene cut, the apologetic extra who'd shouted it explained he'd got carried away because he came from a hanging state.

MR GIMMICK MAN

MACABRE (1958)

New York-born William Castle had been directing unremarkable films for more than fifteen years – mostly westerns and mild dramas – when he suddenly decided on a change.

With *Macabre*, Castle began to reinvent himself as a horror film showman – 'a kind of Alfred Hitchcock of the Z-movie', as one critic put it.

As important as the films, Castle reckoned, were the promotion, marketing and assorted gimmicks he dreamed up to accompany their release. With *Macabre*, he took out an insurance policy with Lloyds of London trumpeting that anyone who died of fright during a screening would get $1,000.

For *The House on Haunted Hill* (1959) he dreamed up Emergo, a rather crude device by which a skeleton was rolled out on wires above the audience. In the same year, *The Tingler* (1959) was enlivened, if that's the right word, by Percepto, for which certain seats were wired to give their occupants a mild electric shock.

Castle then introduced Illusion-O for another haunted-house chiller, *Thirteen Ghosts* (1960). Audiences were issued with tinted glasses known as 'ghost viewers' with one red eyepiece through which ghosts could be seen and a blue one through which they could not.

Probably because of mounting protests from cinema managers about various misfiring paraphenalia, Castle subsequently saved his gimmickry for on-screen employment. *Mr Sardonicus* (1961) had a 'Punishment Poll', a pause in the film during which the audience was asked to choose between alternative endings.

As for *Homicidal* (1961), an oddly effective spin on *Psycho*, there was a minute-long 'Fright Break' just before the bloody climax of the film. If any members of the audience were too frightened to stay, they were now invited to leave and would be refunded the price of admission. 'OK,' a voiceover would intone ominously, 'we're now going back into the house...'

Years after all these cheapo thrills, Castle – immortalised as 'Lawrence Woolsey' in Joe Dante's affectionate 1993 action comedy, *Matinée* – would later be closely involved in one of Hollywood's most successful and effective shockers: as producer of *Rosemary's Baby*.

MONSTER SUCCESS
THE BLOB (1958)

This low-budget pearl of schlock-horror fifties filmmaking began life as the result of an unlikely collaboration between a distributor of crude exploitation films and the Boy Scouts of America.

Jack H Harris, the man behind the release of lurid titles such as *Daughter of Horror* and *My Son, The Vampire*, wanted to be a producer, and he finally got his chance after meeting Irvine H Millgate, head of visual aids for the Scouts.

Harris had the idea for a monster movie about a shape-changing gelatinous alien mass that invades a small American town, and an enthusiastic Millgate wrote a suitable treatment, which he then took to Valley Forge Films, a small production company in Pennsylvania specialising in low-budget TV shows and various 16mm films.

What might have then remained just another routine B-grade gooey chiller suddenly attained lasting fame when Harris decided to offer the lead role of a rebellious high-school teenager to 28-year-old Steve McQueen.

McQueen had had bit parts in a couple of films, but this would be his first starring role in a feature. The film was budgeted at $240,000 with Harris putting up $150,000 of his own money. He offered McQueen either $3,000 up front or 10 per cent of the film's gross profits.

Since McQueen was convinced from the outset that the film would never make money, he settled for the cash. He began to establish his notorious 'bad boy' reputation during shooting and often clashed with his co-star, Aneta Corseaut.

According to Harris, 'They hated each other. The love scene was the very last thing we shot and by that time they were really confirmed in their hatred. Aneta had a bad time, especially since she had a skin blemish!'

Harris surely had the last laugh when his bargain-basement 'baby' went on to earn more than $12 million at the box office. As if being forever connected with this schlock wasn't bad enough, the fact that McQueen missed out on becoming a millionaire in his twenties would haunt the star for the rest of his days.

DYING FOR A BEER
ICE COLD IN ALEX (1958)

One of the most stirring of British war films was notable for the marked absence of battle. This was a story about pluck and endurance, and the longest wait for a well-deserved pint of lager ever captured on film.

The final scene, in which our desert-crossing heroes tuck into their icy-cold Carlsberg lager in an Alexandria bar was even used by the company in the 1990s for a successful commercial.

In some ways the film was a tribute to the skills of its director J Lee Thompson and the script by Christopher Landon and T J Morrison for keeping the suspense bubbling away under so slight a dramatic premise.

John Mills has had few harder roles than that of the stoic, intensely driven soldier who leads his small team across a mined desert during the Battle of Tobruk. Rarely has he gone so far for his art either.

'The thing is,' he explained, 'everything depended on this lager looking great. We got back from the desert and shot that scene in the bar at Elstree. That morning the producer came up and said 'Johnny, we've got a problem.' I asked what and he said it was the lager. They'd tried everything, ginger ale, Andrew's Liver Salts, every damn thing and it just doesn't work.

'He said they'd have to use the real thing. I said, "What's the matter with that, I love the real thing!" But of course we did take one: bang – down it goes. Then they shoot another take: bang – down that one goes.

'And then things started to go wrong. By take fourteen I was absolutely plastered. They had to carry me out of the studio and put me to bed. It was the best morning's work I'd ever done.'

LUCAS AID

THE HIDDEN FORTRESS (1958)

It took Hollywood six years to Americanise Kurosawa's *Seven Samurai* (1954) as *The Magnificent Seven* (1960). It would be nearly twenty years before this action-packed if rather more lightweight adventure by the great Japanese director would prove an inspiration for that otherworldly frontier epic, *Star Wars* (1977).

George Lucas has readily owned up to being strongly influenced by Kurosawa's tale of feudal sixteenth-century Japan, in which a dethroned princess, Lady Yukihime (Misa Uehara), tries to regain her birthright during the country's long and bitter civil wars.

He was particularly struck by a pair of squabbling farmers who help escort the princess though enemy territory; they would become the blueprint for the extraterrestrial droids, R2-D2 and C-3PO, in his sci-fi blockbuster.

Three years later, Lucas was able partially to repay his debt when, with the power and the profits afforded by *Star Wars*, he and Francis Coppola were able to help Kurosawa finance the veteran filmmaker's award-winning, *Kagemusha* (1980)

SMELLS CURIOUS
SCENT OF MYSTERY (1959)

Around the time that William Castle was imposing his outrageous Hollywood gimmicks on hapless horror-film audiences, (see *Macabre*, etc., above), Europe got its own back briefly with a process called Smell-O-Vision.

Filmed in Spain, the world's first, and probably last, 'smellie', a very mild thriller, would have the added thrill of well-timed whiffs appropriate to the plot being sprayed into the cinema via pipes set into the back of each seat.

The sea, tobacco and apricots were among the various odours being perfected by a professor in Switzerland. At a big preview in Chicago, a test audience waited expectantly for each release of aroma-laden air.

The mechanism worked well. The trouble was the result, as every fragrance seemed to smell exactly the same. Like 'cheap eau de cologne', audiences reported.

IMPERIAL CHALLENGE
BEN-HUR (1959)

Clad in helmet and shining breastplate, a bit player had to gallop up to Tiberius, with the whole Roman Forum in the background, and say, 'I come with a message for Caesar.'

After years of silent walk-ons, his big break had finally arrived. In a state of great emotional stress, with a huge crowd cheering in the background and the cameras rolling, he galloped up, tried to rein in and fell off his horse in front of a startled emperor.

'Cut! Cut!' shouted the assistant. 'Everybody back to the start.' With patience, the director William Wyler explained that his final position was critical, as he would end in a big close-up for his lines.

Intended to encourage, this information only increased the hapless actor's anxiety. After several more takes, each ending in the same way, his shining armour began to resemble a battered sardine tin.

'Take it easy, take it easy,' growled the director, trying to subdue his rising tide of fury. 'Just one more time, and it's going to be fine.'

So in galloped the messenger, and this time he came to a halt bang on the required mark. 'I come wi—', at which precise moment the visor on his helmet fell down, totally obscuring his face.

TALKING CURE
THE MIRACLE (1959)

Roger Moore, rising 31, had already appeared in four films and also starred in a 39-episode TV series (as *Ivanhoe*) when he was summoned to a meeting with the director Irving Rapper.

Shooting hadn't started yet on this historical hokum set during the Peninsular War, and Rapper told Moore, playing Wellington's nephew, that he spoke with too exaggerated an English accent – the result, he thought, of mumbling through clenched teeth.

Moore was sent to Warner Brothers' most celebrated dialogue tutor, Joe Graham, for an urgent assessment.

According to the biographer Paul Donovan, Graham 'elicited Roger's admission that the fact he had left school at fifteen did worry him occasionally, and that his lack of formal education and academic qualifications made him feel apprehensive, deep down, of misusing and mispronouncing words.

'These were anxieties with which Roger had never confronted himself, and he came to agree with Graham that he probably did have an unconscious inferiority complex which manifested itself in a desire to keep his jaws together, producing a forced English accent which was nothing more than a defence mechanism.'

Graham slowly began to boost the actor's self-esteem as well as giving him exercises to open those clenched teeth and loosen his jaws. Moore says they opened easily once he got his thinking right.

HAIR-RAISING MOMENT
SOLOMON AND SHEBA (1959)

More than half of this Old Testament epic had been completed in Spain when Tyrone Power, co-starring opposite the busty Italian beauty Gina Lollobrigida, had a heart attack and died.

Power's demise was especially shocking since a recent service medical – he was still an army reserve – had failed to pick up a heart condition when declaring him 100 per cent fit. The actor had even transported his own yacht to the Mediterranean and would fly every weekend from Madrid to the South of France, where the vessel was moored, for a Sunday sail.

There were four options now open to the production team, led by the veteran director King Vidor: scrap the project and collect the insurance; rewrite the script to end the film approximately where the shooting left off; have Power portray Solomon before his father David's death then hire another star to portray him after; start from scratch with a brand-new Solomon.

They opted for the last of these and, emboldened with a record $1.2 million worth of insurance, signed up the world's most famous bald actor Yul Brynner – who reputedly snared most of that insurance money as his hefty fee.

Perhaps the idea was to fool audiences into thinking that Power was still about, because Brynner proved to be almost unrecognisable playing the Israeli king complete with uncharacteristic lush locks – an awesome toupee – and goatee beard.

HEART OF DARKNESS
THE NUN'S STORY (1959)

Playing Sister Luke in the thinly disguised story of a Belgian nun, Marie-Louise Habets, who had renounced her vows after many years working among the lepers of central Africa, would inevitably require some tough location shooting on the Dark Continent for Audrey Hepburn.

To try to make her sojourn in Stanleyville (now Kisangani) a little cosier, the star had a trio of demands: that she be accompanied by a top doctor equipped with all the latest drugs to deal with viral infection; that the Belgian Congo waive its quarantine laws to allow her beloved Yorkshire terrier, Famous, to accompany her; and that a bidet be installed in her African digs.

In the event, she sustained only a single monkey bite. Later, though, back in Rome completing the film's interior scenes, Hepburn fell ill with kidney stones, the result of earlier dehydration. Apparently, Famous remained completely unscathed by its journey into the heart of darkness.

ONE-TAKE WONDER
COMPULSION (1959)

In this fictionalised account of the notorious Leopold-Loeb case – about a pair of rich homosexual teenagers who kidnapped and killed a fourteen-year-old boy for thrills – Orson Welles brilliantly played flamboyant lawyer Jonathan Wilk, styled after their real-life defence attorney Clarence Darrow.

His summation at the climax of the film, containing an impassioned plea against capital punishment, is, at eighteen minutes long, possibly the longest single uninterrupted speech in film history.

Naturally it couldn't be done in one take – there is, after all, only 10 minutes' worth of film in a camera – so the speech had to be broken up into bits and pieces, quite a few of which were, by movie standards, quite long in themselves.

Welles seemed to have no trouble at all with the words delivered without specific eye contact to the courtroom spectators, but, when it came to the parts spoken directly at the district attorney (played by E G Marshall), he was clearly all at sea.

His solution was extraordinary. He asked Marshall and the actors playing the DA's assistants to keep their eyes closed as he clearly found their focus a serious distraction. Since the camera was filming over their backs it didn't prove a problem and Welles breezed through it.

For the last part of the speech, the director wanted to do it in one long three-minute piece. By now, Welles was in a muck sweat ('stage fright', he claimed) and procrastinated constantly about the sequence until it was the day before he was due to finish his contracted stint on the film.

With time running out, the mercurial Welles again provided his preferred get-out. He would rehearse all the moves without attempting a performance but then must be left alone on the set for as long as was required to prepare himself for the actual speech.

The director agreed, nervously. He and the crew were summoned back to the set an hour and a half later. After spurning the idea of yet another technical run-through, Welles emoted perfectly in one take. Cut, print.

THE LAST LAUGH
SOME LIKE IT HOT (1959)

After his first Oscar nomination for the screenplay of *Ninotchka* (1939), Billy Wilder would receive a further, record-breaking nine for writing, actually winning thrice – for *The Lost Weekend* (1945), *Sunset Boulevard* (1950) and *The Apartment* (1960).

They were, in fact, all collaborations, first, most notably, with Charles Brackett and then, in later years, with I A L 'Izzy' Diamond.

In fellow writer-director Cameron Crowe's enjoyable *Conversations With Wilder*, the great man explained how it was difficult to apportion credit for this or that line. Except in the case of perhaps the most famous, certainly the funniest, last line in screen history for this peerless cross-dressing gangster comedy set in the Roaring Twenties.

The final scene was of Tony Curtis, Jack Lemmon and Marilyn Monroe all jumping into Joe E Brown's speedboat. Lemmon still in drag has now to disclose himself as a man to the besotted Brown, who seems quite unfazed by the revelation. But the writers just couldn't think of a line to go with the moment.

Until, suddenly, Wilder recalled the beginning of their discussion when Diamond suggested, 'Nobody's perfect.' Wilder said to his co-writer, 'Let's send it to the mimeograph department so that they have something, and then we are going to *really* sit down and make a *real* funny last line.'

THE 1960s

CURTAIN RAISER
PSYCHO (1960)

When they were filming the notorious shower scene for Hitchcock's most enduringly twisted thriller, Anthony Perkins was three thousand miles away in New York rehearsing for a new Broadway musical called *Greenwillow*.

So who was doubling for main man Perkins, a.k.a. the mother-fixated transvestite motel killer Norman Bates, in one of the most analysed and imitated sequences in cinema history?

The shadowy full-length shots were of a 24-year-old stunt woman, Margo Epper, while the hand holding the knife was Hitchcock's own.

As Perkins himself has pointed out, anyone could tell that, even in drag, the silhouette behind the shower curtain bore little resemblance to the actor, and the knife was grasped in the right hand. Perkins was left-handed.

In fact this wasn't the only occasion that 'Mother' had stand-ins. So as not to betray Perkins's recognisable vocal stylings, the veteran actresses Jeanette Nolan (married in real life to John McIntire, who played *Psycho*'s bucolic Sheriff Chambers) and Virginia Gregg were used at various points, as well as one of Perkins's own young male actor friends, Paul Jasmin.

A TALL TALE
FLAMING STAR (1960)

After decorative bit parts in a handful of British films, Birkenhead-born Barbara Steele was just 21 when summoned to Hollywood for what promised to be her big break.

The tall, dark-haired and very striking-looking actress had been pencilled in to play opposite Elvis Presley in his sixth film, a gloomy, virtually songless, western tale with 'Elvis the Pelvis' (this was before he became the King) as a brooding half-breed.

The producer and director, both concerned that willowy Steele was not only very inexperienced in front of the camera but would also dwarf Elvis, were overruled by the studio.

Wearing a blonde wig and no heels, Steele started filming her role as platonic love interest to Presley's Pacer Burton, but, as soon as the studio started seeing the rushes, they knew that the film-makers had been right all the time.

Steele was duly if gently given her marching orders, to be replaced by authentically blonde and vertically unthreatening Barbara Eden.

Then, in a strange twist of fate creepily to presage the path of her future career, Steele was next called to Rome, where she won the lead role – actually dual roles – in Mario Bava's *La Maschera del Demonio*.

Better known as *Black Sunday*, the witchcraft classic rapidly turned Steele into an icon, the unrivalled Queen of the Screamies. Hollywood's loss was horror's gain.

SNAILS AND OYSTERS
SPARTACUS (1960)

Restoring previously deleted footage has its advantages and disadvantages. What better way of at least belatedly experiencing a director's less-compromised artistic 'vision'?

But what if a key missing scene earmarked for new inclusion had turned up from the vaults minus a usable soundtrack? And what if the main actor in that sequence was now dead?

Even at script stage, the censorship powers-that-be in Hollywood had warned director Stanley Kubrick and his producer-star Kirk

Douglas that their so-called 'snails and oysters' scene was likely to breach the all-powerful Hays Code on 'perversion'.

Set in a lavish Roman marble bathroom at night, the scene was between the aristocrat Crassus (Laurence Olivier) and his new slave boy Antoninus (Tony Curtis). Crassus, who clearly fancies the lad, is trying, in a suggestively oblique way, to discover the sexual lie of the land. 'My appetitite includes both snails and oysters,' half-naked Crassus purrs cryptically to the somewhat bemused Antoninus.

There was simply too much sexual connotation – of (whisper it), homosexuality – for the censors, who were particularly concerned at the word 'appetite'. They did add, however, that the sequence might possibly remain if 'snails and oysters' were replaced by 'artichokes and truffles'.

The scene, along with some gruesome arena and battle footage of spurting blood and a hacked limb, were cut from the original-release print.

Thirty years later, *Spartacus* was being readied for rerelease with the restoration of five minutes of footage along with the original overture and intermission.

The original soundtrack seemed to have survived well, but it related, of course, to the 182-minute-release version of the film. While cutting the new material together, the missing track elements had to be kept in mind. It appeared that none of the missing track had survived and it would have to be produced from scratch. There was music but no effects or dialogue.

New effects had to be created. In the case of the 'snails and oyster' scene, for which new dialogue had to be recorded, the existing tracks for fragments of the scene in the 182-minute version could not be used because the music wouldn't fit.

While the film was being cut, Jim Katz, the producer in charge of the restoration and reconstruction, began to arrange for the completion of the 'snails and oysters' scene. He brought Tony Curtis to Los Angeles to record his lines, as found in Kirk Douglas's original copy of the script.

Olivier had died in 1989 and his widow, Joan Plowright, was contacted to ask if she approved of using another actor to voice her late husband's dialogue, and, if so, could she suggest a suitable candidate?

Her suggestion was Anthony Hopkins, one of Olivier's protégés years earlier at the National Theatre, who also did a wickedly accurate vocal impersonation of his old mentor.

Hopkins agreed and eventually Katz oversaw the recording of his lines in London, referring to a fax from Kubrick as to how the scene should be played. When the dialogue arrived back in LA, it was combined with Curtis's and the scene was reborn.

TROUBLE IN GREENELAND
OUR MAN IN HAVANA (1960)

Apart from the odd hurricane or star tantrum, you can plan for most things when preparing a film. A political revolution is an entirely different matter.

By the time they got round to filming Graham Greene's Cold War satire set on fascistic Batista's Cuba, the communist Castro had swept to power in a popular uprising on the exotic Caribbean island.

The change of regime in the six months between first planning the film and the arrival of cast and crew posed some mundane, if fundamental, problems. Such as how to keep Castro's bearded followers out of crowd scenes, how to make extras wear the hated blue uniform of the Batista police, and how to get the Ministry of Interior's seal of approval on Greene's 30,000-word script.

It seems the book had done the author little good with the new powers in Cuba. In poking fun at the British secret service he had somehow minimised the terror of Batista's rule. But those who'd suffered during the years of the previous dictatorship could hardly be expected to appreciate that Greene's real subject was the absurdity of the British agent and not the justice of a revolution.

Nor did his reasons for changing the character of the head of the secret police from a savage Captain Ventura into a more cynical Captain Segura appeal much locally.

Thirty-nine script changes were required and a censor was assigned to the location shooting. The film company wisely employed a Cuban assistant director, who mustered native stand-by technicians and a large number of extras (with beards suitably trimmed).

The puritanism of the new government also made it difficult to recreate some necessary plot bawdiness and, ever sensitive to its own image, Castro's people even insisted that a bootblack wear clean trousers.

The final 'victim' of the coup was the American actor Ernie Kovacs's facial hair. He had arrived in Cuba wearing a heavy beard to play Segura, but this was considered too much of a symbol of the Castro regime to be worn by a hated character of the past. So Kovacs was shorn of all but a slim moustache.

INSULTING THE CHURCH
VILLAGE OF THE DAMNED (1960)

This modest but rather effective British chiller – based on John Wyndham's *The Midwich Cuckoos* – about the alien 'possession' of a small English village boasted three screenwriters, including its director, Wolf Rilla.

But when the script made its first faltering steps towards a green light earlier in Hollywood, it was entirely the work of one writer, Stirling Silliphant, who had been asked by MGM to pen the leading role for suave Ronald Colman. Unfortunately, the old matinée idol died just as Silliphant was finishing the script.

The studio had gone to a great deal of trouble to buy the original book from Wyndham, to the extent of having microfilm made of each page as he finished typing the manuscript. It was then flown over to MGM.

But, when it came finally to turning in the script, it wasn't to the people who'd gone to all that trouble. It was to a different set of executives, who now seemed 'appalled' to discover what they had bought.

Silliphant, who'd later win an Oscar for *In the Heat of the Night*, told me, 'It was "anti-Catholic", they said. They said, "It deals with the impregnation of women by creatures from outer space thereby paralleling the immaculate conception." They then sent the script to some Catholic advisers who concurred thoroughly, adding it would be "insulting".'

The studio decided to shelve the project 'indefinitely' before suddenly resurrecting it just a couple of years later as a UK-based production, with the equally silver-tongued George Sanders taking on the old Colman role. It would prove to be one of MGM's best-received films of the year.

REACH FOR GLORY
THE ALAMO (1960)

At 57, the Texan actor Chill Wills was far and away the oldest among his four fellow nominees – Peter Ustinov (*Spartacus*), Jack Kruschen (*The Apartment*), Sal Mineo (*Exodus*) and Peter Falk (*Murder Inc.*) – at the year's Academy Awards.

He also probably reasoned that with more than eighty mostly forgettable films behind him – including uncredited work as the voice of Francis the Talking Mule – it was his last chance at glory in his role as Davy Crockett's good-ol'-boy sidekick, Beekeeper.

So Chill – named because he was apparently born on the hottest day of 1903 – decided with the help of a pushy publicist, the splendidly named 'Bow-Wow' Wojeiechowicz, to mount a concerted Oscar campaign to boost his case. Unfortunately, that was where it all began to go horribly wrong.

His first two-page ad listed hundreds of Academy members and said, 'Win, Lose or Draw, You're Still My Cousins, and I Love You All.' Groucho Marx, among those listed, retorted with his own proclamation: 'Dear Mr Chill Wills: I Am Delighted to Be Your Cousin, but I Voted for Sal Mineo.'

But that didn't stop Chill and Bow-Wow. The next ad pictured a large photo of the actor in his trademark buckskins and Davy Crockett hat alongside the message, 'We of the *Alamo* cast are praying – harder than the real Texans prayed for their lives at the Alamo – for Chill Wills to win the Oscar as the Best Supporting Actor – Cousin Chill's acting was great.' It was signed, 'Your *Alamo* Cousins.'

This was the final straw. Even the director and co-star John Wayne, who'd been planning to make the film for nearly twenty years and saw it as a flag-waving antidote to the rising tide of subversive filth currently engulfing Hollywood, was forced to go public with a stern disclaimer.

Mind you, this was a bit rich coming from the Duke, who had helped to orchestrate an ad campaign for his film that seemed to suggest it would be un-American to vote for anything but *The Alamo*.

Overall, the damage seemed to have been done. The film, nominated six times, including Best Picture, won nothing and also proved to be a critical and box-office bust. For the record, Ustinov snatched away Chill's prize on the night.

HOLD THE FRONT PAGE
THE DAY THE EARTH CAUGHT FIRE (1961)

Ask any filmmaker which city has traditionally been the toughest in which to shoot and many, some quite bitterly, will answer even today, 'London'.

So trying to recreate a devastated capital for this surprisingly realistic apocalyptic drama years before computer-generated imagery was even a twinkle in the eye of special-effects wizards must have been a downright nightmare.

For a key scene in what is meant to be a debris-strewn, car-free, deserted Fleet Street, the production was given one early Sunday morning for two minutes' filming at a time between fifteen-minute flows of the normal traffic. Official NO PARKING signs had also been strategically sited between the Law Courts and Ludgate Circus to keep stationary vehicles well away.

At the start of each two-minute session a pair of motorcycle police would accelerate up both sides of the street removing the signs just ahead of an open-backed props truck from which rubble and dust was shovelled into the street.

The operation was disruptive but not more potentially so than when they had to blow clouds of man-made fog, representing a mysterious mist, as people were queuing in Battersea Park for water rations.

A gentle breeze began wafting the fog across the Thames to the Chelsea Embankment and within minutes a police car had roared to the location ordering filming to stop immediately. Apparently the Queen had been trying to opening the Royal Chelsea Flower Show in deteriorating visibility.

FULL OF EASTERN PROMISE
LAWRENCE OF ARABIA (1962)

The familiar, indeed iconic, sight of Peter O'Toole resplendent in his white robes as he leads his Arab forces into battle might never had happened if Albert Finney had been driven more by personal ambition.

It was August 1960 and Finney, 24 years old and rehearsing hard for his new stage role as Billy Liar, received a call to screen-test for the title role in David Lean's new epic which still had the working title, *Seven Pillars of Wisdom*.

Finney, whose own film-starring debut in *Saturday Night and Sunday Morning* was still a few months away from its West End premiere, arrived at MGM's studios in Borehamwood,

Hertfordshire, to find that this was not so much a test as a mini-movie in its own right. More than £100,000 – only £20,000 less than the entire budget of *Saturday Night and Sunday Morning* – had been spent on building quite lavish interior and exterior sets.

The twenty-minute test was shot over four days by Lean and consisted of five scenes – among them, in an Arab tent, a hut and around a campfire against a vivid red sunset. His 'co-stars' were Gregoire Aslan, Laurence Payne and Marne Maitland in parts eventually played by Alec Guinness, Anthony Quinn and Omar Sharif.

At one point Finney had to don the famous white robes, which were being used courtesy of the film project's adviser, Sir Anthony Nutting, an Arab expert and former minister of state at the Foreign Office, who'd been presented with them by a Saudi prince. They'd reappear later in O'Toole's one-day test before being relegated to cushion covers for the Nutting family's dogs.

Nutting felt that Finney would have been a 'marvellous' Lawrence, certainly a very different one from the portrayal that began to emerge when O'Toole, lankier and more outgoing than Finney, began filming ten months later in what would turn out to be an Oscar-nominated role.

Lean's reaction was that Finney 'was rather too young for it ... but the tests weren't half bad'. Producer Sam Spiegel was, however, absolutely convinced, offering the young actor a £10,000 fee for the film and then a contract worth £125,000 over the next five years. To be fair, the various inducements alter endlessly in the telling down the years – from a seven-, to a five-, then a four-year contract with figures of up to £250,000 being bandied about.

What is quite certain was Finney's refusal of any and all offers. He said didn't want to become just a 'property', adding that he 'didn't know where I want to be in five years' time – or tomorrow for that matter. I hate being committed – to a girl, a film producer or to being a certain kind of big-screen image.' Lean's only reported comment on Finney's rejection of the role was that the actor had told him simply that he 'wasn't interested in becoming a star'.

Spiegel had apparently also told Finney that they'd probably want him to change his name. 'Bloody cheek,' thought Finney.

'Why don't you change yours?' He recalled the advice of friends who said to him, 'Nobody can force you to do something you don't want. They can lead a horse to water, but even Spiegel can't make it drink.'

A MILKY DEATH
THE MANCHURIAN CANDIDATE (1962)

Frank Sinatra, who co-starred with Laurence Harvey and Angela Lansbury in this often grim political thriller about Cold War paranoia, often claimed the film to be one of favourites, even if, he'd then confess, he didn't really know what it was all about.

As with all cult movies, audiences tend to interpret the significance of almost every frame and the scene where a man is shot and milk instead of blood comes from his body was ripe for much serious analysis.

The real explanation, the director John Frankenheimer explained later, was 'very simply and prosaic. My problem in the film was the same as that which faces the director of *Hamlet* – both contain an awful lot of corpses.

'I had seven to deal with, and the difficulty was to make the killings different, to prevent it all from becoming monotonous. So I though, why not shoot the old boy through the milk container he's carrying?

'So we did – and got credited with all sorts of symbolic overtones we'd never even thought about.'

TOUGHING IT OUT
CAPE FEAR (1962)

As a fifteen-year-old drifter in Savannah, Georgia, Robert Mitchum had been arrested for vagrancy and sentenced to serve time on a chain gang. Mitchum was just into his forties and a successful Hollywood tough guy when he first learned that the principal location for his latest film would be that very same genteel port town in the heart of America's Deep South.

'F****** Savannah!' he was said to have exclaimed. 'They railroaded me in that town, man. They may still have a warrant out for me ... ' Without much enthusiasm at first, Mitchum was playing the psychopath Max Cady in J Lee Thompson's film of John D MacDonald's pulp thriller, *The Executioners*, originally set in the Carolinas.

Cady, a sexual sadist, is out for revenge against a lawyer, Sam Bowden (Gregory Peck), whose witness evidence had sent Cady to jail eight years earlier. Now the psycho's back in town for payback against Bowden and his family.

Whether it was the surroundings or the fact that he was over-compensating for taking on a role he had originally refused, mercurial Mitchum began to enter into the spirit of the part with an almost manic gusto. 'You know, I live the character,' he told the director, ominously. 'And this character drinks and rapes.'

In a river tussle with Peck – who was also the producer – he all but drowned his co-star. His roughhouse with the actress Barrie Chase, playing a prostitute, was so intense that she threatened to quit the film. And, in the climactic scene where Mitchum terrorises Bowden's wife Peggy (Polly Bergen), members of the crew had to break up the couple after the authentic spilling of blood. 'He just ... lost it,' said Bergen.

Intriguingly, Mitchum and Peck were reunited thirty years on for Martin Scorsese's gorier, more morally ambivalent but much less tense remake of *Cape Fear*.

This time round, in sly cameos (a heavily tattooed Robert De Niro and Nick Nolte were the chief protagonists), they sort of reversed their roles with Mitchum as the amiable local sheriff and Peck as Cady's sleazy lawyer.

THE EYES HAVE IT

MY GEISHA (1962)

This comedy of mistaken identity revolves around an American actress (Shirley MacLaine) trying to fool her director husband (Yves Montand) into believing that she is an authentic geisha girl so she can be with him on location in Japan.

But how could the makeup people transform MacLaine for maximum authenticity? At first they used complicated prosthetic eyepieces, but, whenever she blinked or closed her eyes, the separation between her lids and the plastic was visible. Whatever they tried, the tests were always terrible.

They could disguise her height with camera angles, use brown contact lenses to cover the blue of her eyes and apply rice makeup over her freckles. Yet try as they could they simply couldn't make the shape of MacLaine's eyes Japanese. If the audience didn't believe she was a geisha, how could her husband?

Finally, the veteran makeup man Frank Westmore came up with the solution – condoms. Because the rubber was soft and pliable, he cut out an almond shape and glued it to her eyelids. Applying makeup over the rubber disguised the lines of demarcation.

MacLaine discovered she could blink and even close her eyes without the camera picking up what they'd used. Westmore had, she once wrote, 'made the supreme sacrifice ... safe sex for his art.'

WORD IS HIS BOND

DR NO (1962)

The character of 007 was originated in Jamaica almost exactly ten years to the month before location work on *Dr No*, trailblazer in the James Bond film series, would start filming on that very same Caribbean island.

In January 1952, at his Oracabessa beach home, Goldeneye, Ian Fleming's eye suddenly settled on a coffee-table book called *Birds of the West Indies*. The author was an American ornithologist called... James Bond.

'Brief, unromantic and yet masculine,' Fleming once said about the name for the proposed secret-agent hero of his as yet uncompleted novel (*Casino Royale*), 'written in a moment of intense boredom.'

In June 1961, the producer partners Albert 'Cubby' Broccoli, a gentlemanly New Yorker, and hustling Harry Saltzman, an abrasive Canadian, were still looking for the right actor to play a character, who, according to Fleming, 'likes gambling, golf and fast motor cars. He smokes a great deal, but without affectation. All his movements are relaxed and economical.'

A popular newspaper columnist, Pat Lewis, reported that the producers were having trouble casting the role and that hopefuls should put their vital statistics on the back of a photo and send it to Saltzman's office. Six finalists would be selected for screen-testing.

Lewis penned her portrait of the ideal candidate: '... must be aged between 28 and 35; measure between 6ft and 6ft 1in in height; weigh about 12st; have blue eyes, dark hair, rugged features – particularly a determined chin – and an English accent.'

Selected as 'the man who came closest to' Bond was a 28-year-old professional model called Peter Anthony. The producers were, meanwhile, in final negotiations to snare Edinburgh-born Sean Connery, 31, who'd already had several leading roles in film and TV.

Costing less than a million dollars to make and grossing almost $60 million worldwide, *Dr No* is arguably, dollar for dollar, still the most successful film in the franchise.

More than forty years and twenty films on, the continuing series, the longest in film history, resides with Broccoli's heirs. There have been five 007s in all, but most die-hard fans of the series would still firmly maintain that, of all of them, Connery was born to play Bond.

DEATH ON THE NILE
CLEOPATRA (1963)

Cleopatra, one of Hollywood's most famous flops, and certainly one of its costliest, started filming at Pinewood Studios on 28 September 1960 and was suspended 52 days later, on 18 November. Just under eleven minutes' worth of usable widescreen film was 'in the can'.

With eerie echoes of *I, Claudius* (see page 37), an earlier Roman epic-that-never-was, Pinewood's Nile saga began towards the end of 1959 when 20th Century-Fox sealed a deal with the studio owners, the Rank Organisation, to bring its prestigious production to England.

Why here? Elizabeth Taylor, signed up for the title role, insisted on a European base for tax reasons. Fox was lured here because of potential income from the Eady Fund, which rewarded the box-office performance of UK-produced films.

Whatever the various financial implications, the film would be the biggest ever handled in Britain. The sets alone were to cost more than the entire budgets of the three costliest films made at Pinewood since the studio had opened in the thirties.

Despite a shortage of plasterers – Pinewood had even resorted to advertising on peak-time television for more workers – the paper palaces of Rome and Alexandria began to take shape during the damp, chill summer of 1960. A remarkable set, representing Alexandria harbour, went up on the back lot and some millions of gallons of water went in it, augmented by English rains.

Rouben Mamoulian, the 62-year-old Russian-born director – and no stranger to studio fights, having been fired from both *Laura* and *Porgy and Bess* – had spent a year of preparation on *Cleopatra*. He was said to have been physically sick with apprehension when he first saw the bogus city of Alexandria set in the English countryside. His mood was not improved when he learned that Hollywood was insisting that the Egyptian desert scenes be filmed there too.

When Elizabeth Taylor checked into the studio, trouble followed. She insisted on having her own Hollywood hairdresser, Sydney

Guilaroff. The unions said no. After a dispute that reached out to other studios, the star was told she could have Guilaroff – but only supervising a British hairdresser.

Before a foot of film was shot, the bill had already passed £1 million and there were still scheduled sixteen weeks to come, at the cost of about £120,000 a day.

Shooting finally got under way – with Peter Finch cast as Caesar and Stephen Boyd as Mark Antony – and then came the day for the invasion of five thousand centurions and camp followers for a massive, colourful tableau.

Pinewood management had to lay on 28 tube trains from London and there were 30 buses doing nonstop pick-ups from nearby Uxbridge station to the studios. Mobile lavatories were hired from Epsom racecourse, catering marquees were erected and food to feed the five thousand was created in mountains.

At 8.30 a.m. they were ready to shoot – except that it was pouring with rain and the weather didn't look as if it was clearing up. To cut their losses, the 'call' was abandoned and five thousand extras swept out of the studio, descending on Uxbridge instead for their refreshment. Pinewood's catering, including nine thousand sausage rolls, remained untouched.

As well as the problem of casting huge crowds of Romans, Egyptians and Nubians, there was also the question of Mark Antony and his spectacular horsey stunt. The idea was that the Roman consul, on horseback, would leap from a barge in the harbour onto the landing stage.

The designated stuntman quailed at the thought. Following a brainwave by the horse handler, the powers-that-be contacted the leading showjumper Alan Oliver who raced from his Oxfordshire bed in the middle of the night to complete the stunt early the following morning.

By this time, Elizabeth Taylor was in the London Clinic with a near-fatal illness, eventually necessitating a major operation, and Joan Collins was on standby to take over the role. Fox wisely decided that enough was enough and finally pulled the plug on Pinewood's *Cleopatra* after more than $2 million had been abortively spent on the production.

When it cranked up again the following year in Italy's balmier climate, there was a new director (Joseph L Mankiewicz) and two new actors, Rex Harrison (Caesar) and Richard Burton (Mark Antony) to join a now-recovered Taylor.

In an altogether more cheerful, if rather ironic, sequel to the Fox fiasco, Hollywood's expensive loss proved to be Britain's gain when *Carry On Cleo* – tenth in the comedy film series and certainly one of its best – starting shooting at Pinewood using some of the sets that had been left to rot by Hollywood.

According to the series producer – and Pinewood stalwart – Peter Rogers, who had been amazed by the spiralling costs of *Cleopatra*, 'My basic thought was, Goodness, this is filmmaking gone mad. I really could make a *Carry On* version of this story in the time it took 20th Century-Fox to erect their scenery. My goal was simple – to do just that, in six weeks, under budget.'

BIKER BOYS
THE GREAT ESCAPE (1963)

Steve McQueen was a notorious 'speed freak', officially (but more often than not unofficially) racing cars and motorbikes. On screen, he did much of his own driving for hair-raising films such as *Bullitt* (1968) and *Le Mans* (1971).

For *The Great Escape* – dubbed 'The Great Headache' by the veteran director John Sturges – McQueen personally pitched the idea of his spectacular flight by bike (the original script had him heading out by train before being recaptured).

As Captain Virgil Hilts, the film's 'Cooler King' of Stalag Luft III, he would try to leap the various high fences and wire straddling the border between Germany and Switzerland. Except that insurance requirements absolutely precluded McQueen's personal participation in the eye-catching stunt. That, however, didn't stop him trying a few preliminary runs in third gear.

'I could have bust my melon,' he would say, colourfully, before – one assumes, reluctantly – handing over on-screen duties to his California pal and stunt double Bud Ekins, hair suitably dyed for the occasion, who eventually completed a successful leap over the high wire (in fact a string-and-rubber-band prop) in a single take.

But there was still the problem of the long chase sequence before those climactic leaps in which McQueen, doing his own riding, kept outrunning the German stunt riders in pursuit. The star came up with the solution. He would also play the enemy. Sturges readily agreed, and with clever editing you can't really tell that this was a unique case of McQueen chasing himself.

Velocity also dominated his off-screen moments on the long shoot in Germany, during which McQueen managed to crash his smart Mercedes 300-SL into a tree on the way to work one day and also pick up some 37 speeding tickets in all before the film eventually wrapped.

SELLERS' MARKET

DR STRANGELOVE, OR HOW I LEARNED TO STOP WORRYING AND LOVE THE BOMB (1964)

If the director Stanley Kubrick had got his way, Peter Sellers would have played five of the six main roles in his peerless Cold War satire.

In the finished film we see Sellers as moustached RAF Captain Lionel Mandrake, bald US President Merkin Muffley and, perhaps the most inspired of the three, as the insanely grinning Strangelove himself, the wheel-chaired author and apologist of the impending nuclear apocalypse.

Against his better judgement because he felt he simply couldn't master the Texan accent, Sellers had also started filming the role of Major T J 'King' Kong, pilot of *Leper Colony*, the B-52 bomber unable to be recalled from its misguided mission to nuke the Soviet Union.

When he sprained his ankle in a fall outside a restaurant followed the next day by a tumble while shooting a studio-based scene suspended in the bomb bay, the doctor officially authorised his retirement from the role – much to Sellers's relief.

After John Wayne – apparently Kubrick had written the part with the 'Duke' in mind – and then Dan Blocker, of *Bonanza* fame, turned it down, the former rodeo rider Slim Pickens got his career-making break as Kong.

Sellers would later claim that Kubrick had also wanted him to play General Buck Turgidson, the gung-ho military man so memorably essayed by George C Scott. It seems the actor put his foot down, firmly explaining to the director that 'physically' he couldn't do it and, frankly, he didn't like the role, anyway.

ALL THAT GLISTERS
GOLDFINGER (1964)

The glam actress Shirley Eaton is probably best remembered for her iconic 'death by gold paint' in the third and, arguably, the best of the Bond series.

But, if you look closely at the golden girl in the credits and on the movie poster, that's not Eaton at all but the altogether more voluptuous Margaret Nolan (39–24–38)

It seems that they used Nolan – who also had a short but showy cameo in the film as the masseuse Dink – for paint practice and, so as not to waste any money, kept her, and the gold paint, for the seductive credit sequence.

NOT SO LUVERLY

MY FAIR LADY (1964)

Audrey Hepburn must have known just what it felt like when Julie Andrews missed out on the chance to reprise her career-making stage role as Eliza Doolittle in the film version of Lerner and Loewe's musical.

Hepburn, on the cusp of fame in 1951, when she conquered Broadway in *Gigi*, was passed over in favour of Leslie Caron when Vincente Minnelli directed the film (with music score added) six years later.

Andrews took the decision with typically stiff-upper-lip magnanimity but gently warned Hepburn that she might have trouble with a couple of the songs, which required, variously, 'a lot of power' and 'a great range'.

Hepburn, who had sung before on both stage and in films, asked the director George Cukor at the outset whether they'd use her singing voice here. The answer was a definite maybe.

Her co-star Rex Harrison's refusal to record his songs ahead of shooting certainly didn't aid her cause, because it meant that she would have to perform her shared numbers with him 'live', as it were. And it probably didn't help either that Lerner, the lyricist, had long been a strong advocate of Andrews.

As a precaution – though it seems in fact to have been pretty much a *fait accompli* from the start – Marni Nixon had been hired to record all her songs. Devastated, Hepburn would always feel that she had, effectively, given only half a performance.

To add insult to injury, when the Oscar nominations were announced, *My Fair Lady*'s dozen didn't include one for Hepburn, whereas *Mary Poppins*, Andrews's consolation prize, cited her as Best Actress among its lucky thirteen. The law of Sod did the rest.

TAKING A HIT
KING RAT (1965)

Not for nothing are first assistant directors often regarded as the tough-guy enforcers on a film set.

The British director Bryan Forbes was making his Hollywood debut with this adaptation of James Clavell's novel set inside Singapore's notorious Changi PoW prison during World War Two. On the first day of shooting on a fifty-acre set in the heart of studio-land, Forbes decided to make a welcoming speech to the some seven hundred authentic-looking extras who were permanently to populate the recreated camp.

When one of their number then decided to make a wisecrack at Forbes's expense, up stepped first AD Russ Saunders, an ex-All-American footballer, and knocked him to the ground.

'Anybody else want to be a comedian?' he asked. 'For your information, only one guy makes the jokes on this set, and that's the governor here, so listen to what he has to day and keep your mouths shut.'

The extra was stretchered away and that was the last such incident in the subsequent twelve weeks of filming.

TRAGIC CLIFFHANGER
THE HALLELUJAH TRAIL (1965)

Ten years before this breezy western with Burt Lancaster and Lee Remick, the horse-rider/stuntman Bill Williams was working with Kirk Douglas on another horse opera, *The Indian Fighter*.

Douglas noted that Williams, though clearly an excellent horseman, seemed to be distinctly accident-prone as a stuntman and suggested to him that he stick strictly to riding skills.

Cut, a decade on, to a scene as Williams and another man are riding a horse-drawn wagon towards a cliff. The idea then was that the horses separate, the men jump off and the wagon plunge over the cliff.

With his wife making a home movie at the time of his spectacular stunt, Williams failed to jump clear, went over the cliff with the wagon and was killed.

BATTLE OF THE SEXES

WHO'S AFRAID OF VIRGINIA WOOLF? (1966)

Married and divorced *twice* as well as co-stars in no fewer than eleven films during a dozen stormy years between 1963 and 1975, Elizabeth Taylor and Richard Burton were once the world's most famous, most highly paid and highest-profile twosome on and off screen.

At the time of this memorable adaptation of Edward Albee's savage play about a self-destructive college-campus couple, Taylor and Burton were still in the first flush of their first marriage.

However, their R-rated (this was the first American film ever to receive an R rating) exchanges as Martha (Taylor, 33, made up to look a raddled fortysomething) and George (Burton, already a heavy-drinking 40) graphically signposted their turbulent way ahead. 'I swear if you existed, I'd divorce you,' Martha taunts George.

Taylor would later complain that she was 'tired of playing Martha' in real life, while Burton owned up that he had many of George's worst faults in and out of drink. Both admitted to huge stress as they opened themselves up painfully in the roles under the debutant director Mike Nichols.

Burton, already concerned that the documentary cameraman, Haskell Wexler, would emphasise his pockmarks, was paid considerably less than his wife. When they handed out the Oscars that year, she won (her second) and he didn't.

Along with Peter O'Toole, Burton, who died in 1984, is the most nominated actor (with seven) never to win an Academy Award. At least O'Toole would receive an Honorary statuette in 2003.

MODESTY BLAZED
ALFIE (1966)

Jane Asher was due to play a bedroom scene opposite Michael Caine, as the Cockney Lothario, clad only in one of his shirts, which was about the same length as a trendy miniskirt.

Asher's real-life boyfriend at the time was Paul McCartney and the production was informed that the Beatle was not only concerned about the length of the shirt but also by the acreage of his girlfriend's exposed leg.

Before the scene could be shot, the wardrobe department had to cut up a spare shirt of the same design and then add another foot, which meant it now reached well below the actress's knees.

WORD OF MOUTH
WHAT'S UP, TIGER LILY? (1966)

When Woody Allen made this audacious movie he was already a successful comedy writer and a rising star on the American stand-up comedy circuit.

Using a Japanese B-movie – *Kagi No Kagi* (*Key of Keys*, 1964) – as his starting point, Allen and his collaborators let their comedy imagination run riot through the otherwise mundane espionage tale.

Adding their own dubbed dialogue, they changed the plot of the movie from a spy thriller to a desperate race to find the world's greatest egg-salad recipe.

With his then wife Louise Lasser and sometime co-writer Mickey Rose were Len Maxwell and Frank Buxton, improvising their hearts out in an ever more ludicrous yarn that sees global security hinging on the hero's culinary quest.

The pop group the Lovin' Spoonful made a slightly incongruous appearance in the proceedings, and years before Austin Powers tried a similar gag the two Japanese heroines were renamed Suki Yaki and Terri Yaki. This inspired lunacy helped launch Allen in movies.

OUT OF THE SKY
THE FLIGHT OF THE PHOENIX (1966)

After crash-landing in the Sahara, veteran pilot James Stewart is stranded with his passengers until someone comes up with the bright idea that they could rebuild the aircraft and fly out.

Stunt pilot Paul Mantz, who would be doubling for Stewart in the eponymous climax, decided that the new-look Phoenix was top-heavy, so added rocks and other weights to the fuselage for trimming.

That extra burden was to prove fatal, because, when he responded to radio directions to come in lower at his 80-m.p.h. speed, Mantz couldn't prevent one wing from grazing the ground, which led the plane to smash up. He was killed instantly.

A second stuntman, who'd been uneasy about this piece of action, wisely kept his seatbelt off and was able to leap clear of the craft, sustaining only a broken hip.

BLACK AND WHITE
HURRY SUNDOWN (1967)

Based on a bestselling novel, Otto Preminger's overwrought melodrama of racial injustice in immediate postwar Georgia was a nasty, small-minded tale of bigotry and violence – and that was just when the cameras *stopped* rolling.

Concerned about possible repercussions, the state authorities had denied Preminger permission to film in Georgia, so he relocated to Louisiana.

Their base was a huge hotel in Baton Rouge, which, though accustomed to hosting Hollywood film people on location, was mortified to discover that black stars (Diahann Carroll, Robert Hooks, Rex Ingram) would require accommodation, too. 'Integration' was not in the lexicon of a hostelry that still flew the Confederate Stars and Bars.

The subsequent hospitality was, to say the least, strained, and got worse, especially when they filmed in the small town of St Francisville, which turned out, it seems, to have been the head-quarters of the local chapter of the Ku Klux Klan.

Threatening phone calls, hate mail, tyre slashing and the odd bullet-raking of empty trailers became routine for the duration and Preminger ordered round-the-clock armed guards to protect the cast and crew of what was described locally as 'the nigger picture'.

HOLLYWOOD, ENGLAND
DOUBLE TROUBLE (1967)

Spotted by a Hollywood producer while working on a market stall on Portobello Road, seventeen-year-old Annette Day went one better than Barbara Steele (see *Flaming Star* on page 123) and stayed the course, starring opposite Elvis Presley in this trite travelogue/musical.

Day, along with her British co-stars Yvonne Romain, Norman Rossington, John Williams and Monty Landis, as well as the veteran Aussie actor Chips Rafferty (who Hollywood probably thought sounded Cockney), was meant to convince us that Elvis, as the nightclub singer Guy Lambert, had suddenly landed in Swinging London.

But, as any self-respecting Presley fan knows, the King came this way only once, and that was when he was passing through on his way to GI duty in Germany years earlier.

So scenes of a London discotheque, a carnival in Antwerp, and Bruges had to make do without Elvis. They were filmed by a second unit for colourful scene-setting while the star and cast gyrated in a Europe that was forever the studio backlot in California.

For Telford-born Day, the only English actress ever to play Presley's principal love interest in a film – and given a Ford Mustang by him during shooting – this was to be her only screen role.

BATTLING BACK
YOU ONLY LIVE TWICE (1967)

Johnny Jordan, an experienced aerial cameraman, was in Japan shooting action footage involving a pair of choppers attacking James Bond in his 'Little Nellie' autogyro when disaster struck as he was filming above from a French Alouette helicopter.

A sudden updraught caught one of the autogyros and threw it straight into the path of Jordan's aircraft. One of its rotor blades hit a skid of the Alouette, slicing through Jordan's extended foot.

Apparently, a group of surgeons were holding a symposium not far from where the accident had occurred and Jordan was raced to an operating room being used for demonstrations. There, he had his foot stitched back using comparatively new microsurgery techniques.

After he had been flown back to England, the Bond producer 'Cubby' Broccoli went to see him at the London Clinic.

'Well, Johnny,' Broccoli asked him, 'is there anything you'd like?'

'Yes, Cubby,' Jordan replied, 'I'd like to have this foot taken off. It's still not quite right to me. A friend of mine who went through a similar experience tells me the pain, especially in bad weather, can be quite rough. I'd rather have the thing off.'

Broccoli told him he should think it over carefully, but Jordan was adamant. 'I've done that, Cubby. I really don't want this foot any more.' Two days later, he had it amputated and an artificial foot fitted. Within months he was filming again.

On the next Bond film, *On Her Majesty's Secret Service*, Jordan was responsible for some of the series' most breathtaking footage as he dangled from a helicopter in his own patented parachute rig, swinging through peaks and tall pine forests as he shot some breathtaking Alpine shots establishing villain Blofeld's mountain lair. He also removed his artificial limb and squeezed into a bobsleigh in order to capture some close-up shots on the run as he hurtled around the track at 70 m.p.h.

A year later, the daredevil Jordan was dead. Without a safety harness, he was shooting action footage from a B-29 over the Gulf of Mexico for the film version of Joseph Heller's bestseller *Catch-22*. Another plane passed close by and, as his aircraft banked quickly to avoid a collision, the slipstream drew him out, and he fell two thousand feet to his death.

WHO DARES, LOSES
DOCTOR DOLITTLE (1967)

The world-famous explorer, author and motivational speaker Sir Ranulph Fiennes OBE has never been afraid to make his feelings known, sometimes with disastrous results.

Back in the sixties, while a member of the SAS, 22-year-old Fiennes turned unlikely eco-warrior after becoming deeply disgruntled with the Hollywood film crew that had taken over the Wiltshire village of Castle Combe in order to make this amiable film musical, starring Rex Harrison, Anthony Newley, Richard Attenborough and squads of 'talking' animals.

The picture-postcard village was a perfect setting for the author Hugh Lofting's Puddleby in the film, but the filmmakers found that the location required several changes, including enlarging the local pond for a particular scene.

As far as Fiennes (family motto, 'Look for a brave spirit') was concerned, this was environmental vandalism, so, using all his military know-how, he rigged up explosives on the dam that they had built and quite simply blew up 20th Century-Fox's rural film set.

Such activism did not go unnoticed. Fiennes, under his full name of Lieutenant Sir Ranulph Twisleton-Wykeham Fiennes, was caught and fined £500. The film's American director Richard Fleischer noted, 'English justice must have figured that a name like that was punishment enough.'

Fiennes was also thrown out of the SAS, though he continued his military career for a while by moving to the Middle East as a member of the sultan of Oman's forces.

Unrepentant, he says the dismissal taught him just one lesson: 'Don't get caught.'

GETTING EVEN

IN THE HEAT OF THE NIGHT (1967)

In one of best of many memorable scenes in this compelling thriller set in America's Deep South, Sidney 'They call me Mister Tibbs' Poitier confronts the small town's top employer up at the big house during a murder investigation.

Aghast to be confronted in his own backyard by a black man, the old boy strikes Poitier across the cheek. In the original script, Poitier, accompanied by the racist sheriff, turns on his heel and walks out.

But Poitier, by this time an Oscar-winning star and remembering dark moments in his past when he was hassled by white policemen, 'insisted' on a script revision.

A breath after being slapped, Poitier delivers a flat backhand riposte to the bemused bigwig, who whimpers, 'There was a time I could have had you shot.' Star power at its most effective.

OUT OF THIS WORLD
2001: A SPACE ODYSSEY (1968)

Consider the following exchange of cables.

From Stanley Kubrick's representative to Arthur C Clarke in Ceylon: 'STANLEY KUBRICK – DR STRANGELOVE, PATHS OF GLORY, ET CETERA, INTERESTED IN DOING FILM ON ET'S. INTERESTED IN YOU. ARE YOU INTERESTED? THOUGHT YOU WERE A RECLUSE.'

From Clarke: 'FRIGHTFULLY INTERESTED IN WORKING WITH ENFANT TERRIBLE STOP CONTACT MY AGENT STOP WHAT MAKES KUBRICK THINK I'M A RECLUSE?'

America was still a year away from having a man walk in space, let alone have astronauts set down on the moon, when, in 1964, Stanley Kubrick met the sci-fi writer Arthur C Clarke for the first time in New York and they started planning this visionary extraterrestrial fable.

When the film project was first announced in 1965 – with a release planned the following year – the title was *Journey Beyond the Stars*. This optimistic time frame was, of course, settled before Kubrick's quest for absolute realism dictated a whole new schedule.

With the support of other space writers, scientists and researchers, many of whom were ex-NASA staff, the resources of the space agency as well as IBM, Boeing and Bell Telephone and Grumman were put at Kubrick's disposal.

When the production set up shop at Elstree Studios north of London, where the bulk of it would eventually be filmed, the soundstage was nicknamed 'NASA East'.

The various outside collaborators were said to have been pleased with the final result – all, that is, except for IBM when it was helpfully pointed out that each of its initials was just one notch along the alphabet from each of the letters spelling the name of the computer HAL 9000, the murderous brain of the spaceship, *Discovery*.

But how to voice HAL? Filming began with the British actor Nigel Davenport on set but off screen speaking the dialogue – until

Kubrick felt that an English accent was just wrong. An assistant director then spoke up for HAL for the duration of the shoot.

Later, the American actor Martin Balsam was recorded, then rejected. Finally Kubrick settled on a Canadian, Douglas Rain, whose memorable tones would inspire another extraordinary vocal performance more than twenty years on.

It was recalling HAL – 'like the disembodied voice at the end of a long dream,' as he described it to me – that gave Anthony Hopkins the voice for Dr Hannibal 'The Cannibal' Lecter in *The Silence of the Lambs*.

A TOUCH OF EVIL
ROSEMARY'S BABY (1968)

You won't find his name on the credits, but adding an extra dimension of authentic evil to a very creepy horror film was the imposing figure of 37-year-old Anton LaVey.

Roman Polanski wanted an 'expert' to advise him on matters diabolical and, as founder of the burgeoning Church of Satan, LaVey, bald, black-clad and repellently trendy at the time in a California culty kind of way, was ready, willing and able.

His duties didn't just stop there on the film, for Polanski also invited the man who wrote the Satanic Bible and was known as the Black Pope to play the Devil in a harrowing scene where he impregnates Mia Farrow, as Rosemary, during a shocking rape before a coven of witches.

It was enough to make Farrow look convincingly terrified. But in fact the actress was enduring strife on and off set. Her husband of a year, Frank Sinatra, nearly thirty years her senior, wanted her to co-star in his new film, *The Detective*. When Polanski's film severely overran, Sinatra demanded Farrow should quit straightaway and join him.

She refused, leading to her dismissal from Sinatra's project and the serving of divorce papers on the set of *Rosemary's Baby*. By one of those delicious coincidences, the films both opened on the same day, and Sinatra's cop movie was comfortably eclipsed by his ex-wife's scary blockbuster.

The aftermath for Polanski would prove altogether more shocking when the following year, in 1969, while he was away in London, his pregnant wife Sharon Tate and four others at his rented house in Hollywood were brutally murdered by disciples of Charles Manson, calling themselves 'Satan's Slaves'.

SHOWING SOLIDARITY
FUNNY GIRL (1968)

You have to think someone had a rather dark sense of humour when Omar Sharif was first mooted to co-star opposite Barbra Streisand in her film debut.

After triumphantly playing the Jewish chanteuse Fanny Brice for nine hundred performances on stage, Streisand was locked into the film, but they still needed someone to play her charismatic gambler lover-then-husband Nick Arnstein.

Sharif, who had most of Arnstein's attributes in abundance, and the ability to carry a tune, too, was, however, an Egyptian and in 1967, with the film about to go into production, the tension between Israel and Egypt was at breaking point.

Although Streisand championed Sharif, the predominantly pro-Israel studio honchos were suddenly very nervous about the casting. There was even talk of dumping the actor, until the veteran director William Wyler, a Jew, made it clear that, if Sharif went, he'd go, too.

To raise the bar even further, the Six-Day War broke out soon after shooting began and when, for publicity purposes, Sharif was photographed kissing Streisand, all hell broke loose in his native country.

The actor – nicknamed 'Cairo Fred' by Peter O'Toole during the making of his breakthrough film, *Lawrence of Arabia* – somehow managed to ride out the row, which included threats to revoke his citizenship, and even had an affair with his besotted leading lady during filming.

Streisand's wholehearted support – in every sense – reaped another reward when she and Katharine Hepburn (for *A Lion In Winter*) won Academy Awards, the only Best Actress tie in Oscar history.

FOUR LETTER MAN
HANNIBAL BROOKS (1968)

Like the late Sir Alfred Hitchcock, Michael Winner has been a prolific British director. But there the resemblance ends – apart, that is, from figuring, like Hitch, in *The Penguin Dictionary of Twentieth Century Quotations*.

Winner's entry is gleaned from a 1983 *Observer Magazine* interview in which he said, catchily, 'A team effort is a lot of people doing what I say.' Not a four-letter word in sight, which is what most of his collaborators across forty years of filmmaking – ranging from early highs to recent lows – tend to recall best in their combative dealings with the colourful Winner.

On the set of his most recent film *Parting Shots* (1998) – many still earnestly hope it will be his last – the crew were tempted to have a T-shirt inscribed, 'I'm a f****** moron', because that's what they claim he was always shouting at them.

Winner, an irascible eccentric to some, the rudest man on earth to others, has long been a fertile source of toe-curling stories from his many film sets. The following are just a tiny sample of Winnerisms when he was still in his rampaging pomp making this amusing World War Two adventure.

The day Robert Kennedy was shot they were filming up a mountain and Winner was told the news. Knowing that one of his actors, Michael J Pollard (a gentle flower child who loved the Kennedys and Bob Dylan) would be devastated, he called up to him, 'Michael, Robert Kennedy's been shot – and Bob Dylan shot him.'

On Pollard's birthday during filming, the unit publicist was asked to organise a party for him to take place during the lunch break on location. There was a huge crew of a hundred and fifty so she ordered sixty bottles of champagne to be delivered from the hotel. When they arrived, she found only thirty bottles. Winner had halved the order. She protested that there wouldn't be enough for everyone, whereupon he declared, 'Those at the front can taste it – and tell those at back what it's like!'

They were shooting a scene where Pollard – yes, him again – was playing the leader of a guerrilla band on an Austrian hillside. He suddenly slipped and painfully crashed down several feet. Without waiting to see how the actor was, Winner bellowed, 'Get me another f****** actor!'

Winner was typically tough on everyone, especially the German extras whom he was always shouting at for being 'Nazis'! In one scene the props men were instructed to set fire to the German extras, who were wearing asbestos suits lying on a hillside. The scene took a long time to shoot and the extras became visibly uncomfortable and started to shift a little. Clearly enjoying himself, Winner shouted at them: 'Lie still, you f******, you're supposed to be dead!' and prolonged the shooting even further.

Finally, one of his secretaries on the film took a short break for tea, unfortunately just as Winner was looking for her. When she returned after a few minutes, he told her, 'You can collect your plane ticket – and have your next cup of tea at Fortnum's.'

Don't you love him?

ON THE DIRECTOR'S CHAIR
DEATH OF A GUNFIGHTER (1969)

The pseudonymous directing credit 'Allen [also Allan or Alan] Smithee', which has appeared on more than forty films and television shows over the past thirty years, was first glimpsed by cinema audiences on this very decent sixties western from Universal Studios.

The tale of an ageing sheriff (Richard Widmark), who's 'gotta do what a man's gotta do', was first offered to the veteran filmmaker Don Siegel, but he turned it down, suggesting instead Robert Totten, an experienced horseman who had directed TV episodes of *The Legend of Jesse James* and *Gunsmoke*.

It seems that Widmark took against Totten from the outset and tried to persuade Siegel, with whom he had made the box-office hit *Madigan*, to change his mind. Twenty-five days into shooting on the project, the Universal chief Lew Wasserman contacted Siegel, telling him that Widmark refused to work any more with Totten and would he, as 'a favour', now take over the film, 'starting tomorrow morning?'

Siegel, sensing that Universal somehow blamed him for suggesting Totten in the first place and that his own future at the studio might thus be compromised, reluctantly agreed, although after hastily watching the rushes he was happy to tell anyone who would listen that he thought that much of Totten's completed work was 'excellent'.

Siegel worked on the film for about ten days, contributing principally the opening and ending of the horse opera. To make matters even more embarrassing, Totten remained a regular visitor to the set as he was supervising his two small children, who had minor parts in the film.

When the film was completed, both Siegel and Totten refused to take directing credit, so the Directors' Guild of America came up with the notorious Smithee pseudonym, which is now firmly part of Hollywood lore.

Among Smithee's better-known credits are *Let's Get Harry* (1986, really Stuart Rosenberg), the TV movie *Riviera* (1987, John Frankenheimer) *Catchfire* (1989, Dennis Hopper), *The Shrimp on the Barbie* (1990, Michael Gottlieb), the TV movie *While Justice Sleeps* (1994, Ivan Passer) and *Hellraiser: Bloodline* (1996, Kevin Yagher).

A dire 1998 comedy called *An Alan Smithee Film: Burn Hollywood Burn*, with a cast including Sylvester Stallone, Whoopi Goldberg, Sandra Bernhard, Eric Idle, Jackie Chan and Ryan

O'Neal, endured the ultimate irony when the director Arthur Hiller asked for his name to be removed from the credits after differences with the writer-producer Joe Eszterhas.

THE TWO OF US

ON HER MAJESTY'S SECRET SERVICE (1969)

George Baker – later to become widely known for his role on TV as Ruth Rendell's Chief Inspector Wexford – could have attained screen immortality years earlier had the Bond creator Ian Fleming got his way.

Baker was lunching in 1958 with Robert Clark, head of Associated British Pictures Corporation, when Fleming strolled over to their table and, according to the actor's memoirs, said, 'There you are, Robert, there's your James Bond sitting there. You should turn those books of mine into films for him.'

'Aye, they're good readable books, Ian, but they'll never make pictures, never,' replied Clark, firmly, presaging a similar moment when, twenty years on, a hapless Columbia Studio executive would pass on something pretty worthless called *E.T. – The Extra-Terrestrial*.

History relates that Baker never got the nod, but created a little piece of film history when he signed up for a cameo role in *OHMSS* opposite the series' one-off Bond, George Lazenby.

Baker was required to play Sir Hilary, master of the Royal College of Heralds, whom Lazenby has to impersonate during the adventure. They played their scene together and then, months later, Baker was contacted again, now being asked to dub Lazenby's voice in various scenes, including his own two-hander with 007.

Surely an unprecedented example of one actor providing both performers' voices in a live-action film sequence.

A GAY DAY

STAIRCASE (1969)

The main joke – indeed perhaps the only joke – of this suitably dire adaptation of Charles Dyer's black comedy about a pair of London homosexual hairdressers was its casting of two legendary womanisers, Richard Burton and Rex Harrison, as the ageing gay couple.

The script required a bed scene, the very notion of which truly anguished Harrison, who fought to have it deleted, but to no avail, because it was crucial to the story.

Their London flat had been constructed in a Paris studio – not too far, quite uncoincidentally, from the capital's other studio, where Mrs Burton, Elizabeth Taylor, was starring opposite Warren Beatty in a recreated Las Vegas for *The Only Game in Town*.

Burton and Taylor would take time off from their respective schedules to meet up and co-host lavish lunches, and on this particular day their guests included the Duke and Duchess of Windsor and Maria Callas, as well as *Staircase*'s director, Stanley Donen, and Harrison.

It also just happened to be the day of the big bed scene and, while the brass were away feasting, an elaborate camera rig, comprising a small plank across the bed supported by piles of boxes either end, had been set up by the crew.

Eventually, the stars returned at about 4 p.m. for the afternoon's work. As the well-lunched Burton climbed onto the bed he began to go to sleep while a still-wide-awake Harrison was mortified suddenly to see that the royals, Callas and Taylor had also come onto the set to watch the filming.

Director Donen, sensing that a rehearsal might prove fruitless, ordered they shoot right away. As Burton was jolted out of his slumber, he promptly forgot his lines, which had been the cue to start pulling the camera over the bed.

To get things moving, the camera operator hissed an instruction, at the same time accidentally kicking the boxes at one end so that he, the plank and the camera came crashing down between the actors.

Incandescent with rage and embarrassment, Harrison was now able legitimately to quit this impromptu royal-command performance for the security of his dressing room.

BORN TO BE WILD
EASY RIDER (1969)

Jack Nicholson had already made eighteen films when he became an 'overnight' success at 31, co-starring as the boozy civil-rights lawyer George Hanson in, arguably, the counterculture landmark movie of the sixties.

The director/star/co-writer Dennis Hopper had fought to get Jack into the film – not Nicholson, but Jack Starrett, a former football player from the University of Texas and a seasoned drinking buddy.

Although Hopper and Nicholson were pals at the time – Hopper had appeared in *The Trip*, written by Nicholson – Hopper had written the role of George with his chum Starrett firmly in mind.

'No,' Hopper told me, 'I didn't want Jack Nicholson in *Easy Rider*. The producer Bert Schneider then said he hadn't asked for anything so far but now really wanted Nicholson. I agreed but remember telling him he was ruining the movie.

'Yes, I was a schmuck. Immediately I started seeing the dailies [rushes] I could tell that he was great and from that point on had no problem with what was going on.'

DRIVING INTO LEGEND
THE ITALIAN JOB (1969)

Apart from Michael Caine's immortal one-liner, 'You're only supposed to blow the bloody doors off!', the most memorable thing about this comedy caper was surely its elaborate car chase in Turin, using a team of Mini Coopers.

'This would be the longest commercial for a car ever made,' reflected the director of photography Douglas Slocombe, echoing most of the production personnel, who believed that the Mini's manufacturers, British Motor Corporation, would leap at the chance of being involved in such a high-profile, Hollywood-backed British film.

They thought wrong. According to the producer Michael Deeley, BMC were 'completely uninterested'. Eventually they sold the production six Minis at trade price – the rest they had to buy retail.

How different from the attitude of the Fiat boss Gianni Agnelli, whose enthusiastic support for the project meant that Turin became a viable location after, first, Rome, then Milan were rejected as unsuitable.

Agnelli also offered the film as many Fiats as they wanted, to smash and crash if required, as well as stunt drivers. Despite the apathy of BMC, the offer was rejected, for, as Deeley said, 'The moment you stop the cars being those cheeky little British Minis taking on the might of both the Italian police and the Mafia, there is nothing left.'

However, Agnelli's influence remained firmly on the film with his popular Cinquecento model often littering the frame, and he also provided the production with three Ferrari Dinos, which were used as Mafia vehicles.

As importantly, he also let the filmmakers use the rooftop of his factory buildings and his own test track outside the city for various parts of the spectacular chase.

As the film's historian, Matthew Field, noted perceptively, 'Can you imagine Rover allowing an Italian film crew into Longbridge with a fleet of Fiats to shoot a film that blatantly sneers at Rover and England in general?'

LANGUAGE BARRIER

KES (1969)

Three falcons named Freeman, Hardy and Willis shared the title role in the film about a shy Yorkshire lad (David Bradley) who befriends a kestrel.

The distributors, United Artists, didn't think Ken Loach's film would have much appeal beyond its Yorkshire location and initially opened it only in ten northern cinemas, and then, when they realised it had potential, considered putting out a dubbed version in the south.

When it did open in London in 1970 the poster advertising industry took it upon itself to send men out with buckets of glue and strips of paper to cover up the 'distasteful' words '. . . to you mate!' on billboards showing young Bradley giving a defiant two-fingered gesture.

THE FULL MONTY
WOMEN IN LOVE (1969)

When even the boldest actresses traditionally get nervous about screen nudity, imagine how Alan Bates and Oliver Reed – yes, even Oliver Reed – must have felt about the prospect of filming mainstream cinema's first male full frontals.

D H Lawrence had written about 'the physical junction of two bodies clinched into oneness' as macho chums Gerald Crich (Reed) and Rupert Birkin (Bates) wrestle each other naked in front of a roaring fire.

As the big day approached to shoot the scene, the actors, who had both seemed gung-ho at first about recreating this authentic slice of Lawrentian bonding, were now getting noticeably nervy. Reed developed a limp and Bates sniffled with cold. The night before the big bout, they even produced medical certificates to attest their symptoms and excusing their stripping off.

The director Ken Russell simply ignored all this, told them to have an early night and looked forward to seeing them on set the next day – having wisely prepared an alternative scene in case they funked it.

According to Russell, 'The fateful day arrived with everyone poised ready to rush onto the alternative set in case our two unwilling protagonists should really chicken out.

'But dead on the stroke of 8.30 a.m. they both strode into the baronial hall, where the fight was due to take place, whipped off their dressing gowns without demur and stood there as naked as the day they were born – proud as peacocks.

'So for the rest of the day and most of the next we shot the controversial wrestling scene that made screen history – without any sign whatever of a sore ankle or a single nasal sniff.'

What had caused such a drastic change of mind? Vast quantities of vodka in the pub the night before and possibly in the early hours, too, leading up to filming certainly helped to dull the anxiety.

Reed, it seems, was particularly worried about comparative sizes of manhood but frequent visits together to the loo during their pub binge reassured him on that score. Yet even on set he would still surreptitiously massage himself to retain equality with his co-star.

As for Bates, apart from the physically painful business of tumbling about on hard floors, 'my worst fears were about my mother's reaction – that I really dreaded – but it never bothered her in the least.'

BLOOD FEAST
THE WILD BUNCH (1969)

'We're going to bury *Bonnie and Clyde*,' vowed the director Sam Peckinpah as the cameras started rolling on the ultra-violent, blood-splattered western full of his trademark images of slow-motion death throes.

By the end of the first day's filming in Mexico, the production was completely out of ammo and fake blood, and the first two (of 22 in all) crew members – a special-effects man and a gunsmith – were on their way home to the States in disgrace.

Human replacements arrived the next day, along with more ammunition and fake gore.

During the course of shooting, 'Bloody Sam's' masterpiece would use 239 rifles, shotguns, revolvers and automatics and more than ninety thousand rounds of blank ammunition. 'More than was used in the entire Mexican Revolution!' the film company would gleefully hype.

THE 1970s

BED AND BAWD
PERFORMANCE (1970)

INT. TURNER'S BEDROOM – 8 A.M.

...As she takes off her dress, the two sleepers begin to wake to an erotic reveille shot in slightly overexposed 16mm.

And so begins an extremely raunchy threesome involving Mick Jagger, as the reclusive rock star Turner, Anita Pallenberg and Michele Breton in what some reasonably suggest is the seminal end-of-Swinging-Sixties film, co-directed in London by Donald Cammell and Nicolas Roeg.

The controversial film, also involving James Fox and dealing with, among other things, violence, drugs and sexual identity, ran the gamut of production and censorship problems, some of them stemming from the above stage direction in the script.

What really went on in the bed has since become the stuff of film myth, although versions of it tend to vary wildly.

Chris O'Dell, now a highly successful television lighting cameraman, was employed then by Cammell's commercials company, and worked as a 'runner' on the film.

He told me, 'They had huge script problems and were dealing with artistes, many of whom couldn't basically hang together for more than an hour at a time. The result was the film went massively over budget.

'You may remember there's a scene where some of the characters make a sixteen-millimetre under the bedclothes. So they gave the camera to Mick Jagger and then left him to it. He shot probably ten rolls, some thousand feet, and then the stuff was sent off to the lab. There was, as you might just guess, a huge outcry because the stuff turned out to be pornographic and in those days you could be had up for processing it.

'So one of my jobs was to go round to the lab and witness a man with a steel chisel and hammer chopping up the negative of the porn material. That's how sensitive they were in those days and I can always remember seeing this prune-faced lemon-lipped lab supervisor looking on, too.'

Contrast this with another version of events given to me more recently by the film's camera operator, Mike Molloy, who would also go on to become a successful cinematographer in his own right.

'The facts of the matter are – as I recall – Mick, Anita and Michelle had a threesome under the sheets. Nic Roeg, who was also the director of photography, aimed a couple of big lights at the bed and I got in there with them with a sixteen-millimetre Bolex and started filming.

'When I literally came up to reload the camera, Nic said, "Sod this, you're having all the fun," so he grabbed the camera and dived under the bedclothes himself. Mick was far too busy to do any camerawork himself! I am pretty sure some of the footage was used.'

Molloy confirms O'Dell's story that there was there was 'an uproar at the lab when they saw rushes.'

A recent biography of Jagger and his Rolling Stones colleague Keith Richards reports that uncut footage from the film won an award at a porno festival in Holland.

OUT ON A LIMB
SOLDIER BLUE (1970)

The gory climax of this controversial western – said to be an allegory of atrocities in Vietnam – was an incredibly heavy-handed attempt to recreate the US Cavalry's 1864 massacre of the Cheyenne Indians at Sand Creek.

A 'prosthetics truck' was parked by the set full of decapitated heads, severed arms and detached legs. There were also drawers packed with rubber breasts filled with blood bags for slashing by bayonet.

Paraplegics and amputees were bussed in from Mexico City for the scene. After being fitted with suitable prosthetic devices they were instructed to watch in horror as their limbs were hacked off.

CHAIN REACTION
TORA! TORA! TORA! (1970)

Thirty years after that 'Day of Infamy' when the Japanese mounted a sneak attack on the American fleet at Pearl Harbor, the former enemies decided to pool their creative resources for this powerful re-creation.

Two of the key sequences were to be the USS *Arizona* blowing up at anchor and the fate of the USS *Nevada*, the only battleship that managed to get under way in an attempt to escape the aerial onslaught.

The plan was to tow the production's half-battleship a mile up the channel, then, since it had no engines, take advantage of the tide and the current and let it drift down past five strategically placed cameras.

The channel was filled with dozens of huge water explosions synchronised to go off as swarms of enemy planes released their bombs. Giant firebombs were planted all over the ship to explode at precise moments, at which points scores of stuntmen would be blown overboard.

Sailors would be seen swarming over the decks, fighting back with any weaponry that came to hand, from anti-aircraft guns to hand pistols. The action was framed so that only the built portion of the battleship would be photographed.

Everything was rehearsed and choreographed down to the minutest detail. A system of flag signals was devised to coordinate between the set and the ship because there was concern that a stray radio signal might accidentally trigger some of the explosives.

The battleship was towed to its starting position and tied to a pier. Once it was loosed, the ship would have to travel downstream for nearly half a mile before coming into camera range.

The order was now given for the planes to take off and ready themselves for the attack when given the signal. The director and his producer walked to the first camera position only then to look back and see, to their horror, that the ship was already well under way.

The circling planes saw this as a visual cue and began attacking. At the same time the special-effects men started triggering their explosions while the stuntmen hurled themselves into the action too. All this before the ship had even come within camera range. The battle was almost half over before the cameras starting filming anything.

And there was a worse news to come. A group of sailors had been burned in a fireball explosion after straying into a carefully roped-off area. Shattered, the filmmakers dreaded the official reaction to this near-fatal cock-up.

The next morning they heard by telegram from the head of the studio, who had viewed overnight the retrievable footage. It congratulated them for one of the 'most magnificent sequences ever put on film'.

THE BULLDOG BREED
PATTON (1970)

Boasting some of cinema's most awesomely staged tank battles, this seven-Oscar-winning World War Two epic was filmed on many spectacular locations, including Spain, Greece, Sicily and Morocco. But it was while recreating another, quieter, theatre of war in the unlikely setting of leafy Knutsford, Cheshire, that the filmmakers hit one of their biggest logistical snags.

It's said to be hard to act with animals, but it can be even harder to get *them* to act. The English scenes for *Patton* were filmed in the same town near where the general was stationed and where the American troops used the Old Town Hall as their 'Donut Dugout'.

The main scene was of George C Scott (as Patton) making a speech in front of the Town Hall, in which he insults the Russians by not mentioning them. As he walks to the decorated podium, a bulldog, being carried by a woman spectator and representing the British spirit, was supposed to bark.

On the first take, the dog didn't bark. Nor did it do so on the second or third take. In spite of assurances that the dog was always barking, there seemed no immediate prospect of its doing so, and there was no ready replacement.

Despite his irritation, the director, Franklin Schaffner, took a pragmatic view. He came over and asked the woman to shake it, prod it or do anything that might provoke a bark. All to no avail. Scott looked it in the eye and tried surprising it with a sudden 'Boo!' Not a flinch.

The combined efforts of cast, crew and even a four-star military adviser failed to raise even a growl, let alone a bark.

The makeup man then suggested putting mustard in its mouth and a suitable condiment was obtained from the caterers. With its jaws held open, the mustard was pushed in and everyone awaited the frenzied canine reaction.

The bulldog merely ate the mustard with some relish, licking its lips. By now it had taken at least half an hour and a lot of effort to fail to get the dog barking, and there was even talk of scrapping the shot altogether.

At the last moment, a voice from the crowd of extras piped up with the simple suggestion of blowing at it. Someone did and it barked furiously!

A NOSE FOR TROUBLE
DEATH IN VENICE (1971)

Long before the media made a right meal of Nicole Kidman's new nose (as Virginia Woolf) in *The Hours* (2002), Dirk Bogarde was having serious trouble with his own carefully constructed conk as he prepared to play Mahler in Visconti's lush drama about the ailing composer.

After three hours in makeup to perfect the Mahler 'look', Bogarde arrived on the set for the first day of shooting only to discover that he was unable to move his head or face. The slightest motion caused the nose to crack, which, Bogarde reported in one of his many memoirs, then led to the oozing of an 'extremely unbecoming fluid'.

The nose would have to go and, Bogarde feared, with it, his character. Instead, how about sitting in a wheelchair, bolted by the neck to the headrest? he suggested in some desperation to the Italian director Luchino Visconti. Another makeup man was sent for to give a second opinion on whether the fake proboscis could be usefully resurrected. He also nixed the nose.

Just minutes before Bogarde was due to go before the cameras, he and his minders hastily rummaged for some alternative facial props. They came up with a small, bushy moustache, a rather bent pince-nez, a long beige woolly scarf and a walking stick.

The actor then borrowed his walk 'from my paternal grandfather, heavily back on the heels, no knee caps'. A new character had suddenly come to life.

Bogarde's nasal plight must have almost seemed like the last straw after a string of problems that dogged the production at its outset. The American money didn't want Bogarde anyway and they certainly loathed the idea that his character would be ogling a young boy throughout the story. A young girl would, however, be apparently quite acceptable.

Visconti held firm on both counts, even though his budget was severely shorn as a result. There was even less in the kitty when, just a month before filming, it was discovered that the director didn't actually have the rights to Thomas Mann's classic novella, written in 1912. After they were finally secured, the result was that everyone worked for peanuts – or less.

FLAG OF CONVENIENCE
MACBETH (1972)

Returning to Shepperton one day after lunch at a nearby pub, Elizabeth Taylor became almost apoplectic when she spotted a flag flying over the studio entrance bearing the unmistakable symbol of a *Playboy* bunny.

Taylor, who was filming *Zee And Co.* at Shepperton, demanded to know why that particular logo was blowing in the wind. Because Hugh Hefner's production of *Macbeth*, directed by Roman Polanski, was shooting at the studio, she was informed.

'*I* am working at this studio,' she yelled, clearly unimpressed, 'and *I* don't work for *Playboy*. That f****** flag is coming down or we take this picture out of the studio.' The prominent pennant was furled in double-quick time.

TESTING TIME
THE GODFATHER (1972)

No one had any faith in *The Godfather*. The subject seemed unappealing – using the actual word 'Mafia' was certainly going to be a no-no – filming was stressful and the director Francis Coppola came close to losing his job many times. As for Marlon Brando, he had long since faded from the bright star he was once thought to be.

Certainly nobody apart from Coppola wanted to cast him as the patriarch Don Vito Corleone in the adaptation of Mario Puzo's novel, as many studio executives considered him to be more trouble than he was worth. They would have preferred Laurence Olivier or Edward G Robinson in the role.

The director needed a way of convincing them without getting his proud and perhaps egotistical star to suffer the indignity of a screen test. So one day he suggested to Brando that they try out some of the makeup that would age the 48-year-old actor into the elderly Don he was to play.

Coppola arranged to videotape it for reference, and was delighted to see Brando grow into the role, experimenting with props and exploring the character before his eyes. The plot worked, the execs saw the tape and Brando was cast in the film for which he is probably best remembered.

DEVIL TO PAY
THE EXORCIST (1973)

From lurid tales of a production 'curse' to lip-smacking reports of vomiting, hysteria and fainting among audiences at various early screenings, *The Exorcist* was blessed, if you'll pardon the expression, with the kind of publicity that could only help turn an already spellbinding film into a box-office phenomenon.

Often attributed to the so-called 'curse' was the death of the Irish actor Jack MacGowran soon after he had completed his scenes, as well as other fatalities involving Max von Sydow's brother and Linda Blair's grandmother. Even the co-star Lee J Cobb's demise fully three years on was somehow tainted with the *Exorcist* touch.

Added to these terminal if sometimes decidedly oblique episodes were a traffic accident suffered by Jason Miller's son, a back injury sustained during filming by Ellen Burstyn, the mysterious illness of a production executive and a studio (hell) fire.

According to the film critic Mark Kermode, who describes *The Exorcist* as 'the greatest film ever made', the movie's own publicist purred that 'there were in fact thirteen episodes during the making of the movie that seemed like diabolical intervention'.

It's unlikely he was even counting two of the stranger aspects of filming, which involved an athletic body double and demonic voice stand-in for little Miss Blair, the thirteen-year-old junior high school student from Connecticut, playing the possessed teenager Regan MacNeil.

Second things first. The Oscar-winning fiftysomething Mercedes McCambridge – her voice transformed by the judicious 'swallowing and regurgitation of pulpy eggs', into a horrifying otherworldly obscene bark – helped out with the vocals.

For some of the actual scenes of possession, which included sexually explicit moments that would have been morally reprehensible if undertaken by an underage actress, the filmmakers called in Eileen Dietz, who would, reported Kermode, later – and wrongly, it was officially ruled – claim credit for *all* the possession scenes.

Dietz's contribution also included some of the equally infamous projectile-vomiting sequences – using a mixture of split-pea soup and oatmeal. However, for the much-imitated head-spinning episode, this was achieved by neither performer, rather via the crafty manipulation of a remarkably lifelike Regan dummy created by the makeup wizard Dick Smith.

For the notorious spider-walking scene – excised from the original version but included in the 25th-anniversary rerelease – yet another double was called in, this time the contortionist Linda R Hager.

Whatever the actual extent of McCambridge's and Dietz's involvement – both actresses would variously resort to litigation – the director William Friedkin's 'repeated assertion' at the time that Blair had 'no stand-in, no substitute' was clearly fanciful.

Friedkin also did absolutely nothing then to spoil the useful illusion of a hexed production. The writer-producer William Peter Blatty told Mark Kermode that 'all rumours of a curse were total nonsense. Billy Friedkin had fallen vastly behind schedule and he gave an interview to *Newsweek* magazine blaming it all on devils.'

Years later, Friedkin had radically changed his stance. 'There were,' he now insisted, talking to journalists, 'no unfortunate deaths

173

on *The Exorcist*. We worked on the film for over three years, from its inception to the time it was released. In a three-year period you're going to have some people get sick, get married, have babies and die.

'I worked on a film prior to that called *The Night They Raided Minsky's*, in which one of the lead actors – Bert Lahr (who played the Cowardly Lion in *The Wizard of Oz*) – died during production before he was able to finish his role. So in order to semi-complete what he had done I had to use doubles and shoot over a guy's shoulder. Stuff like that.

'That's a case I hope I never experience again, touch wood, but certainly nothing like that happened on *The Exorcist*. It's all the creation of people with vivid imaginations. Unscrupulous journalists saw in it a way of hyping the whole thing up, especially the Antichrist aspect, and were promoting this theory, with the help of some of the people who'd worked on the film and afterwards said apocalyptic things had occurred.

'But at the time it was no different from any other film. It just took longer to make than most. Yes, Jack MacGowran died shortly after, but he had been very frail and sick when he made the film,' Friedkin added. Methinks he doth...

IN THE FLESH
DON'T LOOK NOW (1973)

Did they or didn't they? One of the most erotically charged scenes in cinema history has to be between Donald Sutherland and Julie Christie as a recently bereaved married couple in Nicolas Roeg's adaptation of Daphne du Maurier's chilling supernatural short story.

The six-minute sequence set in a Venice hotel bedroom cuts craftily between their unbridled naked sex and their getting dressed for dinner.

For the filming, the set was cleared of all but the director and his cinematographer, Tony Richmond, who then, as some have suggested, recorded authentic *flagrante delicto*.

None of the principals has ever confirmed or fully denied it, although Christie is quoted as saying, 'Making love on camera is such hard work that there is no time for the libido to take over.'

For the US release of the film, Roeg had to remove nine frames of the sequence. In the UK the film was passed uncut.

OLD BUT GOLD

THE PAPER CHASE (1973)

There have been older Oscar winners – the current record holder is Jessica Tandy (*Driving Miss Daisy*) at eighty years and eight months – but perhaps none quite so unexpected as the venerable John Houseman.

A distinguished stage – he was co-founder with Orson Welles of the Mercury Theater – and film producer, he was about sixth choice to play Professor Charles Kingsfield, the crusty but benign scourge of the students at Harvard Law School.

His protégé, the director James Bridges, thought he had signed up James Mason for the key role but the actor dropped out at the last minute. With Houseman's help, he then approached Edward G Robinson, who, it transpired, was terminally ill. Names like Melvyn Douglas, Paul Scofield and Sir John Gielgud were then bandied about.

Bridges finally had the bright idea to ask Houseman if the 71-year-old would play the prof. Romanian-born, English-public-school-educated Houseman agreed and, twenty years after his first Oscar nomination as producer of *Julius Caesar*, he won the award for Best Supporting Actor.

Houseman, who had had blink-and-you'll-miss-them roles in a couple of earlier films, was now suddenly a star and appeared in at least a dozen more films before his death in 1988 aged 86. He also reprised Kingsfield in a very well-received US teleseries spin-off of *The Paper Chase*.

LIMP WITH A TWIST
THE STING (1973)

You may recall that Robert Shaw, playing murderous Chicago gangster Doyle Lonnegan, target of Newman and Redford's eponymous 'sting', had a limp and walked with a stick.

This particular characterisation wasn't dreamed up in David S Ward's original Oscar-winning script but, as the result of an accident, which took place just eleven days before filming was due to begin.

Shaw had been playing tennis at the Beverly Hills Racquet Club and, while following that up with a game of volleyball, slipped on wet Astroturf – caused by surface water after a drain had been blocked – and strained the ligaments in his knee.

The studio doctors recommended physiotherapy but declared that Shaw would still walk with a limp for a while. A hasty rewrite was thus ordered to accommodate his temporary handicap. The club was sued and settled out of court for $20,000.

THE COST OF MUSIC
AMERICAN GRAFFITI (1973)

When Ron Howard – then a successful eighteen-year-old actor, now an even more successful director of films such as *Apollo 13* and *A Beautiful Mind* – went to meet George Lucas for an audition, he thought the project was a musical. Lucas quickly reassured him he wouldn't have to sing, but it's true to say that music would play an integral part in the film's phenomenal success.

Effectively recreating some rose-tinted memories of Lucas's own early-sixties adolescence in small-town California, *American Graffiti* – an earlier titling, *Another Slow Night In Modesto* (Lucas's hometown), was sensibly eschewed – cost a measly $700,000.

More than a tenth of that – certainly way more than anything that was paid to the film's young actors (Harrison Ford, Richard Dreyfuss, Howard etc.) – was spent on the rights to some 41 pop songs, which so memorably decorate the soundtrack.

These include rock-'n'-roll classics by Buddy Holly, Bill Haley, Frankie Lymon, the Big Bopper, the Platters and Chuck Berry, which then helped make the soundtrack album – arguably the first of this tie-in compilation kind – such an ancillary hit.

Though Howard wasn't required to sing, Harrison Ford curiously was, baritone-ing his way through a singular version of Rogers and Hammerstein's immortal 'Some Enchanted Evening'.

However, when it came to editing time, Lucas was informed that the rights to the song were suddenly unavailable, so Ford's unique vocal stylings had to be excised (to be restored later for home-viewing consumption).

Incidentally, the film – which went on to make Lucas a fortune and pave the way for *Star Wars* and total filmmaking independence – would have cost even less if it hadn't been for an irate bar owner in San Rafael, doubling for Modesto.

He complained that filming was keeping his customers away and so, after just one night in town, the whole production had to up sticks and move on north to Petaluma, adding another $15,000 to the budget.

OUT OF DEPTH
MAHLER (1974)

Ken Russell should have been prewarned when he agreed to cast the young actor Gary Rich as the youthful incarnation of Gustav Mahler in his typically idiosyncratic biopic of the great Austrian composer.

When he'd hired Richard Chamberlain to play Tchaikovsky in *The Music Lovers* (1970), the actor had assured Russell he could play the piano convincingly. It was only when they started shooting that the director realised that Chamberlain was moonlighting all hours to try to make himself appear a virtuoso.

Young Mahler need to ride, swim *and* play the piano. Before filming was due to begin, Russell would ring up Gary's home to check he was practising hard. The answer was, more often than not, yes, the piano tuition was coming along fine, but the lad was out at the moment, down at the local swimming baths.

Five weeks later, cast and crew were assembled at Derwentwater in the Lake District for a scene in which young Mahler quickly gets into difficulties after boasting to his friends he can swim with the best of them.

Russell and his camera crew were on a small boat getting ready to film Gary when the young man, still shivering in his underwear at water's edge, called out that he hadn't been exactly honest with the director at his audition: he couldn't swim and was clearly terrified at the very prospect.

The yell of 'Action!' eventually stirred Gary's professionalism and he plunged in, only to retreat, quite distraught, back to shore about three yards later. Increasingly desperate to get the shot before the light went, Russell invited Gary into his boat to discuss the situation.

As his boat drew up alongside the director's, Russell offered him a hand to help him across and then claims he lost his balance, at which point Gary was unceremoniously dumped in the water.

As both boats pulled quickly away from him, the camera caught the moment: 'the most convincing drowning scene I have ever seen on the screen,' Russell later claimed, triumphantly.

BOOK OF THE FILM
THE GIRL FROM PETROVKA (1974)

When the actor Anthony Hopkins secured a contract to play a black-marketeer in this Cold War comedy, there was just one problem: he was keen to find a copy of George Feifer's original novel but scoured London's Charing Cross Road bookshops in vain.

Dejected, he returned to Leicester Square station to catch the Tube home. To his amazement, he found a copy of the book lying on a bench in the station.

Two years later, when he was working on the film in Vienna, he was visited by Feifer, who complained that he had lost his only copy of the book after lending it to a friend in London.

It had had particular sentimental value, he explained, because it was an advance copy, which he had marked in preparation for publishing an Americanised version of the English edition, with words such as 'labour' changed to 'labor' and so on.

'Is this the one, with the notes scribbled in the margins?' asked Hopkins, who had been puzzled by the red corrections throughout. It was indeed the very copy, which had gone missing from his friend's car in Bayswater and had never shown up, despite frantic searching and offers of rewards.

Strange coincidence? Maybe, but it is worth just adding that such peculiar happenings seem to dog Hopkins. His fellow actor Simon Ward, who was at drama school with the star, has said that there is something 'deeply strange and mysterious about him... He had the ability to foresee things.

'One evening we were sitting in Bertorelli's eating spaghetti and he suddenly knew something awful had happened back at RADA. One of the students had actually fallen off the stage and broken both his legs. Tony "saw" this happen...'

TURNING ON THE JUICE
THE DIAMOND MERCENARIES (1975)

O J Simpson, a.k.a. the Juice, had switched from American football to film acting when he was signed up opposite Telly Savalas, Peter Fonda and Maud Adams for this bone-headed adventure shooting on location in southwest Africa.

After brief roles in *The Klansman* and *The Towering Inferno*, he was now an authentic co-star – but that didn't help when he tried to check in at Johannesburg's Carlton Hotel. With apartheid still in full cry and WHITES ONLY signs decorating everything from benches to lavatories, O J was politely but firmly refused accommodation.

'One out, all out' was the production's swift response and, with a spectacular international row brewing, the hotel (and the Republic) swiftly backed down, granting O J special VIP and consular privileges.

O J revelled in his newfound status and while on location even defied the arbitrary death penalty by reportedly romancing the film's white leading lady.

SWIMMING WITH SHARKS
JAWS (1975)

Shooting the classic disaster movie proved to be something of a nightmare for its then inexperienced director, Steven Spielberg.

With the idealism of youth, Spielberg had every confidence that the best way to create the shark was not to use a model in a tank – far too simple – but to combine real-life footage of sharks off the coast of Australia with shots of a fin and, for more complicated scenes, film of three life-size mechanical sharks.

All three mechanical monsters were nicknamed Bruce, after Spielberg's lawyer, Bruce Ramer. The problem was that 'Bruce' was designed to work in fresh water. Out in the salty Atlantic Ocean off Martha's Vineyard, he promptly sank and a team of divers had to retrieve him.

Difficulties with the corroding Bruce contributed to the doubling of the movie's budget, but, in the long run, they also helped to make the film the incredibly successful blockbuster it became. With the beast so often out of action, Spielberg hit upon the idea of using the camera as shark and filming from the predator's point of view.

During the editing process, Spielberg concluded that such shots as they had of Bruce were not as convincing as he had hoped, so the shark ended up appearing only halfway through the film, and then just in glimpses.

Undoubtedly, this minimalist strategy paid off, with the audience's imagination left to work overtime, egged on by John Williams's equally minimalist but deeply threatening film score.

These days, a replica of Bruce can be seen at Universal Studios, Hollywood, where he regularly leaps out at tourists. Scary? Not compared with the largely unseen menace that lurked at the bottom of the ocean in *Jaws* and still haunts the imaginations of holiday-makers the world over.

COLD WAR CONFUSION
INSIDE OUT (1975)

The storyline of this fast-moving caper movie, directed by Peter Duffell, was about a group of chancers led by Telly Savalas, Robert Culp and James Mason. They're searching for hidden Nazi gold, which turns out to be buried under a building in East Berlin – in the Russian sector on the other side of the Berlin Wall.

The only people allowed through the infamous Checkpoint Charlie without question were army personnel, and so our heroes plan to pass through in borrowed American Army officers' uniforms.

Local West German filmmakers had advised the producer that it was impossible to shoot night sequences anywhere near the Wall. Any attempt to do so would be faced with floodlights and loud-speaker interference from the Russian side. All previous attempts to film there had ended in total defeat.

The only solution was to recreate Checkpoint Charlie in a nearby street, which looked like the Friedrichstrasse, location of the real checkpoint. So the design department went to work and did just that, and remarkably well, as it turned out. Some off-duty GIs who knew the routine and were happy to cooperate and earn a few dollars were hired to do duty as checkpoint guards.

On the night of the shoot, as the camera rolled and the stars drove up to be saluted by the American guards, a civilian suddenly appeared out of the darkness and staggered towards them, waving his identity papers.

He was an East German worker who had crossed through into West Berlin for a night out with his more fortunate mates who lived there. Being in a state of confused if happy intoxication, he thought he had arrived back at the real Checkpoint Charlie.

As a junior member of the unit pointed him in the right direction, the rest of an amused crew and cast, delighted with this confirmation of authenticity, carried on filming.

THAT SHRINKING FEELING
ONE FLEW OVER THE CUCKOO'S NEST (1975)

The unsung hero of Milos Forman's extraordinary tragi-comedy must surely be Dr Dean R Brooks, superintendent of Oregon's state mental hospital.

The filmmakers were given permission by him to film whatever they wanted wherever they wanted in his facility, with just one proviso: that some of his patients be hired to help out with some of the more mundane tasks behind the camera.

His belief was that having a paid job on a prestigious film production would have a therapeutic effect on his charges. Nevertheless, Forman made sure he had backup crew just in case.

There were also inmates among the extras supplementing a supporting cast of patients, including Danny De Vito, Christopher Lloyd, Vincent Schiavelli and Brad Dourif, all unknown at the time and so authentic that audiences often had real trouble telling them from the real thing.

The director prepared the actors for their roles by having them wander round the wards and observe for hours on end. He insisted they get their own beds in the wards and be issued with the standard gown and shaving kit. He also assigned each one a patient to 'emulate' in terms of his daily demeanour.

As for the good Dr Brooks, he got to play himself in the film, although his character name was Dr Spivey. His scene, admitting Jack Nicholson (as Randle P McMurphy), was improvised.

SLY'S A KNOCKOUT

ROCKY (1976)

Any resemblance between the Bayonne Bleeder and the Italian Stallion might seem purely coincidental – until you realise that BB, alias the real-life boxing no-hoper Chuck Wepner, was the inspiration for Rocky Balboa, and one of the most successful franchises in film history.

With eight unremarkable films behind him as a mumbling young character actor, Sylvester Stallone was a year shy of his thirtieth birthday – the same number as his unproduced screenplays – when he was ringside in 1975 for the World Heavyweight Championship bout between Wepner and the reigning champion, Muhammad Ali.

When the completely unfancied Wepner, not even among the top ten contenders at the time, managed to survive all fifteen rounds and even put down Ali in the process, Stallone was all fired up to write *Rocky*.

The studio, United Artists, loved the screenplay and wanted to have a star actor – James Caan and Ryan O'Neal were mentioned – as the aspiring champ. But Stallone was adamant that it was his material and he wanted to play Rocky.

With the budget cut to the bone, UA reluctantly gave in. Stallone received the standard writer's fee, a miserly $20,000, for playing the lead and, with the studio anticipating just a small box-office return, a cut of the net profits.

The film grossed more than $100 million, a figure predicted long before its release by the disarmingly cocky Stallone. However, like Wepner, in his bid to win Oscars for both writing and acting – he was nominated in both categories – Sly was eventually beaten on points.

THE PLEASURE PRINCIPLE
ANNIE HALL (1977)

Woody Allen's most amusingly autobiographical film, loosely but still very recognisably tracing his love affair with the actress Diane Keaton (née Hall), was originally titled *Anhedonia*.

That may sound like the name of some *mittel*-European principality but is in fact an affliction dictionary-defined as 'the inability to experience pleasure'.

Unsurprisingly, the executives at United Artists were appalled and told Allen that he had to find another title. He refused to budge on the matter. His co-writer, Marshall Brickman, countered with what he considered an equally silly title, *Me and My Goy*.

However, he finally agreed to try out a different name at each of the test screenings. *Anhedonia* was greeted with blank stares. Eventually, it was between *Annie and Alvy* (the name of Allen's character) and *Annie Hall*, which, despite UA's reservations too, got the eventual nod.

TWO OF A KIND

STAR WARS (1977)

John Stears was the special production and mechanical-effects supervisor responsible, among many other clever things, for the radio-controlled robots and droids that were so much a part of the atmosphere of the film.

In the intense heat of the Tunisian desert and salt flats, where much of the location filming was set, Stears was beset with problems caused by the radio signals being sent a bit haywire every now and then.

Sometimes it was extremely frustrating as good takes were screwed up by little vehicles crashing into the set or stopping short of their intended positions. Sometimes, though, the results were hilarious.

At the beginning of the film, R2-D2 and C-3PO are dumped in the desert, having crash-landed their lifepod space vehicle in the sand. C-3PO was standing on a crest of sand and R2-D2 (radio-controlled by Stears) was trundling up behind him on a wooden ramp hidden from the camera by the crest.

C-3PO, looking about him, says, 'What a forsaken place this is. We seem to be made to suffer. It's our lot in life. I've got to rest before I fall apart. My joints are almost frozen. What are we doing here?'

And, with that, R2-D2 moved up behind him as planned, but failed to stop. The radio control had gone AWOL again and he crashed into the back of C-3PO (with the hapless and very hot Anthony Daniels inside) and continued to bash away at his backside with uncontrollable abandon.

Effectively, and to the crew's huge enormous amusement, the two droids were 'at it' in the desert!

MEDICINAL PURPOSES
JOSEPH ANDREWS (1977)

It must have seemed like a good idea at the time. While filming this Henry Fielding novel more than dozen years after his award-laden *Tom Jones*, the director Tony Richardson thought it might be fun to revisit the bucolic character of Squire Western, so memorably impersonated first time round by the boozy Welsh actor Hugh Griffith.

Although some of Griffith's more undisciplined antics had appalled his co-stars, especially Edith Evans and Albert Finney, who had actually punched him out after being cut with a whip, Richardson was still anxious to see if he could get the old actor to reprise the role.

Inevitably, the years had taken their toll, and what now greeted the director was, in his own words, a 'disintegrating wreck of a man'. But once kitted out in his original *Tom Jones* wig and costume, it was as if the years had rolled back. Until it came to the actual performance.

For this, a prop man stood by and before each take Griffith was fed a spoonful of brandy, exactly measured because too little wouldn't have kindled his energy while too much would have put him straight to sleep.

He also had to keep sitting down for take after take, in order to capture a line here, a look there, until Richardson was able to piece it all together into something usable.

AN UNLIKELY SOURCE
HALLOWEEN (1978)

'If not for Michael Myers, I would probably be the manager of the Meltdown Motel at Pico and Sepulveda Boulevards.'

That was the writer-director John Carpenter paying tribute in a 1998 *Guardian* obituary. Michael Myers? The creepily masked serial killer who, in 2002, was still wreaking big-screen havoc in *Halloween Resurrection*, the seventh sequel?

Carpenter, who invented the profitable shock-horror series, was simply giving due credit to the man whose name he nicked to launch a thousand scares.

It was the real-life British film distributor Michael Myers, Hove-born, public-school-educated, who first championed the twentysomething Carpenter, helping turn the young Kentuckian's *Assault On Precinct 13* (1976) into a cult hit. Its success in Britain directly led to the making of *Halloween* and the subsequent sequels.

Carpenter's tongue-in-cheek thank-you was to immortalise him as the unstoppable, apparently indestructible killer who started his 25-year-old killing spree in his home town of Haddonfield, Illinois.

The real joke was that Myers, who ran Miracle Films, was the gentlest and most courteous of men. How ironic that Myers, who died aged 69, should be eventually outlived by his monstrous alter ego.

BIRDS OF A FEATHER
DEEP WATERS (1979)

They were filming on the Isle of Sheppey in Kent for this breezy Children's Film Foundation adventure about birdwatching kids encountering illegal smugglers.

The director suggested that for a future shot it would be wonderful if the sandbank against which the scene was to be filmed could be covered with seagulls. He thought that judicious use of some stuffed seagulls as decoys would do the trick.

However hard the crew reasoned with him that this wasn't going to work, the more he was adamant that they try. The producer said he would order something suitable and in due course a box was delivered all stuck down with brown sealing tape, labelled '*Deep Waters* – Six Assorted Seabirds'. It was put in the prop van and not given much more thought.

The day of the scene in question arrived and the director insisted that the stuffed birds should now be put in position. The prop man was dispatched in a rowing boat with the unopened box. The tides around Sheppey are very strong and with a great deal of effort he eventually beached the boat on the sandbank, some fifty yards away.

He then opened the box and just stood there, motionless, staring into it.

'Put the birds out,' yelled the director.

'I *can't*,' came the reply from across the water.

'Why not?' asked the director.

'I *can't*,' he cried again.

'Put them out,' demanded the director.

A very bedraggled seagull with a broken wing was reluctantly pulled from the box, followed, more hesitantly, by a smaller version with outstretched wings and only one leg.

'Put out the rest!' shouted an annoyed director.

There was another pause on the sandbank and from the box emerged a standing cormorant. Had there been a few rocks, it might have perched quite convincingly but on the sandbank the big black bird looked very out of place beside its motley companions.

The albatross that followed, with one wing outstretched and the other folded, looked completely ludicrous.

'Where are the others?' bellowed a now exasperated director.

'I just *can't*,' cried the mortified prop man.

'Will you please put them out,' insisted the director.

With each bird more disastrous than the last, the rest of the crew could hardly keep straight faces – a situation not helped by the production of the next bird, a puffin, with its brightly coloured beak.

'Where's the last one?' queried the director, by now resigned to the worst.

'*No! I can't*,' pleaded the prop man.

'You must,' commanded the director.

Any final vestige of credibility vanished as the prop man, with great embarrassment, finally held up...a penguin!

GAME FOR A LAUGH
MONTY PYTHON'S LIFE OF BRIAN (1979)

This glorious biblical spoof had a troubled history even before the day the director and co-Python Terry Jones had to motivate a 500-strong crowd of bemused Tunisian extras.

With its financing withdrawn at the last minute by the British media giant EMI because of the script's alleged 'blasphemy' and 'anti-Semitism', a rather unlikely saviour arrived in the person of the ex-Fab Four's George Harrison, who personally guaranteed the film's $4 million budget (and can be spotted in a cameo role as Mr Papadopolous, owner of the Mount).

So there he was in Tunisia pondering the problem of how to get this huge crowd lying on the ground laughing when shy Jones, who always preferred to have his assistant director call 'Action' and 'Cut', knew he had to take the lead.

He told me, 'First we got hold of a Tunisian comedian and had him tell some jokes to the crowd. I then thought, well, I must come out of my shell. So I went up on to a balcony and got the guy with the megaphone to tell the crowd to do exactly what I did.

'I lay on the ground laughing hysterically with my legs in the air. Suddenly there were more than five hundred Tunisians lying on the ground laughing hysterically with their legs in the air as the dust rose everywhere. They were marvellous.'

LIFE AFTER ART
THE CHINA SYNDROME (1979)

Art's imitation of life has been the stock-in-trade of countless films down the years but, as in the case of this chilling 'what if?' cover-up drama about near meltdown at an American nuclear plant, just occasionally the reverse is uncomfortably adjacent.

The film, starring Jane Fonda, Jack Lemmon and Michael Douglas, was riding high in cinemas despite some official rubbishing that the facts depicted had absolutely no scientific credibility.

Then, less than two weeks after its opening, the unthinkable actually happened at Three Mile Island near Harrisburg, Pennsylvania, when the world suddenly heard about America's worst nuclear accident.

An earlier and even more immediately tragic example of the life–art axis came as *Morning Departure* (1950), a stiff-upper-lip drama about a peacetime submarine disaster, was awaiting its London West End premiere.

The submarine HMS *Truculent* was quietly proceeding up the Thames when it suddenly collided in the dark with a large freighter. It capsized, killing all 64 hands below.

SHOCK OF THE NEW
ALIEN (1979)

The terrifying scene in which the snakelike alien bursts forth from John Hurt's chest while he is enjoying a routine dinner with the crew on the spaceship *Nostromo* is one of the most talked-about episodes in Ridley Scott's classic sci-fi horror.

The demise of Hurt's character, Kane, is particularly disturbing, because the audience has been led to believe that he has emerged unscathed from an earlier 'face-hugger' incident in which the alien creature shoots out of a giant seed pod and grabs his head. Up until his death, we have no idea that the alien has implanted itself so successfully.

But it was not just cinemagoers who were shocked by the terrifying 'chest-burster', as it became known on set. Although it is something of a myth that the cast knew nothing about what was to happen, they were certainly kept in ignorance as to the specifics.

According to Sigourney Weaver, 'As I walked on set, I remember everyone [on the crew] was wearing raincoats, which should have given me a hint that something horrible was going to happen. They never rehearsed it. John Hurt started screaming and, because he's such a good actor, all I could think of was, What's happening, not to John, but to Kane?

When Veronica Cartwright was sprayed with blood, her disgusted reaction was absolutely genuine.

Dan O'Bannon, who co-wrote the story, says he was inspired by the spider wasp, which lays its eggs in the abdomens of spiders. The image of their bursting out gave him nightmares, which he put to good use in the film.

However, Roger Dicken, who designed both the face-hugger and the chest-burster, originally wanted something even more horrifying – the creature was to pull itself out of Hurt's body with its own tiny hands. The blood-and-guts explosion was, to his way of thinking, not nearly scary enough.

ROMAN SCANDALS
CALIGULA (1979)

Costing nearly $17 million and starring Peter O'Toole, Sir John Gielgud, Helen Mirren and Malcolm McDowell, as the blood-thirsty, deviant emperor, this scurrilous Roman epic is not only the most expensive but also the most prestigiously cast 'hard-core' film of all time.

Not that the distinguished quartet of British thesps realised at the time of filming in Rome that the finished film was going to be punctuated with explicit sex scenes.

The really dirty stuff, more than six steaming minutes' worth, was added later by the film's backer, *Penthouse* magazine's publisher Bob Guccione, when he felt that the first cut from the Italian director Tinto Brass hadn't fulfilled his original brief.

The film was to prove a minefield for the British censors, who then proceeded to chop more than ten minutes out of Guccione's two-and-a-half-hour movie. Another 55 minutes and 7 seconds was later cut for the current UK video version.

Not that the Brass account was exactly a shrinking violet, gleefully embracing sex and violence – especially decapitations and disembowellings – with undisguised relish.

Gielgud, playing Caligula's haughty servant, Nerva, could hardly believe his eyes most days on the lavish sets as most of the young male and female actors pranced about in the near or full buff.

He'd later recall that the director was a 'very peculiar man' and was a bemused onlooker during a swimming-pool scene in which O'Toole, as Tiberius, rose from the water surrounded by young boys and girls.

Said Gielgud, 'They were splashing about, very good-looking and all stark naked. Then, the moment the bell rang for lunch, they put their hands in front of their genitals and rushed out to have a pizza with their families, who were waiting in the corridors with lunch.'

TOO CLOSE FOR COMFORT
APOCALYPSE NOW (1979)

The central role of Colonel Willard in Francis Coppola's surreal Vietnam War epic not only had Martin Sheen's name on it but also – almost – his number too.

When, first, Steve McQueen, then a series of big-name stars such as Al Pacino, Jack Nicholson and Robert Redford, turned down the part – mostly on the grounds that they didn't want to be stuck away in the Philippines for six months – Coppola's thoughts quickly turned to Sheen, who had tested well if unsuccessfully for Michael Corleone in *The Godfather*.

However, Sheen, though mad for it, was already committed to another project, so Coppola signed up Harvey Keitel to play the Special Forces officer dispatched into the heart of darkness to assassinate a rogue American colonel (Marlon Brando) who'd gone mad in the jungles of Cambodia.

Shooting began on 20 March 1976; a month later Keitel was fired. As the co-producer Fred Roos explained in Peter Cowie's *The Apocalypse Now Book*, 'We know that Harvey's a terrific actor, but he was not comfortable in his skin, or in his uniform or in his role as Willard. He was a city boy.'

By his own admission 'not in great shape', heavy smoker Sheen – born Ramon Estevez, one of ten children to Spanish-Irish parents – was on set in the Philippines just ten days after Keitel was so summarily dismissed.

Ten months later, Sheen and co. – excepting an unexpectedly mountainous Brando, who'd come and gone for three weeks' work at a whopping $1 million a week – were still playing war games in Southeast Asia. As well as Brando's excesses, they'd also survived Typhoon Olga (which had necessitated a six-week production closedown), just one of many costly setbacks that meant that the film was way over budget and schedule. Coppola had also mortgaged himself to the hilt to help pay for the film.

Then, on 5 March 1977, Sheen collapsed early that morning after suffering a heart attack. Five weeks later he was, remarkably, back on set. In his absence, Coppola had decided to press on without a break, and to shoot as much as possible round him, and, wherever necessary, using Sheen's brother Joseph as a double. When Sheen returned they were then able to film close-ups of him to cut into the completed scenes.

Filming, which was originally envisaged to have lasted a maximum of three to four months, finally finished on 21 May 1977. But that wasn't the end for Sheen.

After nearly a year of complex post-production, during which it was decided to add a narration to the soundtrack, he was in a San Francisco remixing studio giving expression to a powerful voice-over penned by a one-time war correspondent, Michael Herr. Despite his heart attack, Sheen was still living life on the edge and after one particularly heavy bout of after-hours drinking was arrested in a local bar.

The first public viewing of the $30 million, 150-minute movie was at the Cannes Film Festival in May 1979, where it shared the Palme d'Or with *The Tin Drum*. In 2001, the now official version of the film, with 47 minutes' more footage, was released under the title *Apocalypse Now Redux*.

Martin Sheen, now 62, survived the whole experience to become America's mostly popular president... in television's hit drama series, *The West Wing*.

THE 1980s

THE DREAMING SPIRES
HEAVEN'S GATE (1980)

The opening caption for this notorious western epic, which effectively wrecked a major Hollywood studio (United Artists), reads, 'Harvard College, Cambridge, Massachussetts, 1870'. We see the sun rising behind a clock tower as a student, played by Kris Kristofferson, runs through an archway.

In reality it was before dawn in Oxford, England, 1979, and this attractive scene-setter for almost twenty opening minutes of college graduation action was being filmed on the sly.

After the excesses of filming in the great outdoors of Montana and Idaho – which had contributed towards spiralling the budget from $7.5 million to more than $30 million – the production decamped for a final couple of weeks in England because Harvard had refused permission to shoot within its precincts.

Compared with the shambolic schedule in the States, this final part of filming – set twenty years before the frontier footage – was to be a model of discipline and rigor: five days, each with a day of preparation.

Unfortunately, the city refused permission for the director Michael Cimino to shoot on a Sunday near Christ Church. However, it was the only day the schedule allowed and was absolutely crucial to the film.

So, as Steven Bach records in *Final Cut*, 'With ingenuity, secrecy and some "persuasion" of university guards, the street and shot were prepared after Saturday midnight, earth was poured to cover asphalt, sixty feet of dolly tracks were laid [for the camera], and Cimino... "stole" the shot at dawn in three takes, wrapped and cleared the site before the authorities were aware it had been used and before the bells rang announcing 8 a.m. church services.'

197

ON THE PROWL
THE LONG GOOD FRIDAY (1980)

After a series of behind-the-scenes rows on this gangster classic, including a drugs-squad raid on his suite at the London Hilton Hotel, the American actor Tony Franciosa flew home to New York only days before he was due to step in front of the cameras.

The producer, Barry Hanson, immediately signed up another craggy American acting stalwart, Eddie Constantine, to replace him as a mobster kingpin.

Veteran Constantine, who died in 1993, was going through one of his worst bouts of insecurity. He'd just finished making a low-budget Continental movie called *Beware of the Holy Whore*. But Hanson was still convinced he could produce the goods.

'Eddie was more off the wall than Franciosa,' he said. 'You weren't sure what you were going to get but at least you were going to get something. Franciosa was a real pain. He had all kinds of problematic baggage, not least his temperament.'

What Hanson didn't bargain for was Constantine's instant sexual obsession with his co-star Helen Mirren, playing Bob Hoskins's wife, as he set about stalking her for seven weeks.

The crew lapsed into quiet bursts of hysterics as he'd use any pretext to enter her caravan. And though he may have been in his sprightly sixties he'd get up to all kinds of mischief once he'd convinced himself she was bound to fall for him during the first week of filming.

He thought, borrowing one of Muhammed Ali's favoured expressions, that 'She will go in seven!' He'd sneak into her caravan and scrawl love notes in verse using lipstick on a mirror. Makeup women would then dash in and wipe off the provocative poetry before she could see his handywork.

Once, Mirren expressed her concerns over what she thought was an on-set Peeping Tom, unaware that it was Constantine again on the prowl.

The director John Mackenzie said, 'Eddie followed Helen around like a lapdog but she never understood what he wanted. He was hilarious. He did most of his movies in France and Germany and they always dubbed him. When I told him he had some speeches, actual dialogue, he went white as a sheet and said, "But nobody ever asks me to say anything!"'

FACING THE WORST
THE ELEPHANT MAN (1980)

Just ten days before shooting was due to start, the film's young American director, David Lynch, excitedly revealed the blueprint for his eponymous character's horrific makeup.

His colleagues were indeed horrified, but not quite in the way Lynch had anticipated. Terry Clegg, the film's production supervisor, recalls, 'It wouldn't have even passed muster at a children's concert. It was rather like someone wearing a pair of long johns covered in rubber latex – a complete disaster.'

Consequently the design was handed over to an expert, Christopher Tucker, who went away to rethink and redesign a head that must be so horrifying as to explain why the unfortunate John Merrick should have been star exhibit in a foul Victorian freak show before later becoming the darling of a curious, prurient society.

While Tucker tinkered with his prostheses, filming had to forge ahead with this unforeseen hitch already responsible for a 20 per cent increase in production costs.

Lynch's original idea was for a kind of organic-looking body suit, which would be worn by the Merrick actor John Hurt. It would take some blending in each day but also, Lynch thought, hopefully avoid a time-wasting five hours daily in the makeup chair.

When Merrick died at the London Hospital in 1890 aged 28, a plastercast was taken of his body, as well as casts of his head, arm and foot. For the first time since Merrick's death, permission was given for the head to leave the hospital so that Tucker could use it at his studio to help fashion more suitably authentic makeup.

Tucker, who would in later years come up with make-up coups ranging from Michael Crawford's stage *Phantom of the Opera* to the monstrous Mr Creosote in *Monty Python's Meaning of Life*, did indeed deliver the goods – even if it did sometimes mean that Hurt would have to spend ten hours daily undergoing the transformation.

The resulting 'look' was also directly responsible for the belated addition of a Makeup Oscar. Because of Hurt's unprecedentedly remarkable appearance there was pressure on the Academy to introduce the category, but it refused. The resulting row led to its introduction the following year – naturally too late for Tucker's masterpiece.

ON THE ROCKS
RAISE THE TITANIC! (1980)

'It would have been cheaper,' the irrepressible Lew Grade said famously of this soggy turkey, which helped sink his film empire, 'to lower the Atlantic.'

If only Grade had trusted his first instincts when he originally turned down the chance to make Clive Cussler's bestseller, thinking it to be yet another yarn about the liner's sinking. But nonsense prevailed and eventually he forked out $400,000 just for the rights.

While they tried to lick a suitable script into shape, there was the matter of making elaborate models and also finding a suitable tank in which to film them. Some eight models in all: the *Titanic* itself, four United States warships, two tugs and a New York Harbor fire ship.

Of these, the *Titanic* replica – at 55 feet long, 12 feet high and weighing 10 tons – was genuinely awesome and the first plan was to build a tank at CBS studios. But, whenever they started to dig, the hole would fill with water. Also, it was never fully appreciated at the outset just how large a tank it would have to be to house a 55-foot model in the simulation of a depth of more than 6,000 feet under the Atlantic. So the CBS scheme was abandoned.

An obvious alternative was the existing tank in Malta – but this was a surface one, for models operated by people standing in the water. However, there was potential. Unfortunately, the prevailing political climate on the island didn't seem favourable.

Requiring a horizon and, for topographical reasons, needing it to face north, Grade's people charged around the Mediterranean looking at Spain, Corsica, Sardinia and even the heel of Italy for a suitable tank site.

Then, with the prospect of valuable film dollars disappearing elsewhere, the Maltese melted and gave Grade the go-ahead to build a brand-new tank so long as he used Maltese labour and a home-grown engineer.

The specifications were crucial: the tank would have to be at least 35 feet deep, saucer-shaped because of water pressure, 240 feet across in order to accommodate the model on the bottom at sufficient depth, and capable of being filled and filtrated overnight so as to be ready for a crew to shoot the following morning.

That would be a fantastic 9 million gallons of water in the tank which meant pumping it in at a rate of more than a million gallons an hour, which in turn meant, apart from anything else – and there was quite a lot else – the necessity of having a super-efficient pumping system.

In addition to the unreliability of electrical facilities on the island, local pipes used for four huge diesel pumps, which had been specially imported from Holland, kept bursting.

Building the tank was an epic in itself. The first sod was dug in November 1978 and the tank wasn't completed until the following September.

Constructed of earth, delivered month after month to the site by a fleet of trucks, it had to be impacted by the biggest bulldozers that could be found in Europe, seven days a week, regularly watered, then faced with tar and finally covered in a sort of tarmacadam material to make it as waterproof as possible.

So the costs began to spiral, not eased by some extraordinarily wasteful diversions, one of them a huge metal gantry, to be suspended over the tank so the main model could be hauled in and out while the tank was emptying.

Aware of the specifications of the gantry under construction back in Los Angeles, the production team in Malta sent telexes indicating that, because of some necessary design changes to the tank en route, the apparatus would also have to be extended by 40 feet.

The design of the gantry was also submitted for some stress tests, and it was declared that not only would the gantry be unable to pick anything up but was also likely to collapse under its own weight. The original gantry duly arrived, 40 feet short. It was never used and subsequently lay mouldering by the side of the tank – a $200,000 mistake.

Then there was the turntable said to be needed to turn the model while it lay at the foot of the tank. The turntable was built to the specification, which entailed its being suspended on wheels and being given a sandy, seabed-type covering. First, a lot of sand fell off the turntable and down into the tracks so it wouldn't turn; then the weight of the water in the tank was so great that the wheels collapsed.

Another brilliant suggestion, sensibly aborted after yet another flurry of telexes, was the construction of an underwater camera house, but this was abandoned when it was realised that no glass in the world could withstand the 17-ton-per-square-foot pressure being exerted by the tank's 9 million gallons.

As the construction proceeded painfully, visitors came and went, including one Grade minion whose brief stay coincided with the emptying of the large tank. Instead, he was directed to a small aquarium nearby. There, lying on the bottom of this glorified fish tank, was a tiny variation of the *Titanic*, whose peace was disturbed only by the periodic intrusion of a large hand reaching in from above with what appeared to be a Fairy Liquid bottle squirting atmospheric bubbles.

For Malta, this new deep-water facility was not just a novelty but was rapidly becoming an item of national significance, so Prime Minister Mintoff felt confident as he demanded Grade also be responsible for properly landscaping the whole area – as aircraft approaching the island's Luca Airport passed over the tank. They obliged. The eventual cost, $3 million, even managed to get its own mention in Malta's national budget of 1979.

It's likely that, even before a foot of film had been turned, around $11 million had already been spent on the project. But still one major logistical problem remained: how did they plan to execute the movie's money shot – the actual raising of the vessel?

A number of highly paid technicians offered their theories on how this could be most effectively achieved. One plan specified a hydraulic system fixed to the bottom of the tank, on which the model could be pushed to the surface.

Another ruled out the tank altogether, opting instead for the nearby sea as the base. The ship would be looped and run up from beneath the waves on a thin steel line – until someone pointed out that the sea off Malta is notoriously dangerous, often subject to a mighty Mediterranean swell.

So how was the $36 million film's most memorable moment (and it *was* memorable, certainly compared with the banality of the rest) executed? They finally got hold of an effects maintenance technician who'd often worked on Grade's films and asked him to come up with a solution.

He reported, 'You won't believe it, but this is what I'd do. We'll build a set of rails up the side of the tank, put the model on a dolly [a wheeled platform used usually by a camera for travelling shots], fix a little ringbolt at the front of the model and then I'll run a cable out to the back of my car and pull her out myself.'

Which was just what happened, the remarkable result then captured for posterity on a high-speed camera, shooting 350 frames per second, fifteen times the normal ratio.

Grade would later blame, rather good naturedly, the failure of his costly film on his brother Bernard Delfont, who ran the rival EMI Films. It just so happened that Delfont had simultaneously sanctioned the production of a four-hour miniseries version of the original *Titanic* story, which then proved a flop on American TV. It was quickly re-edited for cinema release around the world.

By the time Grade's baby (which had overrun its original shooting schedule by a prohibitively expensive four months) finally hit the big screen, the world needed another *Titanic* tale like a hole in the head.

MAP OF WAR
THE BIG RED ONE (1980)

There can hardly have ever been a stranger or more emotional location than the one in the centre of Jerusalem selected for a key climactic scene in *The Big Red One* – a hard-boiled drama recreating the life and times of a frontline unit in the US Army's 1st Infantry Division during World War Two.

With the specific permission of Israel's Premier Begin, the filmmakers were allowed to recreate a Czech-sited German concentration camp in Jerusalem's Schneler base, complete with crematoria and young Israeli soldiers playing Germans, their green helmets perched on top of the traditional *yamulka* (skullcap).

The film, very much an autobiographical exercise for the veteran director Sam Fuller, was originally due to have been shot in Yugoslavia with one final week in Ireland. Eventually, Israel was scouted for the North African scenes.

Finally, the production, starring Lee Marvin and Mark Hamill, was moved to the Holy Land lock, stock and barrel. The upshot was, for example, that one 20-kilometre stretch of coast north of Tel Aviv doubled for the North African campaign, the invasion of Sicily and the D-Day Normandy landing on Omaha Beach.

GETTING INTO SHAPE
RAGING BULL (1980)

Robert De Niro shed 35 pounds to appear like 'a creature of the night' in *Taxi Driver* and learned to play the saxophone in three months – 'The kid plays good tenor sax,' purred his coach, the veteran swing musician Georgie Auld – for *New York, New York*.

So when the same director, Martin Scorsese, signed De Niro up again for *Raging Bull*, the explosive story of the middleweight boxing legend Jake La Motta, the transformation possibilities for the 'Method' actor were boundless.

The script required De Niro to play La Motta as a fearsome, wife-beating 'pug' in his muscle-toned forties' pomp, and then to portray the bloated ex-fighter reduced to a toe-curling nightclub act twenty years later. The challenge was clearly irresistible.

Even before they officially got to the 'fat' scenes, the original schedule was disrupted enough for De Niro – who had eschewed the idea of a 'fat suit' – to have started his eat-athon while still in the midst of the film's earlier scenes. Chocolate milk shakes and cheesecake were consumed to the point of almost constant heartburn.

Scorsese later revealed that when the film closed down for a break so that De Niro could more seriously pursue the poundage, he instructed the actor to 'eat his way through France and Italy'. De Niro returned to the set two months later an astonishing 60 pounds heavier.

'It's very hard,' he was quoted at the time. 'You think the more you eat the more you're going to gain weight. But you have to do it three times a day. You have to get up in the morning and just eat. Eat that breakfast, eat those pancakes, eat lunch, eat dinner, even if you're not hungry. It's murder.'

The resulting 'look' was remarkable and such dedication alone merited his subsequent Oscar for Best Actor. By the time he started his next role, as a conniving Catholic priest in *True Confessions*, the extra weight had been all but eliminated by – you've guessed it – sheer willpower.

CLASH OF THE TITANS
THE JAZZ SINGER (1980)

This second, updated remake of the old Al Jolson classic about a Jewish cantor's son who defies his father to make it big in showbiz pitted Neil Diamond against Laurence Olivier.

As if there weren't enough production problems – which had seen the exit of the original director – the stars couldn't have provided a greater contrast: rock star Diamond, who had never acted before, was underplaying his role almost to the point of inaction, while the veteran thesp often wildly overacted as if to compensate.

Diamond gradually ratcheted up his performance during the shooting but there remained a crucially emotive scene in a sound studio where he had to storm into a recording booth and have a furious argument with his pregnant girlfriend.

In rehearsal, Diamond simply couldn't get up a suitable head of steam, however hard he tried. Diamond was with his band behind soundproof glass and pacing about nervously. 'Action' was called yet again. This time the singer seemed to go absolutely beserk, smashing everything in sight and making his band visibly cower as he crashed into the booth with the cameras rolling.

With the scene successfully captured, Diamond was asked why he had suddenly ignited. He explained that he felt bad he hadn't been able to explode on request, so he had asked the band to play something that would make him suitably angry.

'And what did they play?' the director enquired, politely.

'A Barry Manilow number,' Diamond replied.

BACK TO SCHOOL

FAME (1980)

Alan Parker's exuberant film, and the popular TV series that followed two years later, celebrated the life and times of New York's High School for the Performing Arts.

And yet, oddly, Parker and his production were refused permission actually to use the real school on 46th Street for filming.

Parker explained to me, 'The Board of Education who physically control the school wouldn't let us in there. They had seen the original script and were concerned I didn't appear to show the kids in the light they would like me to show them.'

There were also unhelpful stories in the local press along the lines, 'Alan Parker specialises in films about incarceration. First of all he did Turkish prisons [in *Midnight Express*] and now he's doing New York high schools...'

'Also,' Parker added, 'someone had once borrowed the school and made a pornographic film there. Generally, then, they were paranoid about trusting filmmakers and we suffered for that.

'The great thing was I had the cooperation of the kids them-selves, as well as the parents and teachers in the school, who were very upset we couldn't use the place.

'However, with the help and cooperation of the Mayor's Department in the city and, in particular, its motion-picture section, we recreated the High School in two other empty schools they gave us not under the control of the board.

'We then did the same as we'd done with *Midnight Express* – that is, build onto a real place. The High School had a wonderful feel to it. Its rooms were unique. So we had a great deal of art direction and I think a lot of people thought it was the actual school.'

THE LOOK OF FEAR
THE SHINING (1980)

The convincing look of terror etched on Shelley Duvall's face for the greater part of Kubrick's claustrophobic horror film wasn't entirely as scripted.

For her role as Wendy Torrance, wife of an axe-wielding psychotic husband, Jack (Jack Nicholson), and mother of a creepy psychic son, Danny (Danny Lloyd), Duvall had to endure the worst excesses of the director's legendary 'perfectionism'.

Suffering from ill health for six months during the shoot, Duvall was also a particular victim of Kubrick's passion for – obsession with – repeated takes, sometimes up to sixty or seventy.

A revealing 'Making of' documentary compiled by Kubrick's daughter Vivian shows the director regularly laying into the spindly actress with comments like, 'We're f****** killing ourselves out here and you've got to be ready! Shelley, you're just wasting everybody's time now.'

Duvall's own diplomatic comment on her treatment was, 'Stanley pushed me and prodded me further than I've ever been pushed before.'

She was described memorably by the film historian David Thomson as 'the casting coup of misogyny'.

BIG APPLE BACKLASH
FORT APACHE THE BRONX (1981)

Not even the presence in the cast of the impeccably liberal Paul Newman as a world-weary lawman could persuade the protesters that this taut cop thriller, set in one of New York's more deprived and violent boroughs, was anything other than a monstrous racist diatribe.

So when, rather bravely, the film crew showed up to do some authentic location shooting, the activists were naturally out in force to demonstrate against what they perceived as the film's negative portrayal of the Bronx's citizenry, most of whom seemed to be either black or Hispanic.

As Newman was filming one day, several youths clambered on his car stamping their feet and shouting foul abuse. On another occasion, the production inadvertently set up its cameras right outside the store that was serving as base for the grandiosely titled 'Coalition Against *Fort Apache*'.

Every time the actors tried to began a dialogue scene, the coalition members would shout out, effectively wrecking the soundtrack.

Basing their objections on stories – probably deliberately leaked, for maximum publicity – about the alleged inflammatory nature of the script, several big names lined up to condemn the film.

Among them were Mayor Ed Koch and the radical lawyer William Kunstler, who even helped the protesters file a libel suit against the film. For his part, Newman did his best to deflect the flak by repeating over and over again that the film wasn't racist, merely accurate.

BOTHERING THE BATS
SPHINX (1981)

It may be cheaper, then as now, to make films in Eastern Europe but it doesn't always necessarily make it easier.

Much of this creaking thriller about the search for a mystery tomb is meant to be set inside a steamy Egyptian pyramid, but the shooting on cavernous sets was actually undertaken in a huge warehouse on the back lot of a film studio in Budapest, where the temperature outside was 15 degrees below.

A key scene involved the star – unlikely Egyptologist Lesley-Anne Down – being assailed by bats as she tried the unravel the eponymous riddle.

Dead of winter is, however, hibernation time for bats and, in the kind of Hungarian cold that would make even brass monkeys flinch, live bats were dying in droves as they were ferried from local caves outside the city to the film set in order to flap at doughty Ms Down.

After a couple of tries, for which the only result could be described as Budapesticide, the cameras eventually rolled using mechanical bats and bits of brown paper blown through a wind machine.

However, as countless screen Draculas – including, coincidentally, Ms Down's co-star Frank Langella – will attest, you can't keep a good bat down and enough flying mammals of the authentic kind were finally persuaded to do their stuff and even lived to tell the tale.

BAD-CAR DAY
CHARIOTS OF FIRE (1981)

The powers-that-be at Trinity College, Cambridge, outraged that the script suggested that the then authorities were anti-Semitic, refused permission to let the production stage the film's quad race in its Great Court. Instead, the director Hugh Hudson recreated most of the university scenes at his old school, Eton.

But where to find the ideal venue for the 1924 Paris Olympics? They settled on the Bebington Oval, a local sports ground in the Wirral, across the Mersey from Liverpool, and advertised for a crowd to pack the place one Bank Holiday Sunday.

No one was paid but, as each person arrived, he or she was given a numbered ticket for inclusion in raffles, which would be held every hour throughout the day. The longer you stayed, the better the prizes were, culminating in a Fiat car in the final draw of the day. Because some people wouldn't want to stay the distance, it was announced you'd have to pick up any prize within ten minutes or else it would go back into the pot.

It seems the assembled crowd remained good-natured throughout except for one man, who, while parking his car, reversed too close to a grassy bank and broke off his exhaust pipe. He complained loudly all day and was probably still doing so when he failed to hear an announcement around six o'clock that evening that he'd won the Fiat.

After ten minutes passed, a new number was drawn and this time a woman scooped the car. To complete a very bad day, the chap was done for speeding on his way home.

QUICK AS A WHIP
RAIDERS OF THE LOST ARK (1981)

Unlikely as it might seem now, considering his mastery of the role in this and two sequels – not to mention his uncontestable place among today's Hollywood royalty – Harrison Ford was merely an afterthought for the role of Indiana Jones.

Big, bland Tom Selleck was first choice for the archaeologist/ adventurer, but he was tied into his TV contract as the Hawaii-based sleuth Magnum PI, so Ford got the job instead.

And it's thanks to Ford that the film scored one of cinema's most memorable and oft-imitated scenes. You must remember it: the dusty bazaar of Cairo where Indy is being threatened by a scimitar-twirling native. Without further ado, world-weary Indy simply pulls out his revolver and shoots him.

The original screenplay detailed a three-page whip-versus-sword fight but Ford, suffering badly from dysentery and anxious to get back to his hotel, apparently suggested to the director Steven Spielberg a funny and very effective shortcut.

UP THE WORKERS
REDS (1981)

As co-writer, producer, director and star of this sprawling historical drama set against the backdrop of the 1917 Russian Revolution, Warren Beatty had, it's generally agreed, bitten off more than he could chew.

He was also becoming increasingly unwell throughout the production from a combination of flu and fatigue, not helped by the film's peripatetic schedule, which took the production all over the world – including England, the US and Finland – because Russia (still in the then Soviet Union) had refused permission for filming.

211

He was in Seville, Southern Spain, which was doubling for Baku, and as a 110-degree heat wave raged, Beatty was trying to explain to the Spanish extras through an interpreter what the scene was all about.

He spoke for more than an hour about his character John Reed, the left-wing American journalist who wrote *Ten Days That Shook the World*, which had first fired up Beatty's enthusiasm for the project. He told them that Reed believed the working man was being exploited by capitalists and why they should rise up.

At the end of his speech he called a lunch break, during which some of the extras came to him and demanded a $20 a day pay rise because they felt they were being exploited. Exhausted, Beatty agreed.

VETS IN PRACTICE
FIRST BLOOD (1982)

The violent adventures of the Medal-of-Honor-winning Vietnam 'vet' John Rambo briefly threatened to turn into a series rivalling its star Sylvester Stallone's other franchise, *Rocky*.

But there wouldn't have even been one sequel had Kirk Douglas had his way.

Originally cast as Rambo's long-suffering former boss, Colonel Trautman, in this inaugural tale, adapted from David Morell's novel, the veteran actor had been told he could rewrite his own role.

He wanted his character to kill Rambo, believing him to be a kind of Frankenstein monster that he had helped create back in Nam. When he received what he thought would be a revised script, Douglas was horrified to see that it was actually the script he'd first turned down, co-written by Sly.

Douglas quit, Richard Crenna was hired in his place and Rambo lived on to kill hundreds more in Cambodia and Afghanistan in a pair of increasingly dumb sequels.

THE RIGHT CASTE
GANDHI (1982)

It took Richard Attenborough nearly twenty years to bring his dream project to fruition. From the moment he was first approached in 1962 by a Mahatma devotee, Motilal Khotari, to the completed film's triumphant eight-Oscar scoop of the Academy Awards in April 1983, Attenborough's obsession was not just magnificent but, at times, downright strange.

Nothing was perhaps stranger than his long and at times positively bizarre-minded quest to find the right actor to play one of history's more remarkable and most recognisable little brown men.

Alec Guinness – 'the only star at that time [1963] who bore any resemblance to this distinctive figure', wrote Attenborough – was the first actor approached. He proved extremely reticent from the outset and indeed told the filmmaker that he had grave doubts about the very idea of having a Western actor play this great Indian. Despite Attenborough's continuing entreaties and the support of both Khotari and Prime Minister Pandit Nehru, Guinness said a final no.

Down the years, during which Attenborough had been eventually blooded as a director on films such as *Oh! What a Lovely War* and *Young Winston*, he sent the script to Dirk Bogarde, Peter Finch, Albert Finney and Tom Courtenay. They all swiftly passed.

Anthony Hopkins (long before the days of Hannibal Lecter or, for that matter, *Sir* Anthony) starred in two films for Attenborough and the producer Joe Levine, *A Bridge Too Far* and *Magic*, which he later told me were, he believed, by way of inducements for him to take on *Gandhi*. Attenborough claims that he didn't think of Hopkins for *Gandhi* until *after Bridge* but admitted that 'Joe may have said something'.

After their work together on *Magic*, in which Hopkins played a demented American ventriloquist, Attenborough seemed to be convinced he'd found his man, even publicly announcing his casting coup. 'The long quest,' revealed the *Daily Mail* under the inspired headline A POUND OR TWO TOO FAR, 'to find an actor for the title role of *Gandhi* is over – and, astonishingly, a Welshman has the part... "With careful making up and by losing a little weight, he would be superb as Gandhi," said Sir Dickie.'

'It's going to be a comedy, is it, then?' Dick Hopkins asked his son dismissively on hearing the news.

Years later Hopkins told me, 'What he [Attenborough] got to, for me even to consider it, was my ego. Had I done it, it would have been an act of terrible vanity and really only proving I could cosmetically change myself, lose ten stone, and end up in a coffin. For I would have died. I know that! I looked at myself in a mirror and thought, He's crazy! I can't do *Gandhi*. I can't go through a year of macrobiotic junk. I enjoy my food too much and I'm impossible to live with without it. I mean, I'd die. Attenborough was wonderful; he understood. I wished him luck and hoped it would work out eventually for him.'

'The mistake,' Attenborough would admit to me, 'was, of course, that there are fundamental indigenous attributes within an Oriental which a Causasian European can't really manage. Whereas we were once prepared to watch, say, Burt Lancaster browned up, we're not any more. At the end of the day Tony and John Hurt, another actor I saw for the role, were both absolutely right. They just wouldn't have been convincing.'

By the time cameras finally turned on 26 November 1980, Attenborough's dream project had found its dream actor to play Gandhi: Yorkshire-born Anglo-Indian Ben Kingsley (born Krishna Banji), 36, a pillar of the Royal Shakespeare Company who had yet to make his film debut.

On Oscar night two and a half years later, Kingsley duly picked up the Academy Award for Best Actor portraying a vegetarian pacifist. Hopkins would have to wait fully another decade before snaring his first Oscar – as a serial-killing cannibal.

GENDER BENDING
TOOTSIE (1982)

Somewhere in that high-heeled hinterland between Jack Lemmon's giggling Daphne (in *Some Like It Hot*) and Robin Williams's worldly-wise *Mrs Doubtfire* (1993) totters Dorothy Michaels, another cross-dressing triumph of all-American manhood.

Dorothy – pronounce it with a Southern drawl – was the rather serious-minded creation of Dustin Hoffman, who together with some eight writers (only two were actually credited), dragged her to the screen for this box-office comedy hit.

Making the film was absolutely no laughing matter for all those around the tiresomely picky Hoffman, who surpassed even his usual extreme levels of 'perfectionism' on this particular project.

The character was loosely based on his own mother, who was terminally ill during shooting, but Hoffman – who had been nicknamed 'Tootsie' by her as a child – was determined that this wasn't to be just a cheap drag act.

Playing an out-of-work male actor who has to resort to impersonating a middle-aged woman to get a role in a TV soap, Hoffman wanted the film to reflect everything from noble womanhood to the perils of acting. Happily, it was also very funny.

Two directors came and went before Hoffman finally felt comfortable with Sydney Pollack, who hasn't directed a comedy (or Hoffman) since what turned out to be a stormy if successful collaboration.

As if the director didn't already have enough to do, Hoffman also insisted Pollack play his character's long-suffering agent. How Pollack must have fantasised about firing this particular client.

Hoffman knew he had got the 'look' right when, in full costume, he took his younger daughter, Jennifer, to school one day and told her to introduce him as her 'Aunt Dorothy from Arkansas'. No one spotted the joins.

THE DIRECTOR'S CUT
E.T. – THE EXTRATERRESTRIAL (1982)

Only rarely does an artist get the chance to return to his art and tweak it. Leonardo sadly never had the opportunity to replace *Mona Lisa*'s ambiguous expression with a cheesy grin as he surely intended.

But a handful of modern-day filmmakers who have been successful enough to wield such power have returned to earlier works and given them an overhaul.

In some cases, as with the original *Star Wars* trilogy, there is a sound commercial reason and an authentic artistic one. Special-effects technology had advanced to the point where it matched George Lucas's original vision, so that the late 1990s rereleases of the films featured more dazzling effects and a more gooey Jabba the Hutt.

E.T. was another matter. For years after its 1981 release, it had been the undisputed box office champ, a saccharine fairy tale for a generation of cinemagoers.

Twenty years on, someone decided it was ripe for re-release, something that would first require the original, degradable print to be restored. Digital technology took this challenge in its stride, but then artistic considerations came to the fore.

'I've seen the film many times on videotape with my kids,' said the director Steven Spielberg, 'and I would always flinch at technical flaws that perhaps only I noticed.'

These technical flaws mainly revolved around E.T. himself: the running scene at the beginning of the movie, for instance, and the glow of his heart inside his body as he nears the mother ship. Images with enhanced frames were altered where necessary and previously deleted scenes were returned.

Boldest of all, Spielberg decided to remove the guns from the police and agents chasing E.T. and Elliott during the climactic scenes, something the boffins at Industrial Light & Magic (ILM) achieved by replacing them with walkie talkies.

'I notice some people have accused me of being a Pollyanna,' Spielberg said at the time, 'and I'm sure the National Rifle Association will be angry at me as well. But I stand by this decision.'

Good for him. The only problem is that audiences in 2001 did not flock to the re-release of *E.T.* in the numbers anticipated, perhaps as a result of its earlier massive, global success.

SHIP OF FOOLS
FITZCARRALDO (1982)

In the same way that dog owners can come to resemble their pets, so movie directors can find themselves turning into the characters from their films.

Werner Herzog's labour of love told the true story of an Irishman who decided to bring opera to the South American jungle. Hiring local natives, he presided over an eccentric plan to haul a steamship over a mountain and build an opera house.

But if Fitzcarraldo seems mad, he was no more so than Herzog, who made a decision not to use models or special effects but, like his character, to hire hundreds of Indians to pull a full-sized 320-ton steamship over a small mountain using only block and tackle.

As Les Blank revealed in *Burden of Dreams*, his contemporaneous documentary about the making of *Fitzcarraldo*, from the start, everything that could go wrong did. Forty per cent of the film had already been shot when its star Jason Robards, playing Fitzcarraldo, was taken seriously ill.

The subsequent delays meant that his then co-star, Mick Jagger, was forced to quit. Herzog eventually decided to write out Jagger's character and to hire Klaus Kinski – renowned for his temperamental nature – to play the lead.

When shooting began again, there were interruptions due to violent tribal disputes and torrential rain. Pulling the steamship up the steep hillside proved nigh on impossible. Even when a giant bulldozer was brought in, it proved inadequate and the Brazilian engineer in charge of the operation angrily walked off set saying that lives would be lost.

The problems did not end there. During the production, a plane crash paralysed one of the extras and three others were injured while lugging the boat over the hill.

Yet the more cursed the production seemed, the more determined Herzog became. When Kinski threw a tantrum and threatened to walk out, Herzog said he would shoot him if he did so.

Like Fitzcarraldo, Herzog was obsessed. 'If I abandon this project,' he explained, 'I would be a man without dreams and I never want to live like that. I live my life or I end my life with this project.' The epic drama was to take over four years to complete.

TOO CLOSE FOR COMFORT
TWILIGHT ZONE – THE MOVIE (1983)

Filming on this feature-length spin-off of the cult supernatural 1960s teleseries contained an incident more horrific than anything that was portrayed *on* screen.

The veteran character actor Vic Morrow was playing a racist bigot who after entering the Twilight Zone finds himself successively persecuted by the Nazis, lynched by the Ku Klux Klan and fired on by American troops in Vietnam.

As a final form of redemption, his character tries to rescue two little Vietnamese children after their village is firebombed in an American raid.

During the filming of the scene, directed by John Landis at Indian Dunes Park, about forty miles north of Los Angeles, Morrow and two child actors were dodging explosives when a low-flying helicopter – too low, due to Landis's constant urging, it was later claimed, for proper safety – crashed on top of them. Morrow was decapitated and the children also died instantly.

In addition to various charges filed against certain members of the crew, there were more serious additional charges of manslaughter filed against Landis, the special-effects coordinator Paul Stewart and Dorcey Wingo, the chopper pilot.

After a five-year investigation and a ten-month trial, Landis and his fellow defendants were acquitted. Nine months later, Landis was reprimanded by the Directors' Guild of America for 'unprofessional conduct'.

It was also deemed that the two nonprofessional children had been hired illegally and were used in violation of child-safety laws.

The families of the three victims eventually collected several million dollars' worth of compensation and legal costs. The Morrow sequence remained in the final film.

PICTURE-POSTCARD PLACE
LOCAL HERO (1983)

If they hadn't found a village like Pennan, they'd have had to invent it. In fact, it was so absurdly picturesque, set snugly in a curl of the Aberdeenshire coastline below the main Banff–Fraserbugh road, that a message went out from the art department to 'pretty it down a bit'.

Pennan was required to double for idyllic Ferness, at the centre of the story's gently comic, *Whisky Galore*-ish clash between American big business and rustic Scots cunning.

The filmmakers were hoping for a seaside village and suitable beach combined, but real-life geography rarely suits the vagaries of movie design, so they eventually came up with an intriguing topographical compromise. East coast Pennan played the village while, more than a hundred miles across country, appropriate beaches were discovered at Camusdarrach in Morar near Fort William.

Considerable ingenuity was also required when, after a week's shooting in Houston on the film's American urban scenes, the production lost permission for a crucial big penthouse set in the

Texas city. It was eventually recreated in a distillery in Fort William.

The film's designer Roger Murray-Leach explained, 'We had some really horrendous problems building that far from London, from a studio and proper stage.

'It was the inside of a penthouse suite, a huge composite with a great big sliding roof, various sliding doors with a view straight out over Houston. All this in a distillery warehouse which didn't have enough headroom and, to all intents and purposes, might have been in the Outer Hebrides, the ease we had getting materials.'

MORE IS LESS
THE HILLS HAVE EYES II (1983)

Wes Craven, a former college professor of humanities, had fallen on hard times when he directed this dire sequel to his 1977 horror cult classic. He hadn't made a film for three years and would, he has admitted, have done anything to pay the rent – 'even *Godzilla Goes To Paris*'.

This film must have been written in a couple of hungover days and nights, because the ensuing 86 minutes are a moribund viewing experience.

The movie possibly holds the record for the most flashbacks in a single film (with perhaps the exceptions of *Citizen Kane* and *Ghosts of Mars*). These are all taken from the original picture, and basically recap the whole film in precise detail.

The only highlight, and perhaps a unique cinematic moment in the history of live-action motion pictures, is a flashback experienced by the cannibal family's pet German Shepherd dog, Beast, who survived from the previous film.

This film sat on a shelf gathering dust for over two years, and was not released until 1985 following the huge success of Craven's *Nightmare On Elm Street*.

PIG IN THE MIDDLE
A PRIVATE FUNCTION (1984)

When the producer Mark Shivas and director Malcolm Mowbray started planning their film of Alan Bennett's comic tale about post-war austerity, the prime problem seemed to be whether they could successfully cast a pig.

The plot required the porcine leading lady to wander round inside a house, descend a staircase, rise on her hind legs in a sty and, wonder of wonders, climb into a motor car. And stay there as it drove off.

The filmmakers were recommended a company with the imposing name of Intellectual Animals UK Limited. According to them, training of the animal would have to start immediately to meet the date they intended to shoot.

What's more, the pig could not be more than six months old, otherwise it would be dangerously large and, in all probability, beyond control; it had to be female, as the male of the species is too aggressive; and there had to be three of them in case one of them was sick and the second exhausted, so the third might be in the mood to turn up and perform for the camera.

Turning a blind eye to these grim warnings and undeterred by government regulations that restricted the movement of animals across county borders for fear of spreading disease, they then started the comparatively simple business of choosing locations and casting the humans.

Come the first day of shooting in the North of England, they staged a publicity shot with Michael Palin, Maggie Smith and, on a leash, one of the Bettys, as each of the three animals had to be called. As Maggie Smith looked forward to the weeks to come, she predicted, 'this is going to be a breeze'.

It was Mowbray's feeling as director that, no matter the complications, he couldn't just have cutaways of Betty. She had often to be in the same shot as the actors.

Shivas took up the story: 'One of the first discoveries was that pigs are too smart for filmmaking. The thought of take two, three or four was too much for a creature with such a low boredom threshhold.

'We went to take seventeen with the fruit bowl, and it was tough to get Betty to work on lino rather than carpet, on which she had been "rehearsed".

'Any excuse for the much-trained porker refusing to perform as specified might come into play – it was too hot, there were too many lights, too much noise. She didn't like being laughed at (though who does?). Or we'd changed the scene in some way and Betty couldn't, could she, be expected to improvise?

'Still, our human cast coped bravely, smiling through gritted teeth. Maggie performed an entirely unscripted leap over Betty's back when she found herself trapped by the creature in a kitchen corner. Some of our crew vowed never to eat bacon again; others decided they'd consume enormous amounts in revenge.

'And so, after much shitting, pissing, farting and appalling smells – a few members of the crew pondered putting in for a special clothing allowance because their garments began to reek – we approached the *pièce de résistance* where Betty was to be lured in the dark down a wooded hill covered in wild garlic and into a 1930s motor car.

'As the clock accelerated towards midnight, the increasingly recalcitrant Betty came to the moment of boarding the back seat of the car, which Michael would then drive off.

'But, instead of remaining in the back, Betty suddenly decided she preferred the front, and Michael found himself trapped with Betty's trotters in his lap, supporting, as they did, hundreds of pounds of porker – a moment when he seriously feared that the trotters might put an end to any prospects of his fathering children in the future.

'It was for all of us, but for Michael most of all, a grotesque end to a preposterous and difficult night. The kind of night,' Shivas concluded, 'when you wonder whether shooting films is a proper profession for grown-ups.'

SOURCING SCARES
A NIGHTMARE ON ELM STREET (1984)

Given his screen infamy, which has spawned six sequels and a television series, it's rather surprising to discover that the shock-horror world of razor-taloned Freddy Krueger actually began as some rather innocuous newspaper items.

According to his creator, Wes Craven, the original *Nightmare* was inspired by a series of unnoticed stories in the *Los Angeles Times*, 'unnoticed in that the paper buried them on the inside pages as little two-paragraph stories. They never caught on that they had published another story like it, and, six months later, they would print another one.

'That went on for a year and a half and they went something like this: a young immigrant male, early twenties, usually from Southeast Asia, a son, would have a severe nightmare where he would wake up screaming. The next day he would tell his father that it was the worst nightmare he'd ever had and he had been terribly shaken by it. The next night, when he went to sleep, he died.

'The story was given no significance in the paper, as though it wasn't at all weird. Six months later I looked in the paper and there was another very similar story. I clipped it out, put it with the other one. Then the third one appeared about a year and a half after the first one, this time in northern California. Those elements were the basis for my film.'

So Craven wrote his screenplay – and had it rejected by every major studio in Hollywood because it wasn't scary or believable enough.

THE GOOD DOCTOR
THE KILLING FIELDS (1984)

There may never have been more inspired casting than when Dr Haing S Ngor was selected for the role of the courageous Cambodian news photographer Dith Pran in Roland Joffé's award-laden film about the Khmer Rouge terror.

In fact, extraordinary and moving as Pran's hazardous tale after playing sidekick to *New York Times* reporter Sydney Schanberg was, Ngor's own life story before *and* since the film surely trumped it in spades.

Reel back to the early 1970s when Ngor, holding a French medical degree, was practising successfully as an obstetrician and gynaecologist in his native land. When Pol Pot's troops marched into the cities and started rounding up citizens for relocation in the countryside, Ngor had to forsake politically suspect medicine to masquerade as a taxi driver.

That didn't prevent him from being denounced and he was subjected to slave labour for the next four years, also, periodically, enduring imprisonment and torture. He even had to look on helplessly as his pregnant wife died during premature labour.

In May 1979, Ngor managed finally to escape through mine-fields into neighbouring Bangkok, where he worked again as a doctor in a refugee camp before securing immigration to the US eighteen months later.

Hoping eventually to enrol at UCLA's medical school, he was working as a job counsellor in LA's Chinatown when there were rumours of a film being made about Cambodia's recent history.

Although Ngor believed he was unlikely to get a role because he was, he felt, neither young nor handsome enough, he was picked for Pran (whom he didn't actually meet until filming in Thailand was over) after accidentally meeting the casting director at a wedding.

To compound the fairy tale, Ngor, uniquely for someone in his very first screen appearance, won Academy Awards in America and Britain for Best Supporting Actor and Best Actor, respectively.

The third act of Ngor's life was a mixture of success and, ultimately, more tragedy as he campaigned tirelessly for his fellow Cambodians, wrote a chilling autobiography and appeared in a handful of mostly forgettable films.

On 25 February 1996, aged just 46, the good doctor was murdered while standing next to his car in the garage of his LA apartment block. There were rumours that his killing may have been the work of Khmer Rouge assassins. More likely, it was it a drug-crazed street gang member who got away with just $40.

GORE MAN GHASTLY
THE NEW YORK RIPPER (1984)

The man behind *Zombie Flesh-Eaters* and *Four Gunmen of the Apocalypse* is no stranger to controversy. Born in Rome in 1927, Lucio Fulci, along with his fellow Italian Dario Argento, became known as one of cinema's premier gore directors.

But, while his films consistently shocked and scared audiences and censors with graphic imagery and copious blood, even he finally went too far for the guardians of British morality.

He came to Britain to submit *The New York Ripper* for classification. He was already a well-known figure at the BBFC and pretty well all his previous movies had been cut extensively. Many were even banned following the Video Recordings Act of 1985.

However, Fulci's film was obviously one step too far for the UK censors. Not only did they reject the film, but they had the footage escorted by armed guard out of the country and back to its original supplier, deemed too revolting for public viewing.

The film was eventually released in 2002 on video in Britain, with just 23 seconds cut out.

A BLAZING PREMIERE
AMADEUS (1984)

A little under two centuries after Mozart conducted the premiere (1787) of *Don Giovanni* at the Tyl Theatre in Prague, Milos Forman planned to shoot its re-creation at the very same venue for his film version of Peter Shaffer's play.

But, concerned that the rubbish-strewn place was a potential 'powder keg', Forman decided to stall his idea to light the scene using just candles and torches – as period authenticity dictated – until the very last moment. Firemen were scattered all around the theatre just in case.

Rehearsals went smoothly with the singer playing the Don running successfully through the scene in question. The director now ordered the lighting of the candles and called 'Action!'

The Don emoted away unaware that the long peacock feathers on his hat had actually caught in a candelabra and were beginning to smoke. Yet none of the firemen moved.

The smoke turned into tiny flames and there was still no action from the sidelines until suddenly a young fireman nervously asked the director if he could shout 'Cut!' as one of the actors 'is on fire'.

Forman duly obliged, at which point the firefighters, anxious not to have ruined the maestro's shot, leaped as one on the Don, tore the hat from his hand and stamped out the incipient blaze.

MONKEY BUSINESS
GREYSTOKE: THE LEGEND OF TARZAN, LORD OF THE APES (1984)

Glenn Close, one of the most photogenic of actresses, holds an odd sort of record in that she has provided only her voice in both a live-action and animation version of Edgar Rice Burroughs's jungle adventure.

Here she was required to dub the uncredited newcomer Andie McDowell's dialogue as our hero's genteel lover, Jane Porter. Hailing from the Carolinas, the film debutante McDowell was deemed to havee too Southern Fried an accent so Connecticut-born Close was hired to voice her.

For Disney's cartoon *Tarzan* (1999) Close enjoyed an evolutionary switch, playing the baby swinger's adoptive gorilla mother, Kala.

NO CRUISE CONTROL
LEGEND (1985)

It had taken between forty and fifty craftsmen fourteen weeks to prepare the forest set on the giant 007 stage (constructed originally for *Moonraker*) at Pinewood Studios for Ridley Scott's fantasy adventure.

Enormous trees – some of them as tall as 30 feet with roots 24 feet or more – were sculpted from polystyrene, supported by huge adjustable telescopic stands with metal frames. A greenery company set up its own giant greenhouse on the studio lot, where they grew the grass from seed to assure a constant supply of fresh turf.

To create a cliff-edged pond, a 20-by-20-by-6-foot concrete tank was cut into the floor of the stage, enabling an actor to dive from a cliff without risk of injury.

Then, during the lunch break, with just two days' filming left on the immense set, a fire broke out, destroying the stage, a fortune in technical equipment and the negative from the morning's work. Several million dollars' worth of damage in all, as a result of a freak electrical spark that ignited some gas fumes.

Already a long way from home, Tom Cruise must have thought this was almost the last straw, having earlier hurt his back and been mildly mauled by a fox in his starring role as the cutely clad Jack O' the Green, a sort of woodland sprite. The last straw would prove to be the expensive film's dismal performance at the box office.

Cruise could, however, console himself with the fact that, at 23, he was at least enjoying far and away his biggest-ever payday ($500,000) after just half a dozen roles in Hollywood. A sign of things to come.

THE COST OF WAR
REVOLUTION (1985)

After a poll carried out by Channel 4 in 2003 to rank the greatest 100 film actors (male or female) of all time, Al Pacino was voted top of the pops. Greater than Brando, Streep, Hepburn (K), Hoffman, Gable, Bogart and Cary Grant, who all didn't even make the top twenty.

It's a fair bet that the voters best recalled sixtysomething Pacino as a quintessential twentieth-century – and now twenty-first-century – urban American man in films ranging from *The Godfather* trilogy and *Scent of a Woman* to *The Insider* and *Insomnia*.

It's equally unlikely that these same supporters of the diminutive New Yorker would have remembered his one catastrophic essay into period filmmaking – as the trapper Tom Dobb caught up in events beyond his control in Hugh Hudson's muddled and financially disastrous wannabe-epic set against the American War of Independence.

The devoted father of Ned (played in younger mode by *EastEnders'* Sid Owen, aged thirteen, before he grew into Dexter Fletcher), Pacino affects an accent, described enthusiastically by the director as 'a strange kind of Irish-Scottish-Cockney'. 'New York Cockney', according to the film's well-qualified dialogue expert.

Pacino's disconcerting tones, not to mention his £2.3 million fee excluding lavish expenses – along with villain Donald Sutherland's absurd North Country rasp and the love interest Nastassja Kinski's temperament – were just a small part of a £16 million (rising to £19 million) problem that helped all but bankrupt an important British production company, Goldcrest Films.

To save money – the exchange rate at the time was very beneficial for the Americans – the producers had decided to shoot the film in England: King's Lynn, Norfolk, stood in for eighteenth-century Manhattan, while a number of battle scenes, including Yorktown, were enacted in Devon.

Illness, self-indulgence, adverse weather, huge crowds of extras and the loss of a £250,000 camera crane over a cliff all helped add up to a wildly over budget, overschedule turkey which was ambitious Goldcrest's biggest box-office flop. The film took less than three-quarters of a million pounds at the US box office, at which it had been so squarely aimed. This was the British *Heaven's Gate*.

Part of Pacino's generous performance package, which included a secretary, cook and chauffeur-driven car, was a promise of 20 per cent of the net profits – 20 per cent of absolutely zilch, as it turned out.

The 'greatest film actor of all time', pilloried by audiences and critics alike, didn't make another film for three years. When he returned to the big screen in 1989, it was as a contemporary big-city cop in *Sea of Love*. The film was a palpable hit.

MEAN GREEN MOTHER
LITTLE SHOP OF HORRORS (1986)

She eventually comprised 15,000 hand-made leaves, 2,000 feet of vine, eleven-and-a-half miles of cable – rather more than was needed to build the Brooklyn Bridge – and several hundred gallons of K-Y jelly.

We're talking superplant Audrey II, that 'mean green mother from outer space', the awesome alien centrepiece of Ashman-Menken's breezy film musical derived from their own off-Broadway stage hit.

Originally inspired by a non-musical *Little Shop*, Roger Corman's B'est of B-movies shot in two and a half days on leftover sets in 1960, this altogether more lavish maneater was to be 'like nothing ever seen on this planet', the filmmakers vowed.

The challenge with Audrey II, who would talk, sing and bite the hand that feeds her, was entrusted to the special-effects wizard Lyle Conway, who started his research with field trips to Kew Gardens and the Atomic Energy Authority at Harwell.

Audrey II began as a 'baby' plant resembling a rosebud with lips, modelled after those belonging to Ellen Greene, playing her altogether more sweet-natured human counterpart. Under Conway's supervision, she ended up as something over twelve feet tall and – weighing slightly more than a ton – able to rap, boogie and act homicidal with the best of them.

Crucial to this was Audrey II's lip-synching. 'It had to be perfect,' said Conway. 'Frank [Oz, the director] didn't want big, flapping hamburger buns.' To get the right effect took as many as forty puppeteers.

And Audrey II's voice? That belonged to Levi Stubbs, better known as lead singer of the Four Tops, one of Motown's greatest groups, responsible for sixties hits such as 'Walk Away, Renee', 'Bernadette' and 'Reach Out, I'll be There'.

CONTROL FREAKS
SHANGHAI SURPRISE (1986)

Madonna and Sean Penn had been married barely six months when the happy couple arrived in mainland China to start filming this awesomely awful 1930s-set 'screwball' comedy.

It must have seemed like a good idea at the time to sign up the world's most volatile newlyweds for their first (and last) film together if only to exploit their immense publicity value. A latterday Taylor and Burton? Certainly the ex-Beatle George Harrison thought so when he personally snared the pair for his company, Handmade Films.

Madonna, at 28, two years older than Penn, had already scored nine Top Ten hits in the UK and an admired supporting role in *Desperately Seeking Susan* (1985). Although a very promising young actor – much later to mature into a seriously good director too – two-fisted, arrogant Penn was still best known for his fiery off-screen antics.

From the moment shooting started, with the international press lurking behind every potted plant, it was a just a matter of waiting for things – and mostly Penn – to self-destruct.

When he wasn't constantly undermining the director (Penn would arrive on set with his own viewfinder) and having cast members fired, he was constantly being restrained by minders from hitting various paparazzi.

Location shooting in the Far East was tough enough. When they returned to England, the 'Poison Penns' were inevitably targeted by the tabloids for even closer scrutiny. They often tried actively to provoke the actor into retaliation.

Despite the supposedly surefire casting, the film bombed badly. Two years later, Madonna and Sean Penn were divorced.

REPEAT PERFORMANCE
SEPTEMBER (1987)

Perhaps only Woody Allen and his cottage-industry style of filmmaking could have got away with shooting an entire movie, then, dissatisfied with the result, recasting some of the main roles and shooting much the same story all over again.

Woody's impetus for his 22nd film as a writer-director (though in this case not also a co-star) was to make a small chamber piece on a single set, specifically his then partner Mia Farrow's summer house in the country. But by the time they actually got round to making the film, it was winter, so they had to recreate the house on a sound stage at the Kaufman-Astoria studios in New York.

The original cast for one of the filmmaker's 'serious' films was Farrow, her real-life mother Maureen O'Sullivan, Charles Durning and Christopher Walken. First problems arose when Woody felt Walken was wrong for his role and replaced him with Sam Shepard. During the filming, Woody felt increasingly that O'Sullivan was also miscast.

Second time round – though some of the substitute cast didn't realise they were on this curious roller coaster until well into the shoot – saw O'Sullivan, Durning and Shepard replaced by Elaine Stritch, Denholm Elliott and Sam Waterston.

It was later reported that Woody had regretted not having the chance to make a third version so he could have further developed some of the characters. The reviews suggested that making the film once, let alone twice, was the director's biggest mistake.

IN THE SHADOWS

THREE MEN AND A BABY (1987)

This popular parental comedy is hardly known for its scares, but one story of death and heartache persists from the set. In a scene where Ted Danson and his on-screen mother walk into his bedroom, a figure can clearly been seen standing behind the curtains.

When the film hit home video, so did the rumours about what the figure was, most choosing to believe that it was the ghost of a small boy who committed suicide on the set. Believers said that, if you looked closely, you could see the child holding a shotgun – and, yes, the jagged black outline on the left-hand side could resemble a gun standing on its end.

More fancifully, it was said that the mother of the boy sued the film company for not removing the image from the film and that, after seeing her son in the movie, she went insane and ended up in a mental institution.

Unfortunately, the most likely explanation is that it's actually a cardboard cut-out of Danson himself, who plays an actor in the movie. The figure is supposed to be his character Jack doing a dog-food advert, but all reference to it was cut out of the shooting script. What's more, the scene wasn't shot in an actual house, but on a soundstage in Toronto.

You can see the cut-out again more clearly later in the movie, when the baby's mother comes to collect her child. Danson is standing next to it.

Despite these debunkings, fans of movie-ghost lore persist with their story to this day and it certainly adds a layer to an otherwise breezy but mundane film.

ARMY MANOEUVRES
COMRADES (1987)

Deciding just who could shoot what and when – that applied to lethal ordnance as well as harmless celluloid – was crucially on the agenda when they were filming this epic recreation of the nineteenth-century Tolpuddle Martyrs' story.

The production wanted to use the army ranges at East Lulworth in Dorset for some scenes and, in particular, to build the Tolpuddle set along the old rough road that runs through Tyneham, a village in the middle of the range that was compulsorily co-opted by the army before World War Two.

Only a few cottages and the church, which the army had recently restored for PR purposes, remained standing. The inherent difficulties of army occupation were mostly a blessing, because the beautiful and untouched landscape was devoid of anything remotely modern except one of the earliest Gilbert Scott telephone boxes in the country, erected in the twenties.

This could be easily concealed inside one of the production's cottages – but what were already hidden, and to cause many more problems, were the unexploded devices that lay uncharted beneath the surface of the range.

All negotiations went to plan and they built the set during August, when the army did not fire and the public were allowed to walk on the range. The filming was due to start in September, when they'd be bound by the army's own gunnery schedule.

The Martyrs' tree in Tolpuddle, an old sycamore near the church and under which the labourers met, was by this time nearly two hundred years old, so they need a much younger one to match the period. Luckily, there was an authentic tree only a couple of hundred yards away from the required site, but it would still need a crane to lift it out of the ground and reposition it.

The army, which prohibited the unauthorised use of metal detectors in case a member of the public should unearth something nasty, gave them permission to move the tree, but said they must check first for unexploded devices under the ground. One advantage was that it was the army and not the film crew who had to dig the hole for the tree.

The position of every scaffold tube that secured the cottages and, in fact, anything that was to be driven into the ground required similar checking.

A soldier with earphones scanned the ground and every blip or buzz needed checking out. It might only be a rusty old nail or a brick with traces of iron filings but, on one occasion, the signal was caused by a sinister-looking mortar with vanes, which, to the crew's great surprise, the officer said was only 'one of those' and tossed it over his shoulder.

The basic rule of thumb was: they could shoot when the army wasn't. Ironically, the only casualty turned out to be that rare telephone box. The village set had been left standing over Christmas until the winter gales flattened the cottage along with the telephone box.

RUMBLE IN THE JUNGLE
PREDATOR (1987)

The hunter of the title is now etched in movie history: tall, scary, sometimes invisible, dreadlocks and a maw that's talked about in film-theory classes as being suggestive of a certain part of the female anatomy.

But the seven-foot-two Kevin Peter Hall, who also played Bigfoot in *Harry and the Hendersons*, wasn't the filmmakers' first choice for the dilettante alien who faces off Arnold Schwarzenegger in the jungle. In fact, there were several incarnations of the monster before big Kev came aboard.

At first, the director John McTiernan dabbled with putting a monkey in a red suit (used for the benefit of the optical cameras, which would later add its chameleon-like camouflage) and having it jump around the trees.

But, as McTiernan explains, that idea was short-lived: 'I had them make a suit for the poor monkey, but the problem was, he was so embarrassed by the suit that he hid. He'd go up in the tree and cower and wouldn't do what monkeys do.'

A couple of the movie's shots are also of a gymnast swinging around in a gym in Los Angeles, which were then inserted into the background of the Mexican jungle, where the film was shot.

And then there was a little-known actor by the name of Jean-Claude Van Damme. That's right, the Muscles from Brussels has shared the screen with the Austrian Oak. Well, almost. He lasted only a few days in the role and, of course, there are several stories about why he left.

One is that he got into an argument with the producer Joel Silver over the dangerous nature of a stunt, refused to do it and was fired. Another says that he thought he wouldn't be credited for his work and that he wanted a Hollywood role that would showcase his real face rather than one that looked like a rabid humanoid squid – and quit.

And then there's the story that, after seeing the initial look of the Predator, John McTiernan was so disappointed that he refused to film it and waited while the FX maestro Stan Winston came up with a better design, which ended up being suited to a different actor.

Whatever the case, J-C left Mexico, spotted the producer Menahem Golan coming out of a restaurant and did a 360-degree kick that narrowly missed Golan's head. The producer signed him to his breakthrough role as the lead in *Bloodsport* the next day. And you do see his face.

FROM LITTLE ACORNS
BAD TASTE (1987)

Long before *The Lord of the Rings, Parts I–III*, were even a twinkle in this award-winning Kiwi filmmaker's eye, Peter Jackson, from the age of nine, amused himself and his pals making short films with his parents' Super8 camera. They ranged from comedy and animation to horror and fantasy.

Motivated by the purchase of a 16mm Bolex camera, *Bad Taste* started as a twenty-minute science-fiction comedy called *Roast of the Day*, the simple tale of a charity worker who meets a terrible fate in his small town. A month-long shooting schedule was planned with work taking place only at weekends.

This was October 1983, and, after Jackson's hand-written application for a grant from the Arts Council of New Zealand was turned down, he decided to pay for the production himself out of his wages from working on the *Wellington Evening Post*. Naturally, everyone was immediately placed on a deferred salary.

New ideas extended production from a month to a year and more. By late 1984, Jackson was editing footage on his dining room table. To his surprise, he discovered the film was now one hour long, but it still lacked a climax. The only course of action seemed to be to turn it into a feature and re-title it, *Giles' Big Day*.

An application to the New Zealand Film Commission for funds proved unsuccessful, so Jackson and long-suffering friends pressed on under their own steam.

The next crisis was that the leading man got married. Not only were his weekends restricted as a result, but he also faced a growing moral dilemma over a newly devised chainsaw massacre sequence.

Production stopped until a solution was found – which involved a complete rewrite, using as much of the existing footage as possible. With a new story in place, three extras found themselves promoted to star status and a new character was introduced, played by Jackson himself. The trouble was, he'd now run out of people who would work every weekend without being paid.

Filming got under way after a five-month break. But it still wasn't plain sailing. Two of the cast were in a soccer team, which played every Sunday afternoon, and this meant that all their filming had to be completed by Sunday lunchtime. Only one actor was available for the rest of the day.

By mid-1985, the film was starting to be known as *Bad Taste* and word of mouth was spreading rapidly. By mid-1986, almost three-quarters of the film was shot and edited. Film-industry people who viewed the work in progress encouraged Jackson to go back to the Film Commission, who now invested money to complete the shoot.

The climax underwent a further rewrite and development continued until the shoot was completed in June 1987. More ambitious special effects were developed and several independent filmmakers gave Jackson generous donations of their time and equipment.

After more than four years – Jackson was 22 when he embarked on production – *Bad Taste*, with its eponymous effects-laden blend of cannibalism and gross-out comedy, was launched on an unsuspecting world.

His $300 million *Lord of the Rings* trilogy was still a shelf full of awards and billions of box-office dollars away, but like *Bad Taste*, it has the simple production credit, 'A Wingnut Films Production'.

SWEET SMELL OF SUCCESS
WITHNAIL AND I (1987)

People sometimes say a film feels so real you can 'smell' it. That was often, quite stomach-churningly, the case during the making of the writer-director Bruce Robinson's cult classic set in the late sixties.

It was based on the real-life friendship between the aspiring but constantly cash-strapped actors, Robinson and Vivian MacKerrell (who died three years after the film was released).

The visual sleaze is established from the outset as we meet the pair (Richard E Grant as Withnail, Paul McGann as I) in their unspeakable Camden Town flat, for which the term 'squalid' might almost be a compliment.

The north London abode was created by the production designer Michael Pickwoad and his team in a large house in Bayswater just before it was due for refurbishment.

The vividly disreputable kitchen, into which were put the icons of sixties living, was set up in a room that opened off the living room. There was a gas meter, an electricity meter and a greasy, speckled, grey gas cooker on which sat a dented whistling kettle.

The single light bulb, covered by a paper carrier bag, illuminated an assortment of cupboards, untidy surfaces and, most particularly, a filthy sink under the window with an electric heater for hot water.

The sill was lined with old milk bottles, each with a different level of milk and degree of sourness, that had been bought at intervals over the preceding month and left standing in the prop room.

Since no one in the story ever washed up, the sink had to be filled with a mass of dirty crockery along with the infamous 'matter' in the fetid water.

On the Saturday before filming began, the final dressing was taking place and one of Pickwoad's team was dispatched to buy an eclectic collection of takeaway meals, which were smeared over a variety of plates and bowls and left out on the balcony to dry in the warm afternoon sun.

They were then stacked up in the sink, to which were added the remains of the day's coffee and tea mugs along with dirty cutlery and anything else to hand. It was, Pickwoad recalled, with some understatement, 'beginning to look pretty disgusting when we left that evening'.

They were due to film in the kitchen on Monday, but the schedule changed and eventually the cameras didn't begin rolling there until mid-morning on the Wednesday. The night before, the kitchen was really making its presence felt and by the morning of the shoot there should have been warning signs. It had already been under the heat of lamps for two days and now more were being brought in.

By late morning the camera crew were beginning to retch and threatening a walk-out as the grey waters of the sink slowly bubbled with decomposing material.

Little acting was necessary when the bilious Withnail, like his flatmate, coming down after a sixty-hour bender, claimed the flat was rat-infested.

'I' at least took the precaution of donning a rubber glove before he warily immersed his hand into the murky sink and pulled out a foul mass of congealed sweet-and-sour pork.

GETTING IT RIGHT
THE UNTOUCHABLES (1987)

The preview process by which a cinema audience is recruited, or even sometimes hijacked, for the test-screening of a brand-new film can be painful for everyone from the producers to . . . well, the audience.

At a preview in New York of this Prohibition thriller, starring Kevin Costner, Sean Connery and Robert De Niro, the producer Art Linson spotted a little old lady heading to the ladies' room for the third time.

He was ordered by powers-mightier-than-he to accost the woman on the way back to her seat and discover why she wasn't responding to the film.

'Was there something wrong with the film?' he asked her.

'Huh?'

'There must be something. Was it a little too violent?' he continued.

'No, not really,' she replied trying to move past him. He blocked her path and tried again.

'Well, hell, we need your help. You can't seem to stay in your seat,' he stuttered.

'I quite like it,' she said.

'What made you want to see it? Were you a fan of the TV series?'

'Well, I was invited.'

'Recruited?'

'What?'

'How did you get in here?'

'I am Bob De Niro's grandmother.'

LAW AND ORDER

ROBOCOP (1987)

It was a stand-off worthy of scenes in the film in which the heroic cyborg lawman heads for high noon with the worst human scum of Old Detroit.

But this was before a foot of film had actually been shot showing the gleaming new face of law enforcement in this effects-heavy sci-fi blockbuster.

They'd already been shooting for a fortnight when the elaborate steel-constructed costume finally arrived and tempers were becoming extremely frayed. Starting at four o'clock one early morning in Dallas, Texas, the actor Peter Weller was laboriously shoehorned into his extraordinary robosuit, designed by the effects wizard Rob Bottin.

Twelve hours of 'lugging, fitting and measuring' later, Weller claimed he felt and looked ridiculous in the outfit, comparing himself to the robot Gort in *The Day the Earth Stood Still* (see page 86). Without even the time to acclimatise himself to the suit, the meticulous Weller refused to start filming. He was fired straightaway.

It was now a case of brinkmanship. According to the co-writer Edward Neumeier, 'Peter was the one who fitted the $600,000 suit. The idea that we would let someone else walk around in it was a total fantasy. That dismissal was pure bluff. I do not think anyone, including Jon [Davison, the producer] seriously intended to throw Peter out, but we all pretended we would.

'As soon as the news broke, everyone in Hollywood frantically started looking for a replacement actor, but what they were really looking for was someone with the right shoe size.' Which, of course, remained Weller's.

After a bit of the usual tap-dancing, it was kiss-and-make-up-time. Weller returned to the fold, earned himself a weekend's robosuit practice and by the following Monday was back on the set shooting. He even managed to stick around for the sequel.

THE FRENCH CONNECTION
THE UNBEARABLE LIGHTNESS OF BEING (1988)

This powerful adaptation of Milan Kundera's erotic novel about events following the 'Prague Spring' was released exactly twenty years after the Russians marched into Czechoslovakia.

Unfortunately, because of what was described as 'the stark political explicitness of the film', it was deemed impossible to shoot in the Czech capital. Instead, they chose Lyon in southwest France, whose streets apparently bore an uncanny resemblance to Prague's.

But actually recreating the Soviet invasion was another matter. Genuine Russian tanks in working condition were not to be found

241

through the US Army. In desperation, a replica of a Russian tank was built, but it didn't work.

Finally, Soviet tanks in working order, and other support vehicles located in the French military museum at Saumur, were rented by the production and French soldiers on leave hired to operate them.

As a result, the film of the invasion seems almost indistinguishable from the original newsreel footage with which it was intermingled.

PLAYING ROUGH
THE BEAR (1988)

In 1981, the writer Gerard Brach sent his friend, the director Jean-Jacques Annaud, a book he'd loved as a child called *The Grizzly King* by James Curwood, about a bear cub and a grown bear who were being chased by hunters. Annaud felt the challenge would be to make a film with the story told from the animals' point of view.

In March 1983, Annaud met an animal trainer, Doug Seus, whose main charge was Bart, a nine-foot-six Kodiak bear weighing 1,800 pounds, still wild and untamed.

It was February 1984, and at another meeting in Utah with Seus, Annaud showed him the storyboards explaining what he wanted the bear to do. Bart would have to learn to limp, to wallow in the mud, to catch trout with his paws, to climb steep slopes and to rub his back against trees. Seus's task was to train his bear to recreate on cue the attitudes a wild bear would display under natural circumstances.

In August 1986, having completed *The Name of the Rose*, Annaud was on a promotional tour for the film when he dropped into Utah to check on Bart, who was making great progress and assimilating the actions in the storyboards.

Two months later, Annaud was back in Europe and crossing the Bavarian Alps when he decided these would be the perfect stand-in for turn-of-the-century British Columbia. The following May, Seus's caravan, pulling Bart's cage with the bear that now weighed 2,000 pounds inside it, headed for Los Angeles to catch the plane for Frankfurt.

21 September 1987: Annaud was filming the movie's next-to-last scene. Around 1 p.m. during the lunch break, the director agreed to pose with Bart for press photos of director-with-star. Without apprehension, he entered the forbidden zone closed off by hot wire and sat down with the bear two yards behind him on its hind legs. To add an interesting touch to this special session he put his eye to the viewfinder and turned towards the beast.

Did Bart register this as a hostile move, or did he think the director had just invaded his territory? Suddenly Bart dropped on all fours and started to come towards Annaud. The director froze. He could not mistake the low growl and the jutting upper lip, especially since the day before they had shot the confrontation scene between the bear and the hunter, when for the first time Bart had experienced the thrill of dominance over a vulnerable man.

It was too late for Annaud to escape. The 2,000 pounds of muscle and flesh dropped on him. Bart's roars filled the silence, along with the trainers' yells. Huddled up the best he could, Annaud recalled an excerpt from Stephen Herrero's *Bear Attacks*, a book he read while preparing the film: 'Remaining as motionless as possible – playing dead – seems to have decreased the intensity of injury. A person should assume a position that will minimise exposure of vital areas and parts of the body where such attacks normally focus.'

The bear's jaws tried desperately to break Annaud's neck. Hands behind his head, fingers intertwined, forearms and elbows covering his face, Annaud played 'possum'. Nine seconds ticked by. Suddenly the weight eased off as if Bart's rear end was lifting a bit. Through the thick fur, the director saw a way out and started crawling. His body was intact and in good condition – except for a long trickle of blood from thigh to foot.

Annaud went to the technicians' mess, received first aid, took care of the next shot and then headed for the nearest hospital where there was great interest surrounding the case of a director's rear end being torn up by a Kodiak bear, a case without precedent in Austria.

Two hours later he was back on set, having gone through the only accident to happen on the film during nearly four months of shooting.

Bart, known as 'the John Wayne of bears', went on to co-star in several more films, including *Legends of the Fall*, *On Deadly Ground* and *The Edge*, on which he earned a special end credit 'for his contribution to the film'. He died in 2000 aged 23.

SPIKING HIS GUNS
SCHOOL DAZE (1988)

The pioneering black filmmaker Spike Lee must have thought the gods were with him when he embarked on his second film, a campus comedy about black college life. Lee had invited the Reverend Jesse Jackson to bless the production because he felt it would help underpin the 'historical significance' of his film.

The director was also rather proud of the fact that he was employing an unprecedented sixty black actors and actresses in prominent roles while more than two-thirds of his crew comprised minorities and women.

Unfortunately, none of this seemed to impress the authorities at most of the colleges – including Lee's own alma mater, Morehouse – where they had planned to film all the scenes. They simply disallowed the production to continue on their campuses because of concern over the depiction of black colleges, so Lee rapidly had to find a suitable stand-in.

'It was their prerogative not to let me shoot there,' said a chastened Lee, adding, 'It's an old way of thinking that runs these schools. Nothing could be worked out.'

TAKING FLIGHT
SWITCHING CHANNELS (1988)

While filming this hi-tech remake of that darkly comic journalistic war horse, *The Front Page*, the director Ted Kotcheff was in a Montreal prison researching the kind of items a prisoner might have when he accidentally discovered a crumpled, grimy piece of paper that had been chucked into the corner of an uninhabited cell.

Written out were instructions on how to build a toothpick Eiffel Tower. Curiously moved that some prisoner spending the best years of his life behind bars would indulge in this sort of occupational therapy, Kotcheff set out to discover whether any of the current inmates had in fact constructed such a model.

The only fully assembled toothpick Tower was eventually tracked down and duly donated to the production. In the film, Henry Gibson, playing Death Row prisoner, Ike Roscoe, is seen putting the finishing touches to the intricate model.

Later on during the prison location, there was a rather less helpful, if oddly prescient, footnote to the shooting. In the film, Roscoe manages to free himself from the electric chair and flee the jail.

A real-life prisoner, thinking no one would notice his absence in all the excitement of having a film shot on prison grounds, disguised himself as one of the extras and attempted to stroll out of the front gates. He was nabbed before freedom was embraced.

A WARM WELCOME
STEEL MAGNOLIAS (1989)

The writer Robert Harling's fictional Deep South town of Chinquapin was based on his own memories of growing up in Nachitoches (pop. 20,000), the oldest settlement of the Louisiana Purchase.

What better place then, reasoned the filmmakers, actually to film his sweetly sentimental, loosely autobiographical account of some formidable womenfolk, which had started life as a successful off-Broadway play?

Unsurprisingly, given the warm nature of the material, the good folk of Nachitoches – some of whom were still living on happy memories of John Ford's cavalry western, *The Horse Soldiers* (1959), filmed in the town thirty years earlier – were instantly welcoming to the star-studded production.

However, even Olympia Dukakis was taken aback when she arrived to see a sign on someone's lawn proclaiming 'Michael Dukakis [her Democrat brother] For President!' – especially when it was explained to her by Harling that he knew them to be die-hard Republicans.

Apparently, they just thought it would be 'the neighbourly thing to do'.

FOOD FOR THOUGHT
VAMPIRE'S KISS (1989)

The script called for the character to swallow raw eggs. Instead, and in a move that would become part of the often eccentric actor's enduring mythology, Nicolas Cage opted for a live cockroach.

Cage was playing a deranged Manhattan literary agent, who, after being bitten during lovemaking, becomes increasingly convinced he has turned into a vampire. In Cage's mind was probably the original 1931 *Dracula* film in which the Count's mad henchman, Renfield, was seen catching and eating live insects.

'It was awful,' Cage said later, 'I couldn't really taste it, but psychologically it was murder. I didn't eat anything for three days. I had difficulty sleeping. I rinsed my mouth out with 100 per cent vodka before and after.'

Cage admitted that people continued to ask him about the 'cockroach film'. 'I actually have a fear of bugs and it makes me sick thinking about it. I know the reason the movie is still in video stores is partly because of that.'

BLAST FROM THE PAST
DEAD CALM (1989)

Set on the high seas, this thrilling and suspenseful three-hander, starring Sam Neill, Nicole Kidman and Billy Zane, was the 'sleeper' of its year. But the colourful history of the project, based on Charles Williams's 1963 novel of the same name, is perhaps as intriguing as the fictional story.

It was Orson Welles who first spotted Williams's tale as first-rate subject matter for a film. Welles snapped up the film rights, wrote a screenplay that remained highly faithful to the book (but changed the title to *The Deep*, a.k.a. *Dead Reckoning*) and began production in 1968 off Yugoslavia's Dalmatian coast.

His cast included Jeanne Moreau, Laurence Harvey, Welles's long-time companion Oja Kodar (who performed under the name of Olga Palinkas), Michael Bryant and Welles himself as actor and director.

If the numerous production, technical and financial problems encountered during the two-year-long, on-off-on-again production of *The Deep* weren't solely responsible for its remaining unreleased, the 1973 death of Laurence Harvey certainly acted as a drowning wave, and Welles finally abandoned the project.

Years later Moreau would claim that Welles had actually finished the film, give or take a usable soundtrack, but felt, as he had about his several other ill-fated ventures, that the film shouldn't be presented publicly.

Complete or incomplete, Welles's unreleased version of the film today remains in the vaults of his estate.

THE 1990s

STREET WISE
PRETTY WOMAN (1990)

Hollywood's ongoing love affair (OK, most audiences', too) with Julia Roberts officially began with this shamelessly soft-centred romantic comedy about a beautiful high-priced hooker and her impossibly rich and handsome client (Richard Gere).

It's said that the breakthrough moment came in a scene that was actually improvised by Gere. Showing Roberts a necklace case, he then snapped it closed on her fingers. Her natural reaction was an infectious, trilling (later to become trademark) laugh, which so delighted the filmmakers and, subsequently, preview audiences that they left it in.

The film became a huge hit, revived Gere's flagging career and ignited Roberts's so explosively that more than thirteen years later, she remains the only female star able to command top dollar – $25 million for her latest role in *Mona Lisa Smile* (2003).

How different it might have been had they shot an earlier and much darker draft of the script, then called 3,000 (her price for a weekend's 'escorting') in which Roberts' character was an enthusiastic cocaine user.

BORN TO BE BARD
HAMLET (1990)

Watching a distraught Mel Gibson contemplate suicide in *Lethal Weapon* by sticking a loaded revolver in his mouth, Franco Zeffirelli claims to have cried to himself in the dark: 'To be or not to be...'

For Gibson 'to be' the melancholy Dane was then uppermost in Zeffirelli's mind when he first approached the actor, perhaps best known at this stage of his career as an action star in films such as the *Mad Max* trilogy.

Jack Nicholson, Sean Connery and even Robert De Niro had been considered, then discarded, as being either too old or too vocally challenged for such an onerous classical role.

Gibson had, though, trained as a stage actor back in Australia – indeed, his audition speech was from *King Lear* – and he'd paired with Judy Davis for a successful theatre production of *Romeo and Juliet*.

His agent advised no, and pals warned him he could become a joke. For his part, the veteran Zeffirelli was chastised as 'senile' for even considering Gibbo.

But, after taking stock of his career to date and recalling how Dustin Hoffman had put himself on the line by playing Shylock in *The Merchant of Venice* on the London stage, Gibson decided to go for it and, as they say, properly exercise his 'acting chops'.

At a fraction of his usual megadollar salary and with his own company putting up a slice of the budget, Gibson went to work to a chorus of doubting headlines and the news that Daniel Day-Lewis had recently cracked up on stage while playing Hamlet.

He took fencing and riding lessons, gave up smoking to increase his lung capacity and tore into the text (cut by half for this version), having convinced himself that the character was 'a living time bomb'.

He didn't, however, find his accent until just before the start of shooting at Dover Castle. Just before the end, a friend gave him a present to mark the occasion. It was the shirt, with a bloodstain on the right sleeve, that Olivier had worn in his film version of *Hamlet* more than forty years earlier.

ASSET BUILDING
THE BONFIRE OF THE VANITIES (1990)

As if the production of this misguided attempt to film Tom Wolfe's satirical masterpiece were not already fraught enough, correct continuity should really have been the least of its problems.

Imagine, then, the horror – or perhaps the fascination, judging by her book, *The Devil's Candy*, Julie Salamon's often painfully revealing anatomy of the film – when Melanie Griffith turned up for work at Warner Brothers' studio in Los Angeles.

Griffith was playing Tom Hanks's irresistibly seductive mistress Maria and had completed her New York scenes three weeks earlier. It was immediately obvious following her first costume fitting that this was a new-look Griffith, the recent recipient of a very big 'boob job'.

Nothing unusual about cosmetic surgery, but in this case it was a question of timing. There were scenes Griffith had started in New York that needed to be completed in LA. Would her 'physical realignment' be noticeable?

Luckily not, since the actress was required to be fully clothed in those scenes. Meanwhile, all her sex scenes with Hanks, which required the breast-enhanced Griffith to be down to her underwear, were due to be shot at the studio. Panic over.

FLYING INTO HISTORY
MEMPHIS BELLE (1990)

Of the twenty B-17 bombers still flying at the time they were planning to make the film, eight were located in the United States. Which is why the producers David Puttnam and Catherine Wyler – whose father William Wyler's 1944 documentary about the legendary plane was the inspiration – originally intended to make the film in the US.

But once the decision was eventually taken to move the production to England – from where, after all, the World War Two action originated – it was then a question of mustering enough B-17s to make the film look credible.

The aircraft assembled at Duxford, the Imperial War Museum's airfield in Cambridgeshire, where the only English B-17, the *Sally B*, resides. Duxford is, in fact, only a stone's throw from Bassingbourn, where the original *Memphis Belle* was based.

Two American B-17s made the transatlantic journey, one owned by Catherine Wyler's uncle, David Tallichet, the other by Bob Richardson, who maintained his at the Boeing Field in Seattle.

From France came another brace of B-17s, *Lucky Lady* and *Château de Verneuil*, which, as of 1989, was still the only B-17 in the world actually working for its living. On demobilisation in 1947, the aircraft joined the Institut Géographique National for aerial survey work.

Tragically, on take-off from RAF Binbrook, the film's principal location in Lincolnshire, *Château de Verneuil* developed a swing and veered off the runway, hit a tree and ground-looped severely in a field. Thankfully, the ten people on board suffered only minor injuries, but the B-17 was consumed in the fire that broke out.

In the finished film, Tallichet's plane was *Memphis Belle*, Richardson's played *C Cup*, *Lucky Lady* was *Mother and Country*, while *Château de Verneuil* was immortalised as *Baby Ruth*. *Sally B*, with endless changes in code lettering and nose art, doubled for just about every other plane in the squadron.

As for the real *Memphis Belle*, the first American plane to reach 25 missions, she's permanently sited in Memphis, Tennessee, maintained by her own Memorial Association.

MAGNUM OPUS
QUIGLEY DOWN UNDER (1990)

This sprawling Aussie western was to have provided a rare opportunity for some mass Aborigine employment, but on the day of the climactic scene, which called for a throbbing crowd of three hundred Aborigines, only seventy actually arrived at the set.

Apparently, one of the tribal elders had died and in this official 'sorry time' hundreds of Aborigines from various tribes were in mourning. Time was running out for the production, and there was little room left for flexibility in the schedule.

So one of the producers drove personally from reservation to reservation, met with tribal councils and placed ads on the radio and Aboriginal television pleading for local colour. Without hundreds of native Australians, the drama of the scene would be lost.

Some swift research yielded up the fact that government stipends were due to be handed out imminently. The production hired buses to wait outside the administration offices where the tribes were due to collect their money.

Naturally, hundreds turned up. Then, with the extra inducement of free blankets, billy cans, round-the-clock catering, two days' movie pay and a chance to meet the film's star, Tom Selleck, a.k.a. 'Big Boss Magnum', the buses were quickly filled for the trip to the location. The scene was saved.

A CLEAN BREAK

AWAKENINGS (1990)

Robin Williams once described working with his long-time friend Robert De Niro as 'like hang-gliding over the Grand Canyon. It can be kind of frightening sometimes.'

But whatever warmth existed between the two men seemed to have evaporated, if first reports from the set of *Awakenings*, in which the pair were playing doctor and patient, were to be believed. The story goes that the normally placid Williams had lost his temper and broken De Niro's nose.

The official version is that they were rehearsing a scene when Williams's elbow flew up and hit his co-star's nose with such force that the noise of De Niro's hooter cracking was clearly audible on the soundtrack.

Ever the trouper, De Niro persevered for nine more takes before heading off to have his nose checked. He even claimed that Williams had done him a favour because the blow had helped straighten out an earlier break.

Williams finally defused the increasingly lurid press versions of the incident, explaining, 'If it were true I don't think I'd be here saying, "Let's talk." At least not with my own teeth!'

CAPITAL COINCIDENCES
LET HIM HAVE IT (1991)

There were a number of strange coincidences linking this re-creation of the controversial Craig/Bentley murder case with the real-life events in 1952.

Searching for a suitable warehouse roof on which to film the central scene in which sixteen-year-old Chris Craig gunned down Police Constable Sidney Miles, the locations department were finalising arrangements to visit one of them with the civil engineer attached to the site.

When told it might be used as a film location, he asked about the project and the story was explained to him. 'Oh my God,' he said, and for a moment there was a silence at the end of the phone. 'I was on the jury,' he told them.

A member of the company that was assisting in the copyright clearance of the court material turned out to have been the stenographer during the trial.

Another location, the church in which Miles's funeral was shot, was the church where Sir David Maxwell-Fyfe, the home secretary at the time of the case, who refused all calls to reprieve nineteen-year-old Derek Bentley, had worshipped.

Perhaps strangest of all, and by complete coincidence, the final day of shooting was the anniversary of the day Bentley was hanged: 28 January.

THAT'S SNOW BUSINESS
WHITE FANG (1991)

Snow and Alaska would seem to be synonymous, and, from all historical statistics and local experience, there was every likelihood of cold weather and fluffy precipitation when the filmmakers descended on remote Haines in winter for this adaptation of Jack London's wilderness adventure.

By the time they actually started filming, a strange and completely startling thing happened – the weather changed dramatically. It stopped snowing and started to rain. They'd film one day and it would be snowing right on cue. But then, the next day, when it came to matching the scene, it would be raining. This necessitated reshooting two weeks of material.

Spring had come early to Alaska, and every Sunday for several weeks production crew would get in their cars to scout for new locations further north where the snow was still plentiful. Having decided on the location for authentically treacherous weather, in the end they had to create their own blizzards.

They had to bring in snow-making equipment and the machine would be on the go around the clock in order to blanket the reproduction of the mining town of Skagway.

Finally, the right look was achieved. The man-made snow was in place and the temperatures were adequately cold. Then, the day before shooting, it rained again. The whole town was suddenly covered with brown mush.

In Alaska, you can't make snow out of the usual film-snow substance because it could affect fish-spawning areas. The purest substitute is instant-potato flakes. Unfortunately potato flakes aren't the best alternative either because the wolves – a prerequisite of this epic outdoor tale – eat them and then won't 'act' on a full stomach.

Finally, in order to shroud the brown mush, the filmmakers were forced to bring in an armada of dump trucks loaded with fresh snow from Canada, thirty miles away across the border.

HEADING FOR WAR
FOR THE BOYS (1991)

A very curious case of life overtaking art occurred soon after shooting started on this lavish musical drama about a bickering song-and-dance couple (Bette Midler, James Caan) who entertained American troops for half a century.

Production began at the turn of the year using an Air National Guard hangar in Van Nuys, California, to double as the London airbase hangar where the pair first meet and perform in 1942 for hundreds of World War Two servicemen.

For these scenes, the filmmakers chose extras who were actual servicemen and reservists. Exactly a fortnight after filming started, the Gulf War broke out and the mood on the set quickly took on a bizarre realism. Production was interrupted while cast and crew members were glued to radio and TV coverage of the events unfolding in the Middle East. And, just as quickly, many of those extras who had become part of the *For the Boys* family since 2 January received their orders and were called to active duty.

Before they shipped out, dozens of soldiers who had worked as extras posed for a group photo, which the filmmakers forwarded to each soldier stationed in the Middle East.

The director Mark Rydell said, 'The news that the US decided to bomb Baghdad came as a horrible shock to all of us. It lent an eerie intimacy to our performance. For those kids, it was hair-raising because we all knew they were in danger of losing their lives over there.'

IN A FLASH
BASIC INSTINCT (1991)

The crowds massed at various San Francisco locations for this overheated thriller weren't, in the main, trying to star-spot the likes of Michael Douglas and Sharon Stone.

They were mostly members of various activist groups such as GLAAD (Gay and Lesbian Alliance Against Defamation), Queer Nation, ACT UP and Community United Against Violence, protesting at what they alleged was the film's homophobia. It seems that copies of the script had leaked out and the protesters had concluded from it that the story portrayed bisexual women as psychotic murderers.

The filmmakers agreed to meet representatives of the demonstrators, along with the city's supervisor for homosexual affairs, to see if they could make peace.

When it was suggested by the gay rump that the Douglas role be rewritten for Kathleen Turner as a lesbian cop it seemed clear that there would never be a real meeting of minds.

Eventually, matters turned legal with the Dutch director Paul Verhoeven referring to court the matter of his right to artistic freedom. The demonstrators were ordered by the judge to remain a hundred yards from the locations and the use of torches was also forbidden.

However, when *Basic Instinct* was released, this aspect of the film's controversial sexuality was almost completely overshadowed by what became known as 'The Flash' or, according to one over-excited commentary, 'Three Seconds that Shook the World'.

This was, of course, the police station interrogation of Stone, as ice-cool prime suspect Catherine Tramell, during which she crossed her legs and it briefly became clear (actually, rather shadowy) that she was not wearing any undies.

GOING TOPLESS

FRANKIE AND JOHNNY (1991)

Despite having made more than fifteen films, many of which included steamy scenes, Michelle Pfeiffer was unaccountably nerve-racked this time round. A 'pain in the ass', she later described herself.

In this halting love story about a pair of lonely souls, she was required to bare her breasts to her co-star Al Pacino. The scene took three days and 105 takes to shoot. Pacino reportedly became so tired that his head kept nodding forward into camera view.

To mark the occasion, the director Garry Marshall gave the cast and crew T-shirts proclaiming, I SURVIVED SCENE 105, so at least Pfeiffer could justifiably claim she had been there, done that – and got the T-shirt.

PLAYING BY EAR

RESERVOIR DOGS (1992)

Michael Madsen took Method acting to new and quite nerve-racking heights for his co-star in the scene everyone talks about in Quentin Tarantino's debut movie.

As the psychotic but oh-so-cool Mr Blonde, he got to dance to Stealer's Wheel's 'Stuck in the Middle with You' shortly after relieving a hapless kidnapped cop of his ear.

Kirk Baltz was the actor playing the policeman, Marvin, and he made the naïve mistake of suggesting to Madsen that perhaps he should lock him in the boot of his car for real, to enable him to 'find his character'.

Unfortunately for Baltz, Madsen had already found his, and wholeheartedly agreed. Cruising around LA for over an hour with his co-star in the 'trunk', Madsen practised 45-m.p.h. U-turns, and even stopped off for a burger and a drink along the way back to the location.

'When I opened the trunk Kirk was all sweaty and bruised,' Madsen chuckled later. 'He looked real pissed off. I don't think he took it too well, but I got a real belly laugh out of it. When I told Quentin he laughed for a week.'

When Mr Blonde utters the ominous lines, 'I don't really care about what you know or don't know. I'm gonna torture you regardless. Not to get information, but because torturing a cop amuses me,' before hacking off poor Marvin's ear and dousing him with petrol. The authentic look of fear in Baltz's eyes would have been very understandable.

Spoiler alert: At the end of Tarantino's bravura movie a Mexican stand-off ensues, with various different characters training their guns on each other. A moment later all lie dead from gunshot wounds, despite the fact that one of their number – Nice Guy Eddie, played by Chris Penn – did not have another character pointing a gun at him. Figure that.

BODY BAGS
UNLAWFUL ENTRY (1992)

Researching his role as a Los Angeles beat cop, the tough-guy actor Ray Liotta went for the traditional 'ride-along' with members of the LAPD to familiarise himself with all aspects of lawman protocol.

'The first day I was out on a patrol,' Liotta recalled, 'a furnace exploded. The forensic man was investigating when suddenly he saw me and said, "Oh my God, you're the *GoodFellas* guy. Can I get a picture?"

'As they were taking photographs of the scene, he came over with some body parts in a bag, put his arm around me and I had to smile for the camera.'

That same year he was making the medical drama *Article 99* and this time Liotta found himself at quite literally the cutting edge of surgery in an LA hospital.

'They did the first cut so the body was wide open. I'd already fainted once so now I was queasy. I took off my mask, and they said, "Oh my God, Shoeless Joe [from *Field of Dreams*]!" The next day I came back and they started to take pictures of me as they were opening up more bodies. It was horrible.'

DRESSING THE PART
BATMAN RETURNS (1992)

It was a tough break for the famously free-spirited – some might say eccentric – American actress Sean Young when she had to drop out of *Batman* after being injured in a riding accident. Her role went to Kim Basinger.

Undeterred, she was determined to get back on the Batwagon by lobbying to play Catwoman in this first sequel, which included turning up one day at Warner Brothers' studio dressed for the part.

When she received short shrift there, she went on various television talk shows – most notoriously *The Joan Rivers Show*, once again feline clad – decrying various aspects of 'unfair' Hollywood. The director Tim Burton said, 'She's screaming "Hollywood system" and I'm saying "No, artistic choice."'

The first-choice Catwoman, Annette Bening, had to drop out when she became pregnant, so Burton then successfully cast Michelle Pfeiffer, who had turned down the leading roles in both *The Silence of the Lambs* and *Basic Instinct*.

SIZE THAT COUNTS
WHAT'S EATING GILBERT GRAPE? (1993)

It's one thing to find a young thesp to play a mentally challenged teenager, quite another to try to cast a 500-pound actress as his agoraphobic mother.

With Leonardo DiCaprio as the simple-minded Arnie and Johnny Depp as the eponymous Gilbert, the search was now on for a suitably mountainous 'Momma' in Peter Hedges' adaptation of his own novel.

The Hollywood hype has it that Hedges was watching the popular Sally Jessy Raphael TV 'agony' show when he saw the housewife and mother-of-three Darlene Cates – 500 pounds *and* a former agoraphobic – talking about her personal problems. Texas-born Cates's rather less glamorous version is that the film's casting director rang the programme's producer to check out any likely candidates.

Cates had appeared on the show twice in 1992, making a quite literally massive impression, and so her name was forwarded to the director Lasse Hallstrom.

Married at fifteen to a US Marine, Cates began overeating soon after her husband began long stretches of service overseas. By the turn of the 1990s she was massive, suicidal and had been confined to home for five years. 'God and Prozac' saved her. She eventually managed to reverse the agoraphobia when, with the prospect of her first grandchild's birth, she forced herself out of the house and off to the hospital's delivery room.

For the film, in which Momma was meant to have been housebound for seven years, the impetus was Arnie's arrest and detention in the local police station.

The courthouse in Lockhart, Texas, being used as the location was, coincidentally, the very same place Cates's grandparents had eloped to in order to get married almost exactly seventy years earlier.

A decade on from her very well-reviewed film debut, Cates, now 55, remains as big as ever, although she has added some acting credits along the way, most recently in *Wolf Girl* – as Athena the Fat Lady.

LOOKS FAMILIAR
HOT SHOTS! PART DEUX (1993)

Jerry Haleva was working as a full-time lobbyist to the California legislature when someone remarked on his uncanny resemblance to Saddam Hussein. It was the time of the Gulf War and Haleva was quickly signed up as a celebrity lookalike. This in turn led to his first film – a ten-second appearance as Saddam in the trailer for the spoof comedy *Hot Shots!*. When a sequel beckoned – the film, that is, not the war – the filmmakers decided to bring Haleva back for an extended role as the Iraqi dictator. This included a swashbuckling fight, part *Star Wars* part *Robin Hood*, in Baghdad between Saddam and, presciently, a scarily Dubya-like American president called 'Tug' ('We'll settle this the old Navy way: the first guy to die loses') Benson (Lloyd Bridges).

In subsequent screen stints such as *The Big Lebowski* and *Jane Austen's Mafia!*, Haleva has been used to mock Saddam's image. An exception was *Live From Baghdad*, about CNN and the Gulf War, in which he played it strictly for chills.

At time of writing, further appearances are pending.

BACK TO THE FUTURE
MAVERICK (1994)

The American stunt director (and former stuntman) Terry Leonard might have been forgiven for being a bit apprehensive when asked to reproduce – more or less – one of screen's great stunts from the 1939 western classic, *Stagecoach*.

The original, created and performed by Yakima Canutt, was a dangerous team-to-team transfer set against the backdrop of Monument Valley.

Mic Rodgers, the stunt coordinator/performer for *Maverick*, a big-screen version of the popular sixties television show, explained: 'In order to suit Maverick's character, some twists were added. Normally, he would come out of the coach and go up on top, then jump from team to team.

'But Maverick is more happy-go-lucky and he doesn't really want to get into any trouble, so he has to get there reluctantly by hitting a bump and slipping and falling between the wheels of the coach before getting to the top and doing the transfers. No one's ever done it that way before.'

The complete stunt was actually a combination of two separate feats that many had tried and few have succeeded in doing.

More than a decade earlier, Terry Leonard, working on *The Legend of the Lone Ranger* (1981) – coincidentally another TV spin-off – was shot from the lead horse of a six-horse rig.

Instead of falling off the back, he was to have fallen between the running horses. One of the horses then stepped on him and knocked him loose from his handhold. As a result, both of Leonard's hips were broken when the wheels of the stagecoach ran over him.

Convinced that every element had been thought out as carefully as possible, Leonard and Rodgers, doubling for Mel Gibson, went ahead with the Maverick stunt.

It did not go exactly as planned.

Said Rodgers, 'It's tremendous bad luck to catch both horses out of stride. One may stumble, the other one picks him up. When I jumped from the swing team to the leaders, the left lead horse put his nose in the dirt for about thirty feet.

'I was just waiting for the coach to land on me, for all of them to wad up underneath me. The only thing that kept them up was the four horses behind them, pushing them.'

Luck was with him that day and Rodgers walked away safely, joining an elite group of stuntmen who can claim the feat in their daredevil repertoire.

FLIGHT ARRIVAL
THE DYING OF THE LIGHT (1994)

Peter Kosminsky's film was based on the true story of a young aid worker, Sean Devereux, who was shot and killed while working in Somalia.

There was still trouble in Somalia when they started shooting in neighbouring Kenya some fifteen months after the real-life tragedy. Permission had been given to turn Malindi airport into Somalia's Kismayo airport and an extra storey had been added to the single-storey terminal building.

It had also been suitably distressed with mock bullet damage to make it look war-torn and was finished off with a large sign saying KISMAYO AIRPORT which the production had been urged to keep covered until filming began.

After the early-morning flights had arrived on the day of the shoot, the sign was uncovered and they were just starting to line up the first shot when a halt was called to allow for a late arrival. The flight in question taxied up, the steps were wheeled in and the door opened. The first passengers began carefully to descend, looking down at the precarious walkway.

Then an American tourist stepped out of the aircraft and looked around him, soaking in the early-morning sunshine. Suddenly he gasped and cried out to his wife, 'Gee, honey, do you see where we are?'

The alighting passengers looked up, registering not only the Kismayo sign and the damaged building but also an array of vehicles armed with large machine guns.

There then ensued a general state of panic as the horrified tourists struggled to reboard the aircraft.

MINUS THE MUSIC
I'LL DO ANYTHING (1994)

Many movies end up very different from how they started out, particularly in the era of testing audiences – a process whereby the filmmakers show the film to a variety of focus groups who say what they like and don't like about what they've just seen.

This was an experiment by the much-praised writer-director James L Brooks to make a musical satire about Hollywood, following the fortunes of the unsuccessful actor Nick Nolte and his daughter. Also starring Albert Brooks and Tracey Ullmann, the film featured eight songs written by Prince.

There were also songs by Sinead O'Connor and Carole King, and Nolte and Brooks even did some choreographed dancing.

After the initial nightmare screening, it was shown a further seven times, with new cuts each time, over the next few months, since Brooks always dreamed that they would be able to keep at least a couple of the songs. But, as we know, it was eventually turned entirely into a nonmusical.

Unfortunately for Brooks, while it was filmed as a musical, test audiences indicated that the songs didn't work in the context of the movie and that it would work better as a straightforward comedy-drama.

So that was what they did, excising all the songs and creating in its place a film that was universally labelled as disjointed and strangely cut – unsurprising, considering the manner it was put together.

A similar situation occurred more recently with Disney's full-length animation, *The Emperor's New Groove* (2000).

Originally titled *Kingdom of the Sun*, it was supposed to be a sprawling epic, and Sting worked for more than a year on the score and various songs. However, the Mouse House scrapped the idea, ditched Sting's music (apart from a beginning- and end-title song) and turned the cartoon into a knockabout comedy, arguably one of Disney's most innovative for years.

AUDIENCE PLEASING
FOUR WEDDINGS AND A FUNERAL (1994)

What's in a title? A great deal judging by the panic that ensued when, from America, where the film would be launched first, word reached the filmmakers, as production was nearing its end, that the words 'wedding' and 'funeral' weren't potential audience pleasers.

All kinds of alternatives were dreamed up – including *Toffs on Heat*, *Champagne and Ashes*, *The Serial Monogamist*, *Nuptials and Nightcaps*, *Tailcoats and Confetti*, *Girls in Big White Dresses* and *Weddings A Go Go* – before they eventually settled on a short-list of five.

These were *Going to the Chapel, The Last Bachelor, A Tale of Rings and Other Things, Four Weddings, a Funeral and a Cup of Tea* and *Four Weddings, Some Sex and a Funeral.*

When those finally failed to pass muster too, it became a straight choice between... yes, the original title and *The Best Man.* It was then remembered that *The Best Man* was also the title of a classy 1964 political thriller.

So *FWAAF* it remained without any noticeable damage to the resulting box office either side of the Pond.

REGAL SEQUELS

THE MADNESS OF KING GEORGE (1994)

Fans of Alan Bennett's award-winning stage play, *The Madness of George III*, were somewhat bemused when they queued up to see the film version, whose title had been oddly amended.

Bennett explained in his Introduction to the published screenplay that it was purely and simply 'a marketing decision'. Apparently the American backers of the film felt that, with the roman numerals retained, US audiences might feel they'd missed out on the original and its sequel.

This delightfully daft decision was the result of an equally bizarre survey, which suggested that filmgoers Over There had come away from Kenneth Branagh's film of *Henry V* wishing they'd seen its four predecessors.

As one of the moguls was to tell the director Nicholas Hytner, 'You know, Nick, it could have been like a *Star Wars* trilogy. We could have gone with a prequel and sequel before leading up to the big one. We could have cleaned up!'

KEPT UNDER WRAPS
THE FANTASTIC FOUR (1994)

As an actor, you never know whether your film's going to be successful. But spare a thought for the cast of *The Fantastic Four*, who, despite scoring the leads in this movie version of the famous comic book, were unaware that their work was never actually intended for any kind of public viewing.

The story has to do with copyright. Before *X-Men* (2000), then *Spider-Man* (2002), Marvel's comic-book heroes had barely made a dent at the box office. While the DC Comics heroes Batman and Superman stormed the box office, Marvel flopped with Captain America and The Punisher. The *Incredible Hulk* TV series was their only real success.

This meant that the producer Roger Corman – the man behind some of the most famous low-budget movies in history – was able to snap up the screen rights to the beloved quartet at a bargain-basement price.

However, part of the criteria for movie rights means that you have to go into production by a certain date, otherwise you lose them. Corman, who had the vision to see that the Marvel heroes might one day take off, was in a bind. He had to make a *Fantastic Four* movie, but he had no money. So he did what Corman does best: improvise.

He hired the journeymen actors Alex Hyde-White, Michael Bailey Smith, Jay Underwood and Rebecca Staab to play the foursome and handed the directing reins to one Oley Sassone. However, what the crew knew, but the cast didn't, was that the film was made only for one reason – to hold onto the rights.

Corman never planned to show the movie to anybody. It was made to go into a vault, to surface only if proof were required of his production. So while the actors battle it out with Dr Doom on cheesily cheap sets, with sub-home-movie special effects, Corman was probably looking forward to the moment when he would be executive-producing the $100 million version.

Thanks to bootlegs and the Internet, the film is available on eBay and is worth seeing for the team's hilarious super powers. The

Human Torch shoots the same fireball over and over again, the Thing is a prosthetic construction (played by a totally different actor à la the Hulk), Susan Storm can go 'invisible' and the leader Reed Richards can stretch his body, which involves what looks like a fake hand or foot attached to the end of a long stick.

Meanwhile, thanks to the success of Marvel's recent big-screen crop including *Hulk* (2003), a new *Fantastic Four* movie is in the pipeline, reportedly to star George Clooney.

Coincidentally, a similar situation occurred recently with the pulp-fiction heroine, Modesty Blaise. There was already a cult 1966 movie of that name starring Monica Vitti, Dirk Bogarde and Terence Stamp, but Quentin Tarantino – a long-time fan – was apparently interested in a remake. The rights were snapped up by Miramax, but problems meant the production couldn't get under way in time and they were left having to make a movie or give up the option.

Obviously the lure of another Tarantino film was enough and they knocked out a quickie version called *Modesty Blaise: The Beginning*, in 2002. Directed by Scott Spiegel and starring Alexandra Staden, it is a prequel to the novel's character timeframe.

Shot in Bucharest, the story follows Modesty as a refugee child, who ends up working in a casino and thwarting a gang who try to take it over.

Miramax have been more security-conscious about anyone getting to see it, although the character's creator, Peter O'Donnell, fired off an angry letter to the gossip website, *Ain't It Cool News*, suggesting that he was dismayed by Miramax's approach.

COLOUR-COORDINATED

IQ (1994)

When Stephen Fry made his Hollywood film debut as brainy-but-dull fiancé to Meg Ryan, who was playing Einstein's niece, the pleasures of Tinseltown clearly paled next to the challenge of just trying to keep up with countless script changes.

'It was almost unbelievable', he once told me. 'I don't think anybody except Fred Schepisi [the director] knew what the script was. They have these things called "sides", which are the micro-photocopies of the day's shooting, so that you don't have to carry a script around with you all the time.

'You arrive at your caravan and the sides are on the table; they tell you the scenes you're doing that day. But the actual script itself was being rewritten throughout the production, and each draft had a different colour with a history of the different drafts on the front of it.

'So it starts with "white 1", which was the first shooting script. Then it was "goldenrod 1", which was sort of an orangy colour. Then you had "cherry 1", then "salmon"...and it was a huge list. They went through each colour about four times.

'I sent a memo to the production office suggesting some new colours like "amber glow" and "gay whisper", the sort of things that would just perk up our lives in the morning.

'Every single night you'd get back to your room and there pushed under the door would be rewrites of various scenes on different colours. Unless one was prepared every single evening, to unclip the script and put in the new bits and take out the old pages and then read the whole thing through, you would never know how the whole thing had changed.'

GOTHIC HORROR
THE CROW (1994)

A grim Gothic fantasy adapted from the comic book by James O'Barr, this action tale would echo with tragic irony. At the time, though, it just seemed to be the next step in the developing screen career of Brandon Lee, a 27-year-old actor and sometime martial artist, who was gradually stepping out of the large shadow cast by his father Bruce Lee.

In the film he played Eric Draven, a rock musician murdered alongside his fiancée by a bloodthirsty gang. Resurrected twelve months on, he goes looking for his revenge.

Genuine tragedy struck, however, when a routine action sequence went horribly wrong. A prop gun that contained some wadding and a full charge of gunpowder was fired to produce an authentic sound as well as tragically authentic results, as Brandon Lee sustained an abdominal wound that would kill him.

Much was made of the premature death of the son of a man who had also died suddenly (apparently of a brain haemorrhage aged just 32) and in mysterious circumstances, though it seems that this was little more than a terrible accident during yet another hectic night shoot for a film with a tight schedule and even tighter budget.

Scenes to be completed were filmed using cutting-edge computer graphics, to blend images of Brandon Lee into those parts of the film he never had the chance to do. It has subsequently achieved cult status. Father and son are buried alongside each other in a Seattle cemetery.

PLAYING FOR REAL
AN AWFULLY BIG ADVENTURE (1994)

Some would kill for a role; others are content merely to reinvent themselves. Newcomer Georgina Cates first heard about a proposed film version of Beryl Bainbridge's semi-autobiographical novel when she read about it in a trade paper two years before shooting started.

She then read the book, set in a post-World War Two Liverpool repertory theatre, and kept ringing the production company every three months to find out when filming was due to start. When they finally told her that they were casting, her agents sent off her photograph and CV.

The response was initially good. However, a month later, they replied that, although they knew of her work and thought she was very nice, they were actually looking for a genuine sixteen-year-old Liver girl to play the role of starstruck Stella opposite Hugh Grant and Alan Rickman.

Eighteen-year-old Georgina was doing a play at the time and sought advice from a number of people, asking them, 'If you really wanted something, would you fib and say you were something that you're not?' The general consensus was no. The feeling was that she might never work again if she was rumbled. Later, while appearing in ITV's *The Bill*, she asked the casting director's advice and was again advised against it.

Completely ignoring all the advice she'd been given, Georgina had a passport photo taken with a wig on and penned a letter to *Adventure*'s casting director, Susie Figgis, in the style of Stella. No response. So she finally went and sat for two days on Figgis's doorstep in Soho. This persistence resulted in a meeting with the director, Mike Newell.

She arrived at the meeting using her best Scouse accent, which she'd perfected at the age of seven while playing with two girls from Liverpool on holiday. She was still wearing the wig, as she was worried that Figgis would recognise her as Clare Woodgate, her real name and the name she had been working under as a stage and TV actress.

Georgina wasn't recognised, even when she eventually took off the wig to reveal a particularly bad haircut. An invitation to the screen test made things a little difficult, as she had to spin a web of lies about why she didn't have a phone number in Liverpool.

Newell picked up the story: 'She arrived with a story that she was born in Liverpool and her family were still there, but her mother was both disapproving and unable to handle her ambitions as well as being depressed and agoraphobic. I never found out where her dad was in all this.

'She told me that she'd been coming down to London every Saturday, taking a very early train to attend amateur classes run through the Guildhall School of Music and Drama. I was very impressed that someone would take a train two hundred miles south and two hundred miles north again in order to do a three- or four-hour drama class. That for me signalled real commitment.

'While she was auditioning, I was introduced to her aunt, who came from Essex, with whom she was apparently staying. We all know now she wasn't her aunt: it was her mother who wasn't agoraphobic at all.

'At the audition she had given herself this very weird costume, makeup, haircut, hair dye; she was, in hindsight, very carefully dressed. It was a sort of unsuccessful provincial grunge, which made perfect sense for who she said she was.

'That kid had actually been doing a double performance all the way – she'd been playing Georgina Cates and she'd also been playing the role in the film. It was very, very remarkable.'

Her ruse wasn't without its hairier moments. At her second screen test she'd almost been caught out by a Liverpudlian actor testing for one of the other roles: 'He asked me where I lived in Liverpool and the only road I could remember was Hope Street, which is of course the main street. He said he didn't think there were any houses there so I told him I lived above a fish-and-chip shop.'

Newell admitted that, during shooting, 'everybody felt there was something not right about Georgina – something screwy. When she started work she was clearly obsessed by the notion of being an actress and very obsessed with this part, which she'd studied to the point of insensibility.

'I made a joke in rehearsal that we would probably discover that she was thirty-four and had a five-year contract with *Brookside*. How close to the truth I was!'

After she had managed to keep her secret throughout the production and, indeed, for several months after the shoot, the story of her remarkable deception finally broke in the national press.

Newell wasn't particularly bothered by this belated revelation, adding, phlegmatically, 'She gave a good performance.'

STAR POWER
MUTE WITNESS (1995)

In Hamburg to receive a special Shakespeare prize, Sir Alec Guinness was attending a party given by the British Council when he met Anthony Waller, an aspiring young British director, who was beginning work on a feature film.

Later that evening, Guinness was back at his hotel when the 26-year-old filmmaker came to his table and asked the veteran actor if he'd be prepared to say three or four lines in his 'up-and-coming' new project.

Guinness, who was leaving the city at lunchtime the next day, told him that he had commitments for the next year and a half, to which the persistent Waller suggested they could shoot early the following morning if he was agreeable.

Impressed by his personality and determination, Guinness asked to see a script. Waller disappeared, only to return a few minutes later with some dialogue. Guinness agreed to do the lines but if he hadn't finished his stint by 8.30 a.m. he'd simply walk away.

A team, equipment, film material, location and even a 1938 Rolls-Royce were organised overnight and at 7.45 a.m., sitting in the back of a chauffeur-driven car in a nearby Hamburg garage, Guinness said his 'incomprehensible lines to a nonexistent actor and was finished on time'. He had just one stipulation: that his name should not appear on any cast list or in any publicity.

That was March 1985.

Ten years later, Waller's completed film, a scarily effective thriller about a 'snuff movie' filmed in an cavernous Russian studio, was finally released in cinemas to rather good reviews.

There was, naturally, much interest in the role of the Russian Mafia kingpin known as 'the Reaper', a tiny but effective cameo, who, according to the credits, was played by a rather familiar-looking 'Mystery Guest Star'.

EARLY WARNING
ABOVE SUSPICION (1995)

What might have been a quite reasonable thriller – co-scripted by the ubiquitous character actor William H Macy, no less – took on an eerie air soon after it was completed.

The one-time Superman Christopher Reeve played the brilliant San Diego police detective Dempsey Cain, who is paralysed following a bullet wound to his spine.

Reeve would later describe how he had learned to simulate a paraplegic, discovering how to get in and out of cars and use a sliding board to transfer from a wheelchair on to a mattress in the physiotherapy room.

He spent most of his time with a woman who'd been crushed under a bookcase during a big LA earthquake. As he'd return to his luxury hotel at the end of the day, he'd be thinking, Thank God that's not me.

So it was a grimly ironic real-life twist to this fictitious crime pot-boiler when Reeve later suffered injuries similar to those of his character in a freak horse-riding accident on 27 May 1995, not long after filming was completed.

A little incongruously, the subsequent UK video release was based on the charitable donations that would accrue from sales of a film that had taken on a fresh significance.

Some people point to the supposed curse of Superman – the character who brought Reeve international fame two decades before – which suggests that many of the actors associated with the character and his adventures have encountered tragedy.

The most famous example was the 1950s TV star George Reeves, who, it is believed, committed suicide over the dearth of roles he was offered after his high-profile success as the Man of Steel.

DEEP IN DRINK
LEAVING LAS VEGAS (1995)

The story was simple. A Hollywood screenwriter goes to Las Vegas, where the bars never close, in order to drink himself to death. He meets a hooker, they fall in love but he eventually succumbs to the booze.

The director Mike Figgis based his screenplay on the semi-autobiographical novel by Cleveland-born John O'Brien. An aspiring writer, he had reacted to the seemingly endless series of rejection slips by becoming an alcoholic.

By the time he had achieved a small measure of success with the publication of *Leaving Las Vegas* by Watermark Press, a small Kansas company, and the optioning of the film rights by Figgis, he couldn't stop drinking.

While writing a second book, O'Brien was on the verge of losing both his day job in Hollywood and his wife. In April 1994 he was admitted to a local medical centre in Los Angeles after being beaten up in the street, and was told that such was the nature of his injuries that if he didn't stop drinking he would die.

Three weeks later, O'Brien was dead. Not from drink but as the result of a self-inflicted bullet to the head. This was a fortnight after he had signed the deal for the film. Apparently, his writing hand was shaking so badly he had to hold the pen with his other hand to complete the contract.

A few months after that, production began on what O'Brien's *alter ego* Nicolas Cage – who'd eventually win the Best Actor Oscar for his role as the self-destructive writer – would describe vividly as 'a dead man's suicide note'.

ON THE BUSES
CARLA'S SONG (1996)

This unlikely romance between a fiery Glaswegian bus driver (Robert Carlyle) and a traumatised Nicaraguan refugee takes Carlyle from his bus route on the mean streets of the Scottish capital to the heart of 1980s Nicaragua, at the height of a fierce guerrilla war.

As with any low-budget movie, opportunities had to be taken when they presented themselves, and, while the director Ken Loach and his crew were in their Central American locations, Robert Carlyle was left to face a far more prosaic challenge: passing his bus-driving test.

'I didn't know that I needed to get a bus licence going into the film,' Carlyle explains. 'I could drive of course, but not a bus. So I got enrolled in this course where from Monday to Thursday, nine to five, I was learning to drive this bus.

'Then you sit the test – which takes an hour and twenty minutes – on the Friday. And at that time there was Highway Code questions for twenty minutes after. All the messages coming back were that I shouldn't worry, it was just to get a bit of experience.

'But I passed it, miraculously, and there were celebrations in Nicaragua, where they were filming. It wasn't until I started shooting that I learned if I had failed, there was no film.'

ANIMAL MAGIC
THE ISLAND OF DR MOREAU (1996)

The name of Richard Stanley on the credits as co-writer hardly begins to describe his strange role in this laughably inept (third) version of H G Wells's Gothic horror about a mad scientist and his monstrous mutations.

South African-born Stanley had written and directed two intriguing low-budget sci-fi films (*Hardware, Dust Devil*) when, not yet aged thirty, he was signed up to helm the megadollar *Dr Moreau* with Marlon Brando as the batty boffin.

After spending four years preparing his script, the troubles really began when Val Kilmer, originally cast as the heroic outsider who unwittingly stumbles on the island's terrible secrets, suddenly wanted his role cut by 40 per cent.

They got round this by recasting Kilmer as Moreau's assistant and upgrading Rob Morrow to the hero. As for Stanley's grisly screenplay, this was having to undergo some heavy-duty tampering to make it much more family-friendly.

Eventually he and the cast assembled in a suitably tropical corner of Queensland, doubling as Moreau's 'island of lost souls' somewhere in the Java Sea. After just four days of halting production characterised by frequent altercations between the demanding Kilmer and an increasingly frustrated Stanley, the director was fired. Morrow left soon afterwards.

A fortnight later, veteran John Frankenheimer arrived to take over behind the camera, working with an almost entirely revamped screenplay and a new 'hero' in David Thewlis, who'd been wooed Down Under with pages of Stanley's script.

His credit wouldn't be the last of Stanley's involvement with the finished film. During subsequent shooting, he returned unrecognised to the set and worked as an extra under some heavy-duty makeup as a melting bulldog in a 'humanimal' cave scene with... Val Kilmer.

SHARP AS A BLADE

WHEN SATURDAY COMES (1996)

For the lifelong Sheffield United fan Sean Bean it was a dream role to play Jimmy Muir, a factory worker who gets taken on as a pro by his favourite team. He makes his debut in an FA Cup semifinal against Manchester United, coming off the bench with the Blades (Sheffield) 0–2 down and scoring a hat-trick.

For once Bean didn't have to cover up the 100 per cent Blades tattoo on his shoulder, as he did, for example, when playing an East End hood in *Essex Boys* (for the sake of his art, the actor opted to sport a West Ham emblem instead, but it was only a transfer).

Bean's match-winning penalty was filmed at half-time in a real cup-tie at Bramall Lane against Manchester United. It was not a semifinal, however.

As every football fan knows, they are always played on a neutral ground, but *When Saturday Comes* was, of course, scripted by an American.

FIRE-EATING SCOT
DRAGONHEART (1996)

Most would agree that Sean Connery's vocal stylings are unique. But how did Connery begin to play an 18-foot-high, 43-foot-long, fire-breathing dragon?

Whereas the dinosaurs in *Jurassic Park* were required only to snarl or roar, scaly Draco would have to move his lips convincingly to match Connery's recorded dialogue. This required extremely subtle facial animation.

Connery's voice was recorded prior to filming, and the computer graphics were designed to match not only his voice but also his physical expressions, borrowed from previous acting performances.

To aid the animators in the creation of Draco's performance, the director Rob Cohen created a reference library of Connery film clips. He edited key moments from the actor's extensive filmography, assembling hundreds of images the animators could use for guidance in devising the dragon's various expressions and moods.

'Sean has an incredible body of work,' Cohen observed, 'so I pulled clips from the beginning of his career to his most recent performances, categorising every possible emotion: sardonic, amused, sceptical, critical, charming, seductive, intellectual, introspective and melancholy.

'We broke down his emotional life on film and studied how he used his eyes, posture and body and then applied them to Draco. For example, if we needed Draco to look angry, I could tell the animators, "Go to the 'anger' bin and you will see something Sean does in *The Russia House...*"'

EYE OF THE STORM
TWISTER (1996)

Critics may have rubbished the clichéd plot and characters in this disaster movie about professional tornado chasers, but they and audiences had no reservations about its remarkable BAFTA-winning special effects.

The director Jan De Bont was insistent about creating realistic, documentary-like visuals to simulate the ethereal inception, savage attack and devastating aftermath of a series of ever-larger tornadoes.

One of the more complicated live-action sequences, dubbed 'Hail Storm Hill', concerned two of the main actors, Helen Hunt and Bill Paxton, trying desperately to get their instrument pack in the damage path.

An elaborate set-up was devised that would mimic the wind-whipped, debris-strewn landscape. This meant designing a machine from scratch that would crush ice small enough not to hurt the stars. No detail was overlooked, as even the colour of the hail was altered – in order for it to be seen on film – by the addition of milk to the mix.

Huge blocks of ice were loaded into ice chippers positioned on the back of a forty-foot trailer and the requisite wind was provided by a jet engine from a Boeing 707. On top of that was a garbage popper full of tree limbs, branches, leaves and hay, insulation and painted cardboard.

Consequently, Hunt and Paxton found themselves in the midst of a 200-mile-per-hour whirlwind of ice and debris – not to mention two camera cars with five cameras to each – creating a veritable mini-storm speeding across the Oklahoma flatlands, the heart of the American Midwest's 'Tornado Alley'.

DIGGING DEEP
TWELVE MONKEYS (1996)

The director Terry Gilliam was at first extremely wary of casting major stars such as Bruce Willis and Brad Pitt in his sprawling sci-fi drama (a loose remake of an admired 1962 French short film, *La Jetée*), fearful of losing control over the project.

But, satisfied that Willis had already made enough money to feel secure and had also earned sufficient acting plaudits for his stint in *Pulp Fiction* to want to extend his range still further, he felt comfortable with the *Die Hard* actor.

When it came to casting the pivotal role of the twitchy former mental patient Jeffrey Goines, Gilliam was less than convinced that the hunky heart-throb Pitt could deliver.

When they finally met, Pitt appeared to be more interested in the Willis part but after being told that it was taken he claimed that it was really Goines he wanted. The fact that, like Willis, he seemed desperately to want to prove something beguiled the director, and he signed him up.

Then, said Gilliam, 'we got him together with a voice coach named Stephen Bridgewater. Stephen called me after their first session together, and he said, "What have I ever done to you to deserve this?" He said Brad was incapable of doing it. He had a lazy tongue, couldn't hold his breath for more than five seconds, and had no ability to speak fast or enunciate properly. I thought, That's a good start.

'Little by little, he became a little more confident. Brad was supposed to be sending me tapes of his progress, which he consistently failed to do, which made me even more nervous.

'We were arranging for him to go to psychiatric hospitals, watch schizophrenics and talk to doctors. He even had himself interviewed by a psychiatrist in character. He worked amazingly hard; he's a very diligent, earnest guy.

'Then he arrived on set and he did it. What you see there in that first scene where he's introduced – that was the first day's shooting for him. It was extraordinary. But by the end of the day he was a limp rag because he'd been ticking and twitching and jerking all over the place. He was completely destroyed for the next day's work.'

Twelve Monkeys remains Pitt's first and, to date, only Oscar-nominated performance.

KING OF THE WORLD

TITANIC (1997)

For some people the *Titanic* represented the pinnacle of man's ambition. For others it perfectly represented a suicidal hubris, a vast and unwieldy enterprise that sought mastery over nature and paid the price.

The same could also be true of James Cameron's 1997 film, one of the most written-about ventures in Hollywood history and – as it turned out – one of the most remarkable achievements.

It wasn't just the scale of the film that was daunting. Pitting a human story within this very real and familiar human tragedy and not having it be overwhelmed by all that followed was a major challenge.

Securing top-notch stars such as Leonardo Di Caprio and Kate Winslet did no harm in this respect. Then there were the special effects, which were responsible for pushing the film's already over-stretched budget to over $200 million. But five years of research, visits to the real wreck site and the impassioned energy of Cameron meant that there was simply no turning back.

The main portion of filming took place in Mexico, at 20th Century-Fox's brand-new Baja studios, especially useful because of a 17-million-gallon exterior water tank and a 5-million-gallon tank located inside a 32,000-square-foot soundstage.

Reconstructing the *Titanic*, the filmmakers applied breathtaking attention to detail. The production designer Peter Lamont even managed to find the original manufacturer of the carpeting on D Deck, who were happy to recreate the pattern for the film.

The ship that Cameron had built was only 10 per cent smaller than the real thing, an enormous 775-foot set that inspired awe in all who saw it. And – one supposes – intense hatred.

Days on end spent wet and tired took its toll on cast and crew; an outbreak of food poisoning can't have helped their mood; and both young stars confessed their disillusionment with it all at different moments. But Cameron was a driven man.

'Nobody,' he argued, 'ever walked out of a theatre saying, "That picture sucked but, boy, they brought it in on time and on budget!"'

The release of the film was put back to December 1997 and Hollywood held its breath. Several obituaries had already been written by journalists who saw themselves as the iceberg waiting to sink Cameron's overblown production. But they were the ones to be disappointed. Taking $2 billion at the box office, and winning a record-equalling eleven Oscars, the film was a triumph.

In a neat sequel, Cameron returned to the theme for his documentary film, shot in IMAX 3D, *Ghosts of the Abyss* (2003), which took cameras down to the actual wreck of the real ship that had inspired him as a boy.

Cameron claims that one of his inspirations for making *Titanic* was watching the 1958 film, *A Night To Remember*, as a boy. He even dedicated his documentary to Walter Lord, its original author.

Although low-rent in comparison with *Titanic*, *A Night To Remember* was still a big British film for its day. Authenticity – such as serving exactly the same menu at the captain's table as they had at that last meal in 1912 – rather than scale was the order of the day.

Without the budget to build a replica, the filmmakers found their *Titanic* lookalike in an old ship lying in Gareloch, Scotland, before it was broken up.

These shots would eventually be matched with scenes of lifeboats and survivors slowly coming to terms with the disaster as they prayed for rescue on a millpond ocean. Beneath a similarly starry sky and on icy-cold nights, they filmed not at sea but at the Ruislip Lido, west of London.

HEAT OF BATTLE

WELCOME TO SARAJEVO (1997)

The thinly disguised story of the ITN reporter Michael Nicholson's bid to smuggle an orphan girl out of Bosnia began filming in Sarajevo only months after the Dayton Accord had finally brought peace to a devastated city effectively isolated after four years of armed siege.

Although the city was making a valiant attempt to return to normal, bombed-out buildings and streets of rubble remained everywhere. This allowed the production to give an accurate sense of what life was like for the Sarajevans under siege, but it also meant logistical difficulties.

Power and communications were still sporadic, mail service and telephones were not fully operational. And, most chilling of all, every location had to be checked for landmines before filming could begin.

The filmmakers were sometimes in the strange position of racing against the city's vigorous clean-up efforts. Places like the Holiday Inn were desperately trying to get back to normal, wanting to get rid of the sandbags, broken glass and sniper screens (buses and trams stacked on one another) while the production wanted to keep them.

Recreated warfare in what was once described as 'the fourteenth most dangerous place on earth' was then supplemented with the use of actual news footage from reels of Bosnian TV and ITN coverage.

ALWAYS A SUCKER
SPEED 2: CRUISE CONTROL (1997)

You just can't keep a good Method actor down. In this fairly pointless oceangoing sequel to a breathtaking landlocked blockbuster, Willem Dafoe took over from Dennis Hopper as a psycho ex-employee with a grievance.

Sacked as a designer of computer systems for luxury cruisers because he's terminally ill, Dafoe's character was out for revenge. His disease, some sort of metal poisoning in the blood, requires treatment with leeches, so, along with his secret stash of assorted weaponry, he was also on board with a collection of the nasty little suckers.

The director Jan De Bont explained how Dafoe – who had once endured having hot wax poured on his body by Madonna in that daft erotic thriller *Body of Evidence* – was determined to achieve maximum authenticity: 'I told Willem that I had some little rubber leeches we could stick to his chest, but he insisted on using real ones. When those leeches are put on your skin you can't get them off. I felt terrible putting him through this, because they start sucking your blood straightaway.

'The next problem was that we couldn't get them off – poor Willem! – and finally we discovered the only way to remove them off was with a lot of salt and a lot of hot water. On an open wound that's not very pleasant.

'And once you take them off it keeps bleeding for a long time; it won't stop. So all those spots on his body were very sore. But that's method acting. What can you say?'

GAME FOR A LAUGH
FIERCE CREATURES (1997)

'Dying is easy but comedy's hard' is an oft-used expression, but perhaps never more apt, judging by the reaction of the bemused audience than at an early preview of a rough cut of this 'sort-of-sequel' to *A Fish Called Wanda*.

It became quickly clear that the film, reuniting John Cleese, Kevin Kline, Jamie Lee Curtis and Michael Palin in a tale of an eccentric zoo and corporate greed, 'needed work'.

The official version was, 'Although audiences loved the premise and the characters, they did not find the resolution very funny.' This had apparently involved one of the Kline characters, who was killed by a charging rhino.

Cleese and co. knew all about problems with endings, because they'd had to reshoot the ending of *A Fish Called Wanda* twice.

Cleese himself takes up the story: 'After we finished shooting in August [1995], we started editing the film and I was basically confident that the big, funny set pieces were working. However, at a screening in London in November, I began to have doubts about the ending. When we screened the film again two weeks later, the ending worked much better with the audience so we went off to New York in December with reasonable hopes of success.

'Four-fifths of the way through the New York preview, I was sitting at the back of the audience with a big grin on my face as I thought we were home and dry. But from then on the audience reaction dipped a little, then improved during one very funny scene, then dipped a little and then sank even further in the last two and a half minutes.

'At the discussion afterwards, Casey Silver, chairman of Universal Pictures, said he felt we had a big hit on our hands if we got the ending right but that he felt we needed to go right back to the point in the film [about a quarter of an hour from the end] where one of Kevin's characters was killed.'

Oddly enough, part of the *Wanda* reshooting involved resurrecting the odious Otto, another of Kline's colourfully appalling characters, who had been terminally flattened by a steamroller.

With the studio's blessing and the eager cooperation of the principals, it was decided that the *Fierce Creatures* company would reassemble for additional shooting just as soon as all four leads were available.

However, since Palin was about to embark on *Palin's Pacific*, one of his globetrotting series for the BBC, this wouldn't be for at least another eight months.

Finally, *a full year* after they'd finished filming the first time round, schedules at least briefly coincided, apart from that of the director Robert Young, who was now 'unavailable'.

Cleese, who had been asked by the Australian director Fred Schepisi to play Don Quixote opposite Robin Williams as Sancho Panza, in a new version of the Cervantes tale (a project that eventually came to naught), now approached Schepisi to take on the reshoot.

Says Cleese, 'Once Fred arrived in England, he helped Iain [Johnstone, the co-writer] and me to make the new ending more visual and also encouraged us to reshoot a couple of the earlier scenes, which he felt we could improve by clarifying the motivations of the characters.'

There were to be some twenty days of fresh filming resulting in probably 25 per cent of new screen time. A pale shadow of *Wanda*'s huge success, *Fierce Creatures* probably just about broke even at the box office.

TOO REVEALING

DEVIL'S ADVOCATE (1997)

Pity poor Charlize Theron playing the wife of a hotshot lawyer played by Keanu Reeves. As if filming an intimate sex scene with the devil's spawn in this enjoyably over-the-top thriller weren't tough enough, her naughtiest bits were showing, too.

For nude scenes, they give the actress a 'cloth' – that's a kind of G-string arrangement that sticks to the crotch. So frenzied was the couple's filmic lovemaking that her 'cloth' had been worked off and was lying about ten feet away on the other side of the room.

To her horror, Theron was now totally nude, pubic hair on display. They had to call a halt to shooting and go again with the ever-game Theron saying, 'I'll do these scenes but they've got to work for the film,' adding, '...and they've got to "cloth" me up properly!'

THE REAL THING

THE SIEGE (1998)

After the dramatic events of 11 September 2001, many people commented that the television footage of the collapse of the Twin Towers resembled some apocalyptic scene from a disaster movie.

As the British director Mike Figgis put it, speaking at the 2001 Toronto Film Festival, 'The thing that I kept thinking was, it just looks like a very well-done special effect; I seem to have seen this image so many times before in every trailer of every big movie that comes out of Hollywood.'

Comparisons were immediately made with action blockbusters such as *Die Hard*, *Armageddon* and *Independence Day*, but it was only on quiet reflection that the strange links between 11 September and an earlier film, Edward Zwick's *The Siege*, became apparent.

The picture opens with the kidnapping in the Middle East of a cult religious leader called Sheikh Ahmed Ben Talal, a man who the director Ed Zwick says was modelled on Osama bin Laden. An early shot of the devastation of the 1996 Khobar tower bombing reminds us of this real-life villain's deadly capabilities.

Vengeful terrorists decide to bomb New York into a state of emergency, signifying their intentions by using a suicide bomber to take over a passenger bus. When an old-school FBI agent (Denzel Washington) tries to come up with a peaceful solution, he is swiftly put in his place by a more cynical CIA agent (Annette Bening), who warns him that the terrorists are not about to negotiate. Instead they are 'just waiting for the cameras'. As on 11 September, the whole event seems to have been orchestrated to pick up the maximum TV coverage.

More than anything, *The Siege* perfectly predicted America's reaction to such an assault.

Lines from the film – such as 'The worst terrorist bombing in America since Oklahoma City', 'Make no mistake – we will hunt down the enemy, we will find the enemy and we will kill the enemy' and 'This is a time of war; the fact that it's inside our borders mean it's a new kind of war' – sound eerily prescient now.

Indeed, the reaction of one southern senator in the film – 'Bomb the shit out of them' – echoes almost exactly Georgia's Senator Zell Miller's reaction to 11 September: 'Bomb the hell out of them.'

The Siege imagines that martial law would be introduced in Brooklyn as the government tries to smoke out the last terrorist cell. The internment camp created in a former sports stadium seems now to have uncomfortable parallels with Guantanamo Bay in Cuba.

Somehow, it comes as no surprise to hear the rumour in Hollywood that there was to have been a sequel to *The Siege* featuring Muslim terrorists bombing the World Trade Center. Perhaps it is only natural that those of us fed on a diet of Hollywood action pictures could not help seeing the atrocities of 11 September in those terms.

What is more disturbing to contemplate is the idea that the terrorists themselves may have had the same kind of disaster movies in mind when they worked out their high-profile targets in the first place.

BOWING BOWING
HILARY AND JACKIE (1998)

The actress Emily Watson had played the cello for a year when she was fourteen but now, turned thirty, she was required to provide a convincing close-up musical portrait of the later, great Jacqueline du Pré.

After signing up for the role, she first took a cello to Ireland, where she was filming *The Boxer*, and then embarked on three three-hour lessons each week for eight weeks as well as hours alone in a rehearsal room.

She learned to play some fifteen pieces varying in length from ten seconds to two minutes after devising, with her teacher, a special code to ease learning. The teacher would play the tune on the piano and then Watson would sing it until she'd learned it. She didn't learn scales or read music: instead she interpreted from her own compendium of 'numbers, letters, arrows and squiggles – gobbledegook to anyone else but me'.

It's said that her fingers bled with the subsequent intensity of her cello practice.

Then, during filming, she had to step up to the podium in front of a huge orchestra comprising many musicians who had known and played with the real du Pré. After the first run-through of three minutes of the Elgar Cello Concerto, the orchestra applauded her.

'God knows how Emily does it,' one hard-bitten musician is reported to have said, 'but she had me in tears.' They would actually use du Pré's own peerless recording of the work for the sequence.

STAR MUTINY
SAVING PRIVATE RYAN (1998)

Silver-haired Captain Dale Dye, USMC (ret.) was once a name to strike terror into America's enemies. During thirteen years as an enlisted Marine, he served in Vietnam, surviving 31 major combat operations and earning no fewer than three Purple Hearts for wounds suffered.

Since heading for Hollywood in the mid-eighties as a military adviser/technical consultant on (and performer in) films like *Platoon*, *Born on the Fourth of July*, *Casualties of War* and *Starship Troopers*, he has continued to cause considerable strife – but this time to pampered actors with his own version of 'boot camp'.

Steven Spielberg thought Dye would be just the man to turn the cast – including Tom Hanks, Tom Sizemore, Edward Burns, Jeremy Davies, Vin Diesel, Giovanni Ribisi and Adam Goldberg – into authentic-looking fighting men for his epic tale of the Normandy landings in World War Two.

Dye explained, 'I believe there is a certain core spirit that is common among men and women who fight for their country, and

I think to understand it fully, the actors playing them need to experience the rigours that combat people all over the world face.

'So, to the extent I can, I immerse the actors in that lifestyle: I take them to the field, I make them eat rations, I make them crawl and sleep in the mud and the cold and the dirt. And when they come out, if I've done my job successfully, they have an inkling of what people sacrifice to serve their country in the military.'

What Spielberg eventually got was a mutiny. He told me, 'We required – we didn't ask – that the actors playing the roles spent six or seven days in boot camp in the UK. It happened to be a very bad week where it rained. It was cold and Dale made the guys sleep in their underwear that was wet and cold. They couldn't even put on dry socks. It was awful.

'After two days of this, just about everybody except Mr Hanks was feeling that, as they say, life is too short. It was Tom who rallied the troops and said he was doing it, he was a bigger movie star than any of them and he wasn't complaining. The whole idea here was to get them to respect soldiering.'

Sizemore, one of the erstwhile mutineers, admitted, 'I didn't want to do it. The way I looked at it, just because I had to act like a soldier, why did I have to *be* a soldier?'

Goldberg added, 'If you could imagine Stanislavsky running boot camp, that's what it was like. We were forced to be "Method" whether we wanted to or not.'

Spielberg got the last laugh when Dye presented his director with a unit who were authentically bonded, if only in a common hatred of their taskmaster.

Said Spielberg, 'You can't be a soldier in the USA unless you've had a hundred and twenty days of basic training. These guys had only six or seven days. We were dilettantes here, in uniform. But better seven days of real training than basing their knowledge on John Wayne movies.'

AT THE CONTROLS
SIX DAYS SEVEN NIGHTS (1998)

Strange as it may seem, Harrison Ford may be the first ever major Hollywood star to have piloted a plane *and* conducted dialogue sequences that were filmed from a helicopter.

Playing a grizzled old freight flyer in this romantic action comedy, Ford himself came up with the idea of doing some actual piloting in the film, insurance company permitting.

Ford is an accomplished airman certified to fly a variety of aircraft and helicopters, but it was only after 'long and arduous consultations' that he eventually got the go-ahead.

In return there had to be a safety pilot in the plane – who naturally had to remain hidden away from camera view. Another bonus for the actor was that he got to fly a De Havilland Beaver, the DH-2, for the first time.

Normally, these kinds of sequence are filmed in front of a blue screen, the window images painted in or added on.

THE MANE MAN
SLIDING DOORS (1998)

The former *Bread* actor Peter Howitt had just finished filming a role for the BBC when he heard that the money was finally in place for his writer-director feature debut.

His hair was close-cropped at the time and so he decided there and then not to cut his hair again until *Sliding Doors* – a time-shifting hit rom-com with Gwyneth Paltrow and John Hannah – was complete.

In the film Howitt makes a cameo appearance as 'the cheeky bloke' in a restaurant sequence that was shot on the day of his fortieth birthday.

Looking, in his own words, 'a bit like one of Meatloaf's roadies', Howitt excused himself at the time by saying that at least he could now demonstrate 'how long it takes to make a film – literally!'

SHOT FROM THE PAST
THE LIMEY (1999)

The director Steven Soderbergh intriguingly describes his Los Angeles-based thriller as 'a very simple revenge film with a lot of sixties baggage'.

And he's not just referring to the casting of a pair of sixties icons as the film's chief protaganists: Terence Stamp, as an ex-con Londoner, versus Peter Fonda, as a crooked LA music promoter.

To create an authentic past for Wilson, the Stamp character, Soderbergh devised a unique storytelling device by acquiring the rights to Ken Loach's 1967 film, *Poor Cow*, in which Stamp played a young English thief named, not so coincidentally, Wilson.

He inserted shots of the actor from *Poor Cow* into *The Limey* during the older Wilson's periodic moments of retrospection. Said Soderbergh, 'We thought it would be amazing if we could cut from shots of Terence as he is today directly to the way he was thirty years ago.

'I don't recall seeing that done recently, or maybe ever. I was discussing with Lem Dobbs [the screenwriter] that I would like to find such footage, and he sent me a fax the next day saying he knew exactly what movie to pull it from.'

Since *The Limey*, the same device has been used to great comic effect in *Austin Powers In Goldmember* (2002). For a flashback scene involving Austin's father, the veteran spy Nigel Powers, played by Michael Caine, there's some footage of a golden-curled Caine grabbed from Otto Preminger's overheated 1967 Deep South melodrama, *Hurry Sundown*.

FROZEN ASSET

THE BARBER OF SIBERIA (1999)

On the outskirts of Moscow, where a beautiful old monastery over-looked a frozen lake, about seven hundred extras wandered around this location, all dressed in nineteenth-century Russian costumes as hussars, gypsies, market stallholders and circus performers.

About a dozen large wooden buildings for a winter fair had been constructed on the lake's icy surface. The line producer reassured everyone that the weather had been particularly good recently.

This was actually very *bad* news. The sun was melting the ice fast and the entire, not inexpensive, set was on the verge of sinking. Out of nowhere appeared what looked like a petrol tanker. A truckload of Russian soldiers followed, who leaped to attention, carrying long wooden poles.

Each man grabbing one end of a pole, and with a bucket swinging in the middle of each pole, the troops lined up in pairs by the tanker and filled their buckets from a tap. They then carried these full buckets, which had begun to steam, and poured their smoky contents over the lake.

The tanker was full of liquid hydrogen. The soldiers and the tanker promptly departed as quickly as they had arrived. The Russians had actually refrozen a frozen lake, right in front of everyone's eyes.

STEERING CLEAR

THE THOMAS CROWN AFFAIR (1999)

One of Pierce Brosnan's most successful non-007 outings came in this classy remake of a 1960s hit. The role of Thomas Crown was, however, originally created by the writer Alan Trustman with another Bond in mind – Sean Connery. Failing Connery, then Rock Hudson or Jean-Paul Belmondo.

Connery kept the producers and the director Norman Jewison dangling right up to a month before shooting – and then said no.

'I wouldn't have touched this film if Sean Connery had been the original Thomas Crown,' Brosnan explained. 'I think that would have been rather foolish. Comparisons are odious at the best of times, but in the case of Bond you just live with them. You need broad shoulders for that.

'But I didn't know that Connery was offered the role by [director] Norman Jewison until we were well into the picture. That was ironic.'

In the end, after everyone else turned the part down, Jewison turned reluctantly to another iconic actor, Steve McQueen, who starred alongside Faye Dunaway. Thirty years on, Dunaway took a cameo role in this remake, playing a therapist who probes the inner workings of the billionaire thief Crown's mind.

WEB WONDER
THE BLAIR WITCH PROJECT (1999)

In the age of the Internet, this bargain-basement filmmaking phenomenon was the first cinema hit to be created with worldwide webpower.

It started out with a pair of young filmmakers, Eduardo Sanchez and Daniel Myrick, thinking it would be 'cool' to make a horror film that was formatted like a documentary, 'the kind that creeped us out as kids. We came up with this premise of these three filmmakers being lost in the woods, then needed a reason for them to be there and why they were shooting a film.'

So they finally came up with the fictitious Blair Witch legend and the folklore behind it.

'It kind of grew and evolved from there' – thanks, they might have added, to the establishment of a compelling Internet website – www.blairwitch.com – that a number of Hollywood chiefs have since credited with starting a sea change in film marketing.

By the time *Blair Witch* hit the cinemas, it seemed hardly relevant that the result was just a moderately exciting, if for some almost unwatchably wobbly, 'shockumentary'. A kind of mass hysteria had set in that was to prove unstoppable.

Although technically now overtaken by *My Big Fat Greek Wedding* (2002) as the biggest-grossing independent film ever, dollar for dollar – it cost $22,000 and made back more than $240 million – *Blair Witch* must surely still be the most successful film of all time.

THE 2000s

DESERT ISLAND FLICK
CAST AWAY (2000)

What if a modern man were stranded alone on a remote desert island? That was the germ of a new film idea mooted by Tom Hanks to the screenwriter Bill Broyles when they were working together on *Apollo 13* in the mid-1990s.

Broyles had himself cast away briefly on an island in the Sea of Cortez off Baja, Mexico, to try to get acquainted with the business of survival – 'to figure out where to get water, how to make a knife out of stone, what to eat...'

Then together with the star and the director Robert Zemeckis, with whom Hanks had made *Forrest Gump*, he began concocting a suitable script.

A year before production started in January 1999, the search began in the South Pacific for 'Chuck's Island', where Hanks's character, a time-driven FedEx employee called Chuck Noland, is trapped for four years.

The filmmakers eventually settled on the uninhabited tropical island of Monu-riki in the northwest section of the Fiji Islands group. Permission was granted with, for the first time ever in those parts, an environmental code of conduct built into the temporary lease.

Cast Away had one of the more unusual schedules in recent filmmaking history. For a start, beginning with a location in Red Square, Moscow, it was to be filmed for the most part in strict story order.

Then, perhaps uniquely, it was decided to shoot the film in two sections with a year's hiatus in between. This break, at the point in the story when Chuck is cast away after his plane crashes, was designed to give Hanks the time effectively to complete a physical transformation for the character that in one visual would show the ravages of his long deprivation.

In April 2000, the cast and crew returned to Monu-riki and then went on to other islands, where Chuck/Hanks, now 55 pounds lighter and four years into his exile, would attempt to make his escape on a crudely constructed raft.

If Hanks had been busy during the break working on, among other things, looking authentically haggard – 'a kind of life spark was out of Tom's eyes,' Zemeckis claimed when they all reconvened – the director was no less so.

Zemeckis, together with some of the same key crew members, had been in leafy Vermont making a very different film, the suspense thriller, *What Lies Beneath*.

STAYING COOL
SAVING GRACE (2000)

For this Cornwall-set comedy about a debt-ridden widow (Brenda Blethyn) who swaps her prizewinning orchids for a profitable marijuana crop, the filmmakers were anxious to ensure a certain authenticity.

'I think,' recalled the writer-producer Mark Crowdy, 'we're the only film to get Crown dispensation to use real marijuana plants. The Ministry of Agriculture allowed us to use this very low-THC-content hemp.

'We had a hundred and fifty plants and they'd arrive in a secure van every day, accompanied by two representatives from the Ministry. At the end of each day, they had to be stored in a secure building, so the local police station agreed to look after them.

'They were delighted to help and told me when I first called up, "No problem, they'll be perfectly safe with us though you might not get them all back."

'The super buds were made for the film by our amazing art department, as we would never have been allowed the real ones. They said they did a lot of research – they just can't remember where,' he laughed.

FOREIGN TONGUE
CROUCHING TIGER, HIDDEN DRAGON (2000)

Michelle Yeoh, who played famous sword fighter Yu Shu Lien in Ang Lee's hit film, had anything but an easy ride when it came to shooting this blockbusting martial-arts epic.

Not only did she have to conquer her fear of heights to perform complicated aerial fight scenes, but the former Bond girl found herself out of action for a month after she tore a ligament in her knee during a stunt sequence.

Oddly enough, though, it was not these problems, nor even the inhospitable locations (ranging from the Gobi desert to freezing Beijing), that posed the greatest challenge for her when making the film. Having grown up in an English-speaking household in Malaysia before moving to Hong Kong, where she spoke Cantonese, Yeoh was in the tricky position of not being able to read or speak the Mandarin language necessary for her part.

Using a dialogue coach, Yeoh had to start from scratch, learning the language phonetically. As Mandarin has four very specific tones, she found that, if she did not hit exactly the right tone, she could find herself saying something completely different, as Mandarin-speaking Ang Lee would immediately point out.

The exhausted star told journalists, 'It's like speaking Shakespeare. I literally had to memorise sounds. I went around the set murmuring to myself all the time. I don't remember ever being such a hard worker even when I was studying!'

SUDDEN DEATH
GLADIATOR (2000)

There were just five days' shooting left in Malta on Ridley Scott's epic re-creation of revenge in Ancient Rome when 61-year-old

Oliver Reed keeled over and died in a Valletta bar while drinking with friends on his day off.

The legendary hellraiser had almost – but not quite – completed his role as Proximo, a grizzled old ex-gladiator who teaches Russell Crowe's Maximus the tricks of the trade.

In the original version of the story, Proximo was a survivor. After Reed's sudden demise Scott decided to amend the script to give the character a decent death.

But how to complete the late actor's portrayal. According to his biographer Cliff Goodwin, 'Two earlier scenes were adapted to allow Oliver's head to be computer-grafted onto the body of an acting double and hi-tech imaging was used to change his expression and add shadows and wrinkles to his face.

'Additional appearances, filmed weeks earlier, were clawed back from outtakes and already discarded sequences. One entire scene is a repeat of a previous one, but with Oliver in different clothes, against a different background and uttering different words. Proximo's death, for reasons of tact, was shot carefully from behind.'

The film is dedicated to Reed.

SWIMMING STAR

THE BEACH (2000)

'Wet she was a star', they used to say of Hollywood's favourite aqua actress Esther '*Million Dollar Mermaid*' Williams. With a suitable gender adjustment the same could have been said for Leonardo DiCaprio after *Titanic*, which would go on to become (to date) the most successful box-office film of all time.

There was certainly no getting away from *Titanic* when DiCaprio turned up in Thailand for this soggy adaptation of Alex Garland's best-selling novel about paradise lost. Even in the middle of apparent nowhere, star-struck locals would come up to him and say, 'Jack Dawson!'

In *Titanic*, DiCaprio's character finally perished beneath the waves. Here he needed all his survival instincts for real when the production was struck one day with what the director Danny Boyle described to me as 'a terrible boat accident'.

He explained, 'One of the themes of the film is that you waltz into nature and think you can conquer it and it bites back. We were filming on a very flat sea, an absolutely perfect sea, and suddenly, for reasons we found out later, there were eight- and ten-foot waves above us.

'And it's extraordinary. It's not like the movies where people shout and yell and get into lifeboats. It is just silent. People just look at each other and you can tell all at the same time that the boat's going to sink.

'They couldn't get near us with the safety boats. Because there were so many people in the water and so much equipment just being swirled around like a big washing machine, the safety boats were frightened if they came near their propellers would chop up somebody. And if they turned the propellers off they'd also be thrown into the water.

'What it was, the tide was changing from going in to going out, and we happened to be above a sand bar which we didn't know about, which then turns into this great threshing mill.

'The good swimmers, like Leo, helped people, but we were very frightened. Fortunately, there was a diver who screamed at everybody to swim out to sea. Everybody was swimming to the shore, which was a long, long way away, and we weren't getting anywhere because we didn't know the tide was going out.

'But he knew this for some reason; so we swam out to sea, which is completely against what your brain's saying. Then it was calm and the boats came and picked us up.'

HOME MOVIE
ZOOLANDER (2001)

Hollywood has never been a place to shy away from nepotism, but even by its own incestuous standards, the director Ben Stiller's casting of his hilarious fashion spoof must take some beating.

As well as helming (and co-writing), Ben was also firmly front of camera as a male catwalk idol, Derek Zoolander. Then, in no particular order, his father, Jerry Stiller, played his shell-suited agent Maury Ballstein, his mother, Anne Meara, was an awards protester, his sister Amy essayed a member of his main rival's fashion posse, and his wife, Christine Taylor, co-starred as a dogged investigative reporter.

Last but not least, for a night-time image of a Pennsylvania coalmine, Ben required a dog wandering through the shot. So up stepped the Stiller pet, Kahlua, a chocolate Labrador, to complete the family album.

GIVING DUE CREDIT
ROAD TO PERDITION (2002)

After the main credits have rolled and before the obligatory source-listing of songs and music, there's a handful of 'Thanks to', leading off with 'Anthony LaPaglia'.

Film fans will need no introduction to the Australian-born tough-guy actor, who has impressive track records in film and TV, including *Lantana*, *The House of Mirth* and *Murder One*.

He's also no slouch when it comes to playing colourful Italian-American gangsters – witness Barry 'The Blade' Muldano in *The Client*, Charles 'Lucky' Luciano in *Lansky* and the eponymous *Frank Nitti: Enforcer*.

Now, many will know that Nitti was right-hand man to Al 'Scarface' Capone – especially those who saw *Road to Perdition*, in which Stanley Tucci etched a memorable cameo of the thirties' mafioso.

But where was Capone then in Sam Mendes's exquisite re-creation of Chicago mobdom? The answer was in a 'wonderful' (said Mendes) performance by LaPaglia, which sadly never progressed beyond the cutting room.

Mendes told me, 'Anthony did a day for us as Capone for one scene. In the end, we decided that Capone felt like a much more frightening and mysterious figure when he was only referred to; it was as if he was hanging there like a shadow.'

The two-minute scene would, Mendes promised LaPaglia watchers, be one of the 'deleted scene' highlights of the DVD. Meanwhile official 'Thanks to' had to suffice.

At least LaPaglia's efforts will have seen some light of day. Until Robert De Niro finally committed himself to playing Capone in *The Untouchables* (1987), Bob Hoskins had been on standby for the juicy role. His consolation was a $200,000 pay-off.

CREATURE FEATURE
THE LORD OF THE RINGS: THE TWO TOWERS (2002)

Fully computer-generated characters in films have ranged from *Jurassic Park*'s scaly monsters to the woe-begotten house elf Dobby in *Harry Potter and the Chamber of Secrets*.

But none surely have quite attained the 'How did they do that?' sophistication and sheer appeal, enjoyed by critics and audiences alike, of slithering, sibilant Gollum, the deformed, mind-warped ex-Hobbit and former Ringbearer.

The director Peter Jackson was anxious that the character must seem entirely authentic, a presence that would carry as much reality and emotional weight as a live actor.

So, although Gollum is a completely digital creature, Jackson was determined to get an actor actually to create the character. The result is probably the most actor-driven digital creature ever used in a film.

He found a willing ally in 39-year-old West London-born Andy Serkis, whose live-action credits on stage and screen include *Topsy-Turvy* and *Death Watch*.

As Jackson and his cinematographer Andrew Lesnie supervised Serkis's performance on set, the animators studied the resulting performance to remake it digitally, using his movements and facial expressions to animate the Gollum that would ultimately 'act' in the scene.

His body and voice design were then taken further into an animated world through motion-capture photography, computer-generated imagery and digital sound mixing.

Jackson explained, 'Obviously Andy created the character through the voice. But also we did a lot of it as motion capture, which is where Andy wore a skin-tight suit covered in these little dots and he performed Gollum. He said the dialogue, playing out the scenes just as he would, and then the computer was able to capture his movement and translate that to the digital version of the character.

Starting with sketches by the film's conceptual artists, Jackson's vision for Gollum was ultimately sculpted into a Plasticine maquette, which was then scanned into the computer.

According to the creature supervisor Eric Sainden, 'There are around three hundred different muscles or more on Gollum. He has a full skeleton and a full muscle system that's all driving what you see on his skin. One of the greatest challenges is his face. He has to act with the other actors. The facial system we're doing has about two hundred and fifty different face shapes that we're working in between.'

But it was the voice that became Serkis's touchstone and key to the character. 'In just doing the voice,' said the actor, 'I immediately got into the physicality of Gollum and embodied the part as I would if I were playing it for real.

'It was really quite bizarre,' he chuckled, 'because my character has two sides to his personality, Smeagol – who he once was – and Gollum, who he became. When I saw the new design, Gollum was like my dad and Smeagol was like my two-year-old son!'

SAVING THE DAY
BLOOD WORK (2002)

So willing was the actor Jeff Daniels to support his director and co-star Clint Eastwood's vision while making this rather routine thriller that his efforts nearly spelled disaster for the production while shooting a driving sequence in the desert.

Daniels recalled, 'It was my second or third day of filming, I was driving, Clint was sitting in the passenger seat and the camera and operator were positioned in the back seat.

'The sun was going down and I was manoeuvring the car along this curvy road as we're playing the scene and trying to nail the shot before losing the light.

'The car's side mirror was catching a reflection of the camera, so they asked me to adjust it. As I'm fixing the mirror, I see Clint reach across me, grab the wheel and turn it just slightly.

'I looked up and realised he had very calmly avoided a head-on collision with a minivan coming round the turn. I froze, thinking, I almost killed him! I almost killed Clint Eastwood.'

VIRTUAL BEAUTY
SIMONE (2002)

The eponymous heroine of Andrew Niccol's entertainingly satirical sci-fi fantasy about Hollywood is a computer-generated sex goddess who never argues with her director, worries about her salary or checks the length of her trailer.

To create his digitised 'synthespian', Niccol mostly used the stunning Canadian model Rachel Roberts. But at the end of the film he also 'thanks the following for their contribution to the making of Simone'.

In order they are: Lauren Bacall, Ingrid Bergman, Mary J Blige, Ernest Borgnine, Marlene Dietrich, Claire Forlani, Greta Garbo, Rita Hayworth, Audrey Hepburn, Katharine Hepburn, Grace Kelly, Veronica Lake, Sophia Loren, Jayne Mansfield and Marilyn Monroe.

Hang on! Was that *the* Ernest Borgnine in among that roll-call of screen pulchritude? The same pug-faced veteran symbol of macho Hollywood man?

Niccol's explanation was, to say the least, enigmatic: 'I've always felt that every beautiful woman should have a little Ernest Borgnine in them.'

TILTING AT WINDMILLS
LOST IN LA MANCHA (2002)

From Orson Welles's famously unfinished *Don Quixote* (started in 1955) to Terry Gilliam's $32 million epic, *The Man Who Killed Don Quixote*, aborted after just six days shooting in Spain, there seems to be something truly fated about Cervantes' absurd, questing hero.

Keith Fulton and Louis Pepe's award-winning documentary about the 'unmaking of a major motion picture' is all the more poignant because of unprecedented access granted them by Gilliam, starting during preproduction in March 1999. Two months later, Gilliam's finance collapsed.

A year later, Gilliam called to say the project was on again and they were invited to Madrid to start observing eight weeks before shooting was even due to begin.

Their fly-on-the-wall camera captures mounting problems such as a multilingual crew struggling to communicate detailed ideas, actors remaining absent as they run overschedule on other projects, untrained horses and a sound stage that isn't soundproof.

Uncomfortable with the nature of what they were capturing on tape and with the strange looks they'd receive from members of the production team whenever they pointed their lens, Fulton and Pepe took their concerns to Gilliam. He assured them that they should document whatever might happen, no matter what transpired in the course of the following weeks.

'This project has been so long in the making [Gilliam's first attempt had been in the early nineties] and so miserable that someone needs to get a film out of it. And it doesn't look like it's going to be me,' Gilliam told Fulton and Pepe.

The subsequent illness of his leading man (Jean Rochefort) and a catastrophic flash flood were the final straws. The curse of Don Quixote had struck again.

FOOTBALL HEROICS
BEND IT LIKE BECKHAM (2002)

The task of selling this hit British film to American audiences might, at first sight, have seemed insurmountable. Not that the Cinderella-style story of an Anglo-Indian girl who goes against the wishes of her parents to pursue an impossible dream did not have broad appeal.

But for a country that mistakenly imagines football to be a game in which feet are only peripheral to the action, and for whom David Beckham is an obscure chap married to Posh Spice, it was tricky to say the least.

Despite this, Gurinder Chadha's feelgood movie performed incredibly well at the US box office, benefiting perhaps from its novelty value but also meeting some of its apparent disadvantages head on.

Never mind that US audiences wouldn't know who this Beckham guy might be, or just how or why he should want to bend 'it', the film's resourceful distributors recruited the services of a high-profile female American soccer star to help sell the film. This was a logical step, given the aspirations of the young women in the story who dream of a professional career in America.

That the film opened successfully in Britain was not such a surprise. That it played well in America is a very pleasant one. And in an ironic twist, after the filmmakers had feared that this high-profile footballer might object that his name was being used to sell a mere movie – the film has helped to sell 'Becks' to US audiences.

In the aftermath of the sleeper success the film enjoyed at the box office, one of the few national newspapers in the last significant soccer-free zone on Earth had an extraordinary front page. *USA Today* carried a picture of David Beckham over the headline HE'S THE MOST FAMOUS ATHLETE IN THE WORLD (EXCEPT IN THE USA). Truth and fiction have rarely enjoyed so fruitful a collaboration.

POWER TO THE PEOPLE
CRADLE 2 THE GRAVE (2003)

In the red corner, Beijing-born Jet Li, aged forty, four-times national wushu champion, who, when only eleven, performed a two-man fight for President Nixon on the White House lawn. He's five foot six.

In the blue corner, Mark Dacascos, aged thirty-nine, from Hawaii, a tournament winner from the age of eight and in 1982 European kung-fu and karate champion. He's five foot nine.

Here was a big-screen showdown surely just waiting to happen.

Both men had parlayed their early martial artistry into screen success: Li in films such as *Shaolin Temple*, *Once Upon a Time In China*, *Lethal Weapon 4* and *Romeo Must Die*; Dacascos with *Only the Strong*, *Crying Freeman* and *Brotherhood of the Wolf.*

So who was actually responsible for finally matching these chopsocky wizards in a glossy all-action Hollywood film?

In an intriguing twist on the old casting couch it was actually down to the paying customers, in particular the many aficionados of Jet Li. The little master explained, 'We did a survey through my website. We asked my fans who they'd most like to see me fight on screen, and the overwhelming response was Mark.'

Interestingly, Dacascos had been a fan of Li's for more than fifteen years and so his preparation for this first-ever clash of the furiously fisty Titans was extra special for him.

Though the two men had never before met on screen, they also shared a history of lost roles. Li was said to have been first choice for the Chow Yun Fat part in *Crouching Tiger, Hidden Dragon*, while Dacascos was considered for Bruce Lee in his biopic *Dragon – The Bruce Lee Story*.

WHAT'S IN A NAME

THE TRUTH ABOUT CHARLIE (2003)

As if remaking *Charade* (1963) weren't bad enough, devotees of one of Hollywood's best – and surely unrepeatable – romantic comedy thrillers must also have been a little bemused by one of the screenplay credits for a certain 'Peter Joshua' on this pointless facsimile.

It was, of course, one of the many pseudonyms used by Cary Grant as he and Audrey Hepburn embarked on their twist-packed adventure in the original film.

This time round, it was utilised to mask the identity of *Charade*'s screenwriter, the late Peter Stone, who'd been employed to do some work on the dismal remake, co-starring Mark Wahlberg and Thandie Newton.

At least the pseudonymous Joshua wasn't likely to be asked to go up on stage and collect a screenwriting Oscar.

So just imagine what might have happened if, back in 1985 at the Dorothy Chandler Pavilion in lovely downtown LA, Michael Austin and P H Vazak had been announced as the winners for their script of *Greystoke: The Legend of Tarzan, Lord of the Apes*.

Vazak was, in fact, the alias of Robert Towne, who was reportedly so dissatisfied with the finished film that he decided to take the name...of his beloved pet sheepdog!

AN IMMATERIAL GIRL
SWEPT AWAY (2003)

The date above refers not, as has been the practice in the rest of this volume, to its cinema release in the UK. Why? Because it simply never happened, despite it starring the pop diva Madonna under the direction of her British husband Guy Ritchie, he of *Lock, Stock & Two Smoking Barrels* (1998) fame.

Madonna, no stranger to box-office turkeys – *Shanghai Surprise* (1986) and *Who's That Girl?* (1987), to name but two – might have thought that at the age of 44 she deserved more respect in her adopted country than to suffer the indignation of straight-to-video.

The idea of being bitchy and nude must have appealed to Madge – and to her fans she doubtless surmised – when the happy couple decided to remake Lina Wertmuller's delightfully titled Italian sex comedy, *Swept Away...By an Unusual Destiny in the Blue Sea of August* (1974).

However, even with a shorter title and running time than the original, the result did absolutely nothing to prevent an onslaught from US critics, which resulted in just two paltry weeks in American cinemas.

Fearing the inevitable backlash, the British distributors simply cut their losses and decided to usher Mr and Mrs Ritchie 'straight to radio', as it's drolly dubbed.

CUTTING TO THE CHASE
THE MATRIX RELOADED (2003)

Aside from the massive weight of expectation – from the studio as well as audiences worldwide – the Wachowski Brothers laboured under more pressure than many would find bearable to bring their latest film to the screen.

For one thing it was shot right up against its own sequel, *The Matrix Revolutions*: seven weeks' work in California, then 270 days of principal photography in Australia, finally more than a year of postproduction.

The sheer scale, scope and size of these films is exemplified by such single-minded determination, and is illustrated by the decision to build an entire mile-and-a-half-long section of freeway – complete with a nineteen-foot-high wall and two over-passes – on a disused airforce base in Alameda, California, at a cost of $2.5 million.

Speed (1994), an earlier example of motorway mayhem, had at least the advantage of being able to utilise an unopened section of Los Angeles' Century Freeway.

Here, on their bespoke road, the Wachowski Brothers and their close-knit team of collaborators committed to film what may yet go down in history as the most spectacular car chase sequence ever.

Car smashes, truck surfing and even a kung-fu battle on top of a barrelling big rig are merely the menu items of a protracted pursuit of our heroes by bad guys with the power to infiltrate any car – or driver – they wish.

It lasts more than fourteen minutes on screen, and the whole thing took a mind-blowing 45 days to film – not counting all the time-consuming computer-generated imagery that came later.

There are, it should be noted, classic movies that have been made in their entirety in this time.

When the production left Alameda, the freeway set was pulled apart, leaving behind a mile-and-a-half's worth of pristine timber and plywood. Rather than be scrapped, it was all sent to Mexico, where the wood was used in the construction of a hundred low-income family homes.

Not just a sequel but also an object lesson in another kind of crafty recycling.

RULES OF THE GAME
FULL FRONTAL (2003)

They called it with, one suspects, a certain lack of Nordic humour, 'The Vow of Chastity'. This was the umbrella title for a set of spartan filmmaking rules in a ground-breaking manifesto called Dogme 95, headed by the award-winning Danish directors Lars von Trier and Thomas Vinterberg.

There were ten rules in all. One read, 'Shooting must be done on location. Props and sets must not be brought in (if a particular prop is necessary for the story, a location must be chosen where this prop is to be found).' Then there was, 'Music must not be used unless it occurs where the scene is being shot.'

The Vow concluded with this portentous (or perhaps that should be pretentious) affirmation: 'I swear as a director to refrain from personal taste! I am no longer an artist. I swear to refrain from creating a "work", as I regard the instant as more important than the whole. My supreme goal is to force the truth out of my characters and settings. I swear to do so by all the means available and at the cost of any good taste and any aesthetic considerations...'

There have been, to date, more than thirty mostly forgettable films produced in the Dogme style (you feel that word is probably *verboten*), such as *Festen*, *The Idiots*, *Mifune* and *Julien Donkey Boy*, from an admirably cosmopolitan bunch of filmmakers.

To all intents and purposes, *Full Frontal*, shot minimalistically in eighteen days on film and video, appears to be Hollywood's belated response to Dogme. When Steven Soderbergh, better known for directing big-budget films such as *Erin Brockovich*, *Traffic* and *Ocean's 11*, sent out the script to his preferred cast, it too came with a set of rules:

1. All sets are practical locations.
2. You will drive yourself to the set. If you are unable to drive yourself, a driver will pick you up, but you will probably become the subject of ridicule. Either way, you must arrive alone.
3. There will be no craft service, so you should arrive on set 'having had'. Meals will vary in quality.

4. You will pick, provide and maintain your own wardrobe.
5. You will create and maintain your own wardrobe.
6. There will be no trailers. The company will attempt to provide holding areas near a given location, but don't count on it. If you need to be alone a lot, you're pretty much screwed.
7. Improvisation will be encouraged.
8. You will be interviewed about your character. The material may end up in the finished film.
9. You will be interviewed about the other characters. This material may end up in the finished film.
10. You will have fun whether you want to or not.

Unlike Dogme 95's Vow, this asceticism Tinseltown-style did at least seem to have a sense of humour. What made it also extremely newsworthy was the fact that Soderbergh's cast was firmly from a usually pampered A-list: Julia Roberts, David Duchovny, Catherine Keener, Mary McCormack, Blair Underwood, David Hyde Pierce and Brad Pitt.

How wonderful it would be to report that this brave experiment in slumming it proved a rip-roaring success. Critics mostly slaughtered *Full Frontal*, calling the film a 'vanity production' and a 'show-off stunt'. Its box office barely registered. But that hardly mattered, as the film cost only in total $2 million in total, a twelfth of Ms Roberts's usual asking price.

Will this West Coast austerity become a template, Dogme 95 style? You suspect not – especially if the stars' agents have anything to do with it next time round.

ON THE ROAD AGAIN
A MIGHTY WIND (2003)

Proving there is 'mockumentary life' after the classic *This Is Spinal Tap* (1984) comes this hilarious and even rather poignant reminder of advancing years and changing musical tastes.

But can it really be that same absurdly hairy trio who heavy-metalled up a storm twenty years ago as Spinal Tap now demonstrating varying degrees of baldness and rather gentler string-picking ability as the Folksmen?

Thanks to the versatility of Christopher Guest, Michael McKean and Harry Shearer, Tap's Nigel Tufnel, David St Hubbins and Derek Smalls have transformed into Alan Barrows, Mark Shubb and Jerry Palter, whose jaunty showstopper, 'Old Joe's Place', once got to number seventeen in the charts.

Directed and co-written by Guest, *A Mighty Wind* takes the form of a spoof documentary tracing the reunion concert of the Folksmen, the New Main Street Singers and the troubled double-act Mitch and Mickey in tribute to their late manager, one Irving Steinbloom.

However, unlike Spinal Tap – who actually began performing live after the success of the film – the Folksmen were already a fact of musical life before the decision to immortalise them on film. Messrs Guest, McKean and Shearer in the trio's guise had actually been the opening act for some of their own successful Spinal Tap gigs.

Guest insisted the actors perform their own music, which was all recorded live. 'That was the point from the start: to play music in a movie.'

IN THE BUFF

CALENDAR GIRLS (2003)

'It was,' confessed the director Nigel Cole, 'the hardest thing I had ever done.'

If you thought it was hard for him, then spare a thought for a bunch of middle-aged British actresses including Helen Mirren, Julie Walters, Penelope Wilton, Annette Crosbie and Celia Imrie who had all agreed to strip off for their art.

Their full monty was required for the re-creation of a heart-warming true story from 1999 about members of a local Women's Institute in Yorkshire who decided to raise money for leukaemia research by posing nude for a calendar.

The eye-catching achievement of the Rylstone and District WI spread as far as Hollywood, so it was a just a matter of time before a film followed. But would the actresses go, as they say, all the way?

'Many of the actresses had never taken off their clothes on screen on in public,' said Cole. 'Many are considerably older than actresses who are prepared to take off their clothes on film, and we couldn't and didn't want to use body doubles.'

When the moment arrived, the actresses stepped up to the mark. They described the experience as 'intimidating and liberating'.

Julie Walters explained, 'If the original women could do it, how could we not do it? They were the brave ones, the pioneers, not us. And being part of a group made a big difference. By the time we got round to doing the group photo, we were all quite blasé about it.'

Annette Crosbie added, 'We were apprehensive, partly because we had to take off our clothes not in front of just one man, but in front of the whole crew.

'Strangely, during the taking of the group photo, a man whom I'd never seen before kept appearing behind me. It turned out he was the man in charge of the gas fire. There must have been something seriously wrong with the fire because he came back three times to look at it!'

DOUBLING UP

ALEXANDER THE GREAT (2004)

You'd think filmmaking was sufficiently expensive without also wishing to turn it into a kind of race for most cinemagoers' already seriously limited attention span.

Is, for example, the world really ready for a pair of megadollar epics about the exploits of a pre-Christian imperialist conqueror from Macedonia, even if he happens to look like Colin Farrell or Leonardo DiCaprio?

Farrell is starring in Oliver Stone's version of those historical BC events, which will probably hit multiplexes some months ahead of Baz Luhrman's account, with DiCaprio.

Not that there's anything new in this kind of rather reckless competition. At the turn of the sixties, Peter Finch was the clear winner over Robert Morley in simultaneous films about Oscar Wilde; in 1965, there were a pair of biopics about Jean Harlow with, respectively, Carol Lynley and Carroll Baker; in the 1980s, *Dangerous Liaisons* trumped *Valmont* for awards and box office; and in the 1990s, Kevin Costner's blockbusting *Robin Hood: Prince of Thieves* trounced Patrick Bergin's lower-budget man in Lincoln green.

SIGN OF THE CROSS
THE PASSION (2004)

This compendium of Strange But True could almost be said to have come full circle with Mel Gibson's bold new version of the last twelve hours in the life of Christ.

Gibson, staying firmly behind the camera, decided to shoot his epic in Aramaic and Latin, the two languages extant in Jerusalem in Jesus's time.

He has also said that he will, if at all possible, eschew the use of subtitles, effectively relying on visuals only, recalling the silent days of cinema when celluloid tales of the Christ first became popular.

On location in Italy, Gibson told the *New York Daily News*, 'Subtitles will somehow spoil the effect that I want to achieve. It would alienate you and you'd be very aware you were watching a film if you saw lettering coming up on the bottom of it.

'Hopefully, I'll be able to transcend the language barriers with my visual storytelling. If I fail, I fail, but at least it'll be a monumental failure.'

Gibson shot the crucifixion scenes in Matera, where Pasolini filmed *The Gospel According to St Matthew* (1964), still regarded by many as the best-yet account of Jesus's last days.

To play Jesus, the director chose the intense American actor Jim Caviezel, like him a devout Catholic. Aged 33 when Gibson first offered him the role, Caviezel claims his performance will be 'divinely inspired'.

Reports from the set suggest he endured fifteen days on the cross as well as long hours in ropes and chains being whipped and scourged. He even battled through the pain of a dislocated shoulder to carry on filming, said his director proudly.

Last word goes to the actor who clearly felt authenticity was, as they might say, good for the soul: 'By the time [audiences] get to the crucifixion scene, I believe there will be many who can't take it and will have to walk out – I guarantee it. And I believe there will be many who will stay and be drawn to the truth.'

OK, that's a wrap!

SELECT BIBLIOGRAPHY

Andersen, Christopher, *Citizen Jane*, Virgin, 1990

Attenborough, Richard, *In Search of Gandhi*, The Bodley Head, 1982

Berg, A Scott, *Goldwyn*, Hamish Hamilton, 1989

Bergan, Ronald, *Anthony Perkins: A Haunted Life*, Little, Brown, 1995

Bogarde, Dirk, *Snakes and Ladders*, Chatto & Windus, 1978

Box, Betty, *Lifting the Lid*, Book Guild, 2000

Bragg, Melvyn, *Rich*, Hodder & Stoughton, 1988

Bright, Morris, and Robert Ross, *Mr Carry On*, BBC, 2000

Broccoli, Cubby with Donald Zec, *When the Snow Melts*, Boxtree, 1998

Brown, Peter Harry, and Pat Broeske, *Howard Hughes: The Untold Story*, Warner, 1996

Brownlow, Kevin, *The Parade's Gone By*, Columbus Books, 1989

Brownlow, Kevin, *David Lean*, Richard Cohen Books, 1996

Butler, Ivan, *The Making of Feature Films – A Guide*, Pelican, 1971

Caine, Michael, *What's It All About?*, Arrow, 1992

Cammell, Donald, *Performance*, Faber, 2001.

Challis, Christopher, *Are They Really So Awful?*, Janus, 1995

Christie, Ian, *Gilliam on Gilliam*, Faber, 1999

Clarke, T E B, *This Is Where I Came In*, Michael Joseph, 1974

Cohen, J M and M J Cohen, *The Penguin Dictionary of Twentieth-Century Quotations*, Penguin, 1995

Crowe, Cameron, *Conversations with Wilder*, Faber, 1999

Davidson, Bill, *Spencer Tracy: Tragic Idol*, Sidgwick & Jackson, 1987

Deans, Marjorie, *Meeting at the Sphinx*, Macdonald, 1946
Dewe Matthews, Tom, *Censored*, Chatto & Windus, 1994
Dougan, Andy, *Robert De Niro Untouchable*, Virgin, 1996
Dougan, Andy, *Robin Williams*, Orion, 1998
Dwyer, Roland, *Lethal Hero*, Oliver Books, 1993
Eastman, John, *Retakes*, Ballantine, 1989
Eberts, Jake, and Terry Ilott, *My Indecision Is Final*, Faber, 1990
Field, Matthew, *The Making of the Italian Job*, Batsford, 2001
Flamini, Roland, *Thalberg*, André Deutsch, 1994
Fleischer, Richard, *Just Tell Me When To Cry*, Souvenir Press, 1993
Forman, Milos, and Jan Novak, *Turnaround*, Faber, 1974
Freedland, Michael, *Some Like It Cool: The Charmed Life of Jack Lemmon*, Robson Books, 2002
Gifford, Denis, *The British Film Catalogue 1895–1985*, David & Charles, 1986
Gillett, 'Mo', *Light 'Em Up*, Book Guild, 1996
Glen, John, *For My Eyes Only*, Batsford, 2001
Goodwin, Cliff, *Evil Spirits: The Life of Oliver Reed*, Virgin, 2000
Griggs, John, *The Films of Gregory Peck*, Columbus, 1984
Guinness, Alec, *My Name Escapes Me*, Hamish Hamilton, 1996
Guest, Val, *So You Want to Be in Pictures*, Reynolds & Hearn, 2001
Harris, Marlys J, *The Zanucks of Hollywood*, Virgin, 1990
Higham, Charles, *Hollywood Cameramen*, Thames & Hudson, 1970
Hughes, David, *The Complete Kubrick*, Virgin, 2000
Huston, John, *An Open Book*, Columbus, 1988
Kermode, Mark, *The Exorcist*, BFI, 1997
Kulik, Karol, *Alexander Korda: The Man Who Could Work Miracles*, Virgin, 1975
Knight, Vivienne, *Trevor Howard: A Gentleman and a Player*, Sphere, 1988
Leaming, Barbara, *Katharine Hepburn*, Weidenfeld & Nicolson, 1995
Linson, Art, *A Pound of Flesh*, André Deutsch, 1994
McCabe, John, *Cagney*, Aurum, 1998
MacLaine, Shirley, *My Lucky Stars*, Bantam, 1995
Medved, Harry, with Randy Dreyfuss, *The Fifty Worst Movies of All Time*, Angus & Robertson, 1978

Miller, Frank, *As Time Goes By*, Virgin, 1992

Neame, Ronald, with Barbara Roisman Cooper, *Straight from the Horse's Mouth*, Scarecrow Press, 2003

Parker, John, *Polanski*, Gollancz, 1993

Pendreigh, Brian, *The Film Fan's Guide to Britain & Ireland*, Mainstream, 1995

Richardson, Tony, *Long-Distance Runner*, Faber, 1993

Robb, Brian J, *Nicolas Cage: Hollywood's Wild Talent*, Plexus, 1998

Roberts, Randy, and James S Olson, *John Wayne American*, Free Press, 1995

Robertson, Patrick, *Film Facts*, Billboard, 2001

Rose, Simon, *Classic Film Guide*, HarperCollins, 1995

Russell, Ken, *Directing Film*, Batsford, 2000

Salisbury, Mark, *Burton on Burton*, Faber, 1995

Sandford, Christopher, *McQueen*, HarperCollins, 2001

Sellers, Robert, *Always Look on the Bright Side of Life*, Metro, 2003

Server, Lee, *Robert Mitchum: 'Baby, I Don't Care'*, Faber, 2001

Siegel, Don, *A Siegel Film*, Faber, 1993

Spada, James, *More Than a Woman*, Little, Brown, 1993

Spada, James, *Streisand, The Intimate Biography*, Little, Brown, 1995

Spoto, Donald, *Stanley Kramer Filmmaker*, Putnam, 1978

Tims, Hilton, *Once a Wicked Lady*, Virgin, 1989

van Scheers, Rob, *Paul Verhoeven*, Faber, 1997

Victor, Adam, *The Complete Marilyn Monroe*, Thames & Hudson, 1999

Walker, Alexander, *Audrey – Her Real Story*, Weidenfeld & Nicolson, 1994

Waterman, Ivan, *Helen Mirren*, Metro, 2003

Watkin, David, *Why Is There Only One Word for Thesaurus?*, The Trouser Press, 1998

Weddle, David, *If They Move, Kill 'Em*, Grove Press, 1994

Young, Freddie, *Seventy Light Years*, Faber, 1999